THE PLAYFUL ENTREPRENEUR

THE PLAYFUL ENTREPRENEUR

How to Adapt and Thrive in Uncertain Times

Mark Dodgson and David M. Gann

YALE UNIVERSITY PRESS
NEW HAVEN AND LONDON

For information about this and other Yale University Press publications, please contact:
U.S. Office: sales.press@yale.edu   yalebooks.com
Europe Office: sales@yaleup.co.uk   yalebooks.co.uk

Set in Adobe Caslon Pro by IDSUK (DataConnection) Ltd
Printed in Great Britain by TJ International Ltd, Padstow, Cornwall

Library of Congress Control Number: 2018938631

ISBN 978-0-300-23392-6 (hbk)

A catalogue record for this book is available from the British Library.

10 9 8 7 6 5 4 3 2 1

For Oliver and Michael

Contents

Prelude

In 1762, the Swiss philosopher Jean-Jacques Rousseau wrote an influential book called *Emile*. The book was stylistically rather strange and, as we shall see, was written by an extremely peculiar man. Some of the views in the book were so subversive it was banned and even publicly burned. Its ambitions were no less than understanding the nature of mankind, and how education can encourage innate human goodness.

The eponymous Emile is an imaginary child, and Rousseau writes about how early education should encourage his ability to carefully observe the world around him. Having made an 'active and thinking being', the latter part of Emile's education is completed by making a 'loving and feeling being – that is to say, to perfect reason by sentiment'. A key to Emile's learning, which we call 'Emile's gift', is the way he combines his work and his play.

> Work or play are all one to [Emile], his games are his work; he knows no difference. He brings to everything the cheerfulness of interest, the charm of freedom.[1]

The gift of combining work and play is the core of this book. The wide range of entrepreneurial people and organizations whose stories we tell show the importance of merging play and work in today's uncertain world. They show us the behaviours of entrepreneurs that allow everyone at work to express the cheerfulness of interest and enjoy the charm of freedom. With so many people working in circumstances that are volatile, stressful and unrewarding – and where new technologies can seem so threatening – new approaches to work are needed that bring the pleasure, fun and meaning back to this important aspect of our lives. Emile's gift is to show us the virtue of playful work and how its helps us survive and thrive in our jobs in a turbulent and unpredictable world.

Acknowledgements

We have worked together for nearly thirty years, researching and teaching and writing numerous books and articles. We have argued a lot, learned much from each other, and have had tremendous fun. In short, we have collaborated productively and happily through what shall be described in this book as play. That play has had serious intent – we're both very clear about what needs to be done to succeed in our careers and have often been single-minded in their pursuit – and it has been energizing and hugely enjoyable. We laugh a lot: mainly at each other.

Trying to understand play has taken up a fair proportion of our thinking time the last decade or so, and it has been a fortunate privilege because it has allowed us to research some amazing and inspiring people and organizations. We're very glad we didn't choose to study misery.

As well as the immense debt we owe to the people we interviewed for the book, we have also benefited enormously from discussions and feedback from colleagues and friends. Our deepest thanks are accorded to: Gerry George, Nelson Phillips, Martin Wardrop, Jonathan Weber, Geoff Garrett, Jack Dodgson, Amy L'Estrange, Tim Kastelle, Philip Pullman, Martie-Louise Verreynne, Robert Skidelsky, Paul McDonald, Kirstin Ferguson, John Bessant, Nancy Pachana, Kate Dodgson, Kristien de

ACKNOWLEDGEMENTS

Wolf, Sheridan Ash, Andrew Scheuber, Mike Steep, Irving Wladawsky-Berger and Leslie Butterfield. Rosie Dodgson showed us how to combine one of the at once most playful and responsible jobs in the world, operating the bungee jump in Queenstown, New Zealand.

Our great thanks go to Tim Brown and Dave Webster and the people at IDEO for giving us a wonderful week.

Some have progressed beyond the call of duty and have read a draft of the book in its entirety. We especially acknowledge Anne Asha, Maryam Philpott, Diane Moody, Jeff Rodriguez, Anna Krzeminska, Peter Childs and James Stanfield. In the spirit of playfulness, all shortcomings in the book are entirely their responsibility.

We are grateful to our employer institutions – University of Queensland and Imperial College London – for providing the environment within which we and our colleagues can play with ideas and the time and space to think and reflect on them.

Thank you, Paddy O'Rourke, for showing us what it is to be noble.

Our gratitude goes to our agent, Maggie Hanbury, for her good judgement and perseverance.

Our greatest debt is to Sheridan and Anne for all their grace and fortitude.

PART 1

Why be playful?

1

Work

Work helps give life purpose. As well as providing the means to pay our way in the world, it is through work that we express our personality, engage constructively with others and contribute to the communities of which we are a part. What work we do and how we do it helps define our society, the organizations to which we devote our efforts and our roles and identity as individuals. The purposeful effort of work is one of the most rewarding, meaningful and time-consuming activities in all our lives.

More than ever before, work is surrounded by opportunity and besieged by uncertainty. People are working hard, putting in long hours, but see few non-pecuniary returns and more and more stress. Secure, full-time employment is becoming rarer. Portfolio careers, where people work in many different fields, are more common and the freelance 'gig' economy extends from low-skilled jobs to a wide range of professional occupations. Pressures are ramping up in all forms of work, with demands for greater efficiency, quicker returns, more accountability. At the same time as increased competition in the private sector and reduced budgets in the public sector add to workplace anxiety, new technologies compound the uncertainties confronting us all.

Almost every workplace is affected by continually changing technologies. New developments in artificial intelligence (AI) and machine learning are asking profound questions about how we work and how we co-exist with these powerful new technologies. On the one hand, these technologies create many exciting prospects, resulting in useful new organizations and valuable jobs. On the other hand, companies can swiftly go out of business, and skills once in demand can quickly become redundant, meaning people can rapidly find themselves unemployed, or in the most unexpected of jobs, and few can predict how their careers will pan out. As computers, robots and algorithms become more powerful and intelligent their greater incursion into more areas of working life will lead to massive disruption, producing opportunities for stimulating new work and affecting how, and how much, we work.

We recently asked a group of senior executives how many of them were in jobs they expected to have when they began their working lives. No hands went up. Then we asked these people, at the pinnacle of their careers and right at the top of their organizations, whether they knew what jobs they'd have in five years' time. Again, not one person claimed to know. Such uncertainty is typical in our experience, and it confronts everyone.

There's plenty of evidence of this degree of churn. A Harvard Business School study on the lifetime employment model of the US's top 1,000 executives, for example, found the percentage of top leaders who spent their entire careers at one company dropped from half in 1980 to less than one-third thirty years later.[1] In the UK, Deloitte estimates that automation threatens one-third of UK jobs by 2034,[2] and in the US, the median job tenure is around five years for employees over the age of twenty-five. More philosophically, Roman Krznaric writes of the affliction of the modern workplace as 'a plague of job dissatisfaction, and a related epidemic of uncertainty about how to choose the right career. Never have so many people felt so unfulfilled in their career roles, and been so unsure what to do about it.'[3]

When organizations are not continually changing and adapting, they eventually go bust or are superseded, people lose

4

their jobs and stakeholders lose their investments. When faced with uncertainty at work people can watch and helplessly let changes happen or they can do something by actively trying to create the future they want. They can reconsider how we work, and look for admirable ways of working that can help us improve the work we do now and the work we aspire to do in the future. It is helpful to look at those people who thrive on uncertainty and technological change, who work hard and also reap extraordinary rewards from their labour.

There is a group of people who don't sit by and powerlessly observe the world change around them: they mould opportunities to their advantage. These people – innovators and entrepreneurs, leaders of change – show determination and resilience in the face of the most extreme uncertainty. Indeed, they embrace instability and complexity, and are comfortable in confusing and unpredictable circumstances. Such people show how it is possible to assert ourselves in the face of changes to working life, turn things to our advantage and find elements of stability and contentment in so doing. They succeed because of what we call *play*.

This is a book about why and how innovators – people who put new ideas to good use – and entrepreneurs – people who see opportunities and take risks – play at work. Play is something creative, intuitive and instinctive, helping innovators perceive opportunities and at the same time revealing the features of humans that machines will find hardest to replicate. Play in our sense is about the liberty to explore and tinker with ideas to be applied at work, pushing ourselves and having fun at the same time. In the fourth century BCE Plato said we should live out our lives playing,[4] and play is a crucially important contributor to modern societies and organizations where learning and knowledge are the key to progress. This book will tell of how inspiring designers, philanthropists, financiers, engineers, scientists, politicians and businesspeople play. These extraordinary achievers show how play generates personal, organizational and social development in a wide range of activities. They reveal how, by fulfilling Rousseau's ambitions for Emile, play at work helps people to advance their careers while enjoying themselves at the same time. Their lessons apply to every person wishing to have greater choice and input into how they work in the future. They show why you should play at work, what play looks like and how to encourage playfulness in individuals and organizations. Their message is that everyone can develop entrepreneurial behaviours at work that give advantages over and alongside the technologies and other uncertainties that change jobs.

Play is fun, and bringing more pleasure and enjoyment into the workplace is important, but that doesn't mean it involves any less effort at work. Consider the greatest players in a sport, or actors in film and stage (also known as players), and then think of their personal attributes. They will include dedication, perseverance, determination and risk taking, where failure is a distinct possibility. The players are highly competitive and preoccupied with performance. Very few succeed all the time, and great players use their losses and failures to build their resolve, learn and improve. Their achievements have been built on sheer hard work and commitment, and occasionally almost obsessive single-mindedness, but there is joy and reward in what they do, because their efforts are directed to a purpose and meaning of their own choosing.[5] Top players can thrill, inspire and reward those playing with and watching them. So it is with the entrepreneurs and innovators in this book, who can do all these things. Their work animates and energizes. They work hard and play hard, and the two are often indistinguishable.

The behaviour of some famous entrepreneurs and leaders may make readers feel uncomfortable with the idea of looking for lessons in how they work. The book and film *The Wolf of Wall Street* shows the decadence, corruption and fraud associated with the entrepreneurship of Jordan Belfort. In the earlier film *Wall Street*, Gordon Gecko, the character played by Michael Douglas, uttered the immortal line: 'The point is ladies and gentlemen that greed, for lack of a better word, is good.' Gecko, a fictional character, has many counterparts in reality. Think of the Enrons of the world, where lies and deceit are part and parcel of the pursuit of personal wealth, or Bernie Madoff accumulating $1 billion by defrauding his friends and family. The impression given in TV programmes such as *The Apprentice* and *Shark Tank* is that success lies in hyper-competitive, winner-takes-all behaviours, while modesty and sharing are seen as weaknesses. These representations of business behaviour for entertainment purposes, which also regularly appear in the autobiographies and biographies of corporate figures found in airport bookshops, paint a bleak picture of what is necessary to get on in the modern world. But what can we possibly learn from such acquisitive, obsessive, self-interested and self-serving people? We don't deny that these behaviours sometimes typify particular innovators and entrepreneurs, but we counter this with numerous examples of those who take of a different view. These people demonstrate that there is nobility in the work of entrepreneurs, and it is possible to be highly successful and be a decent human being.

The innovators and entrepreneurs whose stories we tell are successful people who are respectful and inclusive, and whose motivations extend well beyond financial wealth. Some are wealthy and are putting that wealth to good use, but that is not the lesson they offer. The people we write about have succeeded in their chosen field – which may or may not involve becoming wealthy – by enjoying their work's contribution through worthy methods and laudable purposes. They provide valuable insight and act as role models for those who want to thrive in the modern world without trampling over others. They receive immense pleasure and reward in play and the behaviours that support it, as well as enjoyment from its results. These people spend a lot of time, effort and money *giving back* in various ways. They have a sense of fun, as seen in the case of a successful Silicon Valley venture capitalist who happily describes herself as Chief Yoga Officer. Wanting to enjoy their work does not limit their ambitions. When asked if the eventual intent was for Google to buy his well-credentialled company, the CEO of a thirteen-person start-up responded rather that it was his intent to buy Google.

These inspiring people help us to reassess and improve ways to work and, by bringing more play into what we do, put us in a better place to shape the world to our own and others' advantage.

Why 'play'?

It might seem strange to place such importance on 'play' at work, as play is usually connected with children, and playing games is both entertaining and important for their learning and development. But this book is about play and adults, developing means to learn, progress and enjoy. It might be thought a little ill-advised to refer to innovators and entrepreneurs who play as 'players'. There are some very negative connotations with the term – negativity we aim to overcome. When thinking about a 'player', one generally thinks either of sport – a great tennis player or footballer – or its pejorative association with gamesmanship and deviousness in politics or dating. Players are referred to here in the noble sense: think Roger Federer, not *House of Cards*. The innovators and entrepreneurs move play from the schoolyard and games console to the workplace, rescuing 'player' from its occasional association with gambling and poor masculine behaviour to a virtuous role to be widely celebrated and encouraged. We use 'player' as shorthand for playful worker. James March, one of the world's most venerated organization theorists and a renowned poet, says play is an instrument of intelligence rather than self-indulgence, and the focus of this book is intelligent play at work.

The arguments about play at work can be simply summarized. Play is an effective way of benefiting from, and dealing with, the uncertainty, unpredictability and turbulence surrounding the world in which we work. It expresses freedom and fun and inspires the exploration and experimentation that encourages our curiosity and the collision of different ideas. It challenges established practices, mitigates boredom and monotony and provides the capacity for people and organizations to adapt and change. We can learn much from innovators and entrepreneurs because uncertainty and change is their world. As Lord Robert Skidelsky, Keynes's most eminent biographer, put it: 'The more unstable the parameters in the world you find yourself in, the more the insights or intuition of the entrepreneur matters.' Entrepreneurs' play is supported by a number of behaviours that inspire, motivate, fashion and sustain it, and outlining these will comprise the major part of this book. The virtues of play cannot be extolled without describing the conditions that encourage it. Play can be fostered in a range of places and is rewarding at many levels. In essence, playful people are highly productive and valuable in the modern workplace, and playfulness is something to which everyone can aspire and which organizations should promote. Play at work brings progress, enhances our humanity and adds to the distinctiveness of what we can contribute as humans compared to machines. Our argument is that work in the future, where technology will assume an even more important role, needs to become less machine-like and more playful.

A stimulus to our interest in play was a book called *Think, Play, Do* we wrote some years ago with a colleague, Ammon Salter, on how large companies innovate.[6] Organizations come up with ideas, select the best by playing around with them through prototyping and testing, and then put the best ones to use. We spoke to a lot of people about this idea and it was the notion of play that interested them the most. There was especial interest among the largest and most bureaucratic organizations we talked to, because they somehow felt that play was important, and suspected their organizations and the people in them had lost the ability to do it.

Our interest in play is also based on our experiences at work. Between us we have worked in a wide range of jobs, including: builder; drayman; lorry driver; toy-factory worker; civil engineer; labourer; loudspeaker manufacturer; aluminium-ladder factory worker; animal-feed maker; marketer for an international hotel chain; shop assistant; picture framer; borough surveyor; furniture manufacturer; entrepreneur; university professor; adviser to governments and mayors; and consultant to companies all around the world. We have started and run three companies, and been on the board of directors of multibillion-dollar firms. Some of these jobs have been miserable drudgery, draining our energies and spirits, while others were among the most enjoyable and rewarding experiences of our lives.

The more case studies of innovators and entrepreneurs we collected, the more it became clear that play is the antidote to many of the things that prevent us, as individuals and organizations, from being imaginative and welcoming of innovation. Organizations develop antibodies – rules, policies and procedures – that kill playfulness; they become clogged up, inward-looking and cautious. Notoriously, Kodak invented the digital camera but failed to progress with the idea, leading to the company's eventual demise. Organizations develop bureaucracy and practices that limit ambitions and the discretion of workers to make decisions. Individually, it is easy to be set in our ways, grow comfortable with processes and procedures that tell us how to behave and become fearful of any risk and disruption. Yet in the globalized, technological world of today there is nothing more predictive of personal and organizational redundancy than being oblivious to the need for change.

People have widely different experiences of new technologies at work. Some see them as providing nothing but intriguing and exciting opportunities and have thrived using them in confusing circumstances; at the same time there is a great deal of apprehension at all levels of organizations. Everyone is working harder, it is said, and yet people feel more insecure about their future at work. Authors such as Erik Brynjolfsson and Andrew McAfee outline the profound challenges of work brought about by technological change; they argue in their book *The Race Against the Machine* that many workers are losing the race, and demand more consideration of how to cope with the effects of digital technologies. In *The Rise of the Robots* Martin Ford is even more pessimistic, painting a picture of a world with fewer jobs and growing pressure on professionals and workers in manufacturing, as machines take over more and more tasks.[7] These tensions underlie much of the growing disenchantment and resentment among many electorates in the developed world.

Steven Johnson has written a book called *Wonderland: How Play Made the Modern World*, in which he shows how play in a variety of contexts has led to profoundly important social and technological innovations.[8] He writes about play in a range of areas – fashion and shopping, music, taste and especially our enthusiasm for spices, illusion, games and public spaces – and traces their connections to modern life. The development of software is connected to playing musical machines; public limited companies to the spice trade; cinema to the entertainments of optical illusions; computers to games such as chess and dice; eighteenth-century coffee houses to public museums, insurance companies, formal stock exchanges and weekly magazines. Johnson writes how play creates innovations because they emerge from 'a space of wonder and delight where the normal rules have been suspended, where people are free to explore the spontaneous, unpredictable, and immensely creative world of play. You will find the future wherever people are having the most fun.'

We agree absolutely with Steven Johnson about the results and consequences of play, and are full of admiration for the brilliantly playful way he makes his case. Where we differ is in his belief that play is something separate from work, and his view that progress and innovation 'more often than not ... do not unfold within the grown-up world of work'. Johnson shows how play leads to innovation; in writing this book we focus on how being playful can help people gain and contribute more in their everyday work experience.

We explore what play means in the world of work and why it is important in expanding our choices. We asked why and how people play at work. We read about famous entrepreneurs, past and present; interviewed individuals who have been remarkably successful; and studied several organizations renowned for their playful workplaces. Although we draw lessons from players today, many robust insights are offered from players and playful organizations in the past, and this book includes a mixture of historical and contemporary examples. All reveal why play and the behaviours that support it can make work more resilient and satisfying in the face of the uncertainties and challenges that confront it, and why play is so personally, organizationally and socially progressive. Play, essentially, is the means by which people and organizations compete and perform, and undertake successful and rewarding work, in the face of endemic and persistent uncertainty.

Playful entrepreneurs welcome change, are keen to seize new opportunities and are prepared to take risks. They are bold and different; they can buck the system and shake things up. They are the opposite of the grey bureaucrat cautiously complying with procedure. Such people have imagination; they see things others don't and do things others do not dare. And they very often display an abundance of good humour even when faced with adversity. Play underlies a great deal of creativity and innovation. It is not the frivolous enjoyment of indulging in hobbies or immersion in computer games; it is intelligent because it improves cognizance, understanding and knowledge. Being a player is exciting and stimulating because there is risk involved: money and reputations can be made and lost; great ideas are successfully applied or wither on the vine. When entrepreneurs play they are expressing their freedom. They are showing they want to control their destiny, to decide and not be told, and to have some fun along the way. Brian Sutton-Smith, a leading play theorist, says play constructs a more fulfilling sense of self than simply doing what we are told.[9] Play is a way of displaying curiosity, and it frames the ways players engage with their work and with others.

Players play when they challenge and disrupt the status quo. And yet they also play within a system of social rules. When great sportsmen and women display their individual genius, doing things others can't or wouldn't dream of, they do so within the rules of their game, often in consort with others. Innovators and entrepreneurs are the same. They are driven often to extreme acts of self-expression and belief, yet they operate within boundaries of established behaviours and relationships. Players are also team-members, and none really succeed on their own. Play's social purpose is to provide opportunities to 'play together', creating cohesion and a sense of belonging.

Players make serious contributions. They make new things happen. Some make themselves and others wealthy, and the best make the world a better place. Play is important because it allows them to do serious things in the way it balances freedom and fun, on the one hand, with order and purpose on the other. People are playing when they are enjoying themselves, and sometimes also when they get stuck with a problem and need to solve it. As with Emile, this can be childlike in the pleasure in adventure and discovery it brings, but it is not foolish. And here lies the paradox of play: it is about enjoyment with serious intent.

When we refer to players we are talking about anyone in any organization who is, or has the capacity to be, playful. Players can be business or social entrepreneurs, work in the government and public sector, charities and non-governmental organizations, or indeed be freelancers or employees in large organizations. The insights from the innovators in the book are valuable to those in a wide range of work and with a broad span of objectives. They hold lessons for those wishing to replicate their success by becoming innovators, entrepreneurs and leaders, and those who simply wish to develop better approaches to dealing with, and benefiting from, uncertainties at work. Our argument is that the ways innovators and entrepreneurs play, and the behaviours that support that play, provide an opportunity for everyone to think about behaviour at work. They can encourage reflection on current work and help stimulate aspirations for different and better work in the future.

We are not psychologists or moral ethicists measuring or analysing personality or character: this is a book about behaviour. These behaviours may reflect an individual's character or values, but we do not delve into these. We focus on what people do when they play at work. There is no prescription – in a new-age or management-guru mode – for a series of steps to a more fulfilling life and successful career. Instead, various examples show how play allows us to move away from being passive observers and become more capable of making things happen to our advantage. We are interested in what players do to motivate themselves and those around them, and what influences and shapes their conduct as they make things happen.

Perhaps the most important element underlying the success of innovators and entrepreneurs is sheer hard work. As J.R.D. Tata, a pioneering entrepreneur and the man who built one of India's great corporate conglomerates, said: 'Nothing worth-while is achieved without deep thought and hard work.' Elon Musk, of PayPal, Tesla and SpaceX fame, extols the virtues of 'working super hard'. Visiting one of his factories, we were told that Musk boasts his engineers are like Spartans, requiring one engineer for other companies' hundred. Certainly they work hard. A senior manager there said some time ago he was stretched to his absolute limits and really enjoyed it: 'There's something about being tested to the extreme and coming out the other end.' Few innovators and entrepreneurs will have succeeded without dedicated, and often single-minded, commitment to their objectives. But this is not the tedious and mind-numbing hours of repetitive and meaningless work. As Malcolm Gladwell puts it, hard work is a prison sentence only if it doesn't have meaning. Playful work is work with a purpose; it is enjoyable, rewarding and deeply satisfying. Joseph Schumpeter (more of whom later) said the entrepreneur 'seeks out difficulties, changes in order to change, delights in ventures' and revels in 'the joy of creating, of getting things done, or simply exercising one's energy and ingenuity'. Work in these circumstances has blurred boundaries with play, and just because work is playful does not imply it involves any less commitment and exertion.

As well as showing us what play at work is and what it contributes, the innovators and entrepreneurs in this book tell us about the broad behaviours that support it. They display what we call 'noble' behaviours that endorse, stimulate and guide play. Playful work is supported by fortitude, craft, ambition and grace. It is these behaviours that underpin play, encouraging it and making it manifest.

Noble behaviours

Distinguished by virtue of intelligence, knowledge, or skill. Of a deed or action: illustrious, renowned, celebrated.[10]

We do not use noble in the sense of the titled aristocracy, but as something that is earned through effort and experience and displayed in behaviour at work. It is something distinguished, elevated and worthy of celebration. It demonstrates gravitas. A robust language is needed to describe these noble behaviours, one that uses traditional vocabulary but at the same time resonates with modern idiom, without using deplorable 'management speak'. In the end we selected slightly antiquated terms, hoping optimistically that their contemporary relevance could be elucidated. So, what follows is discussion about play, its importance and its relationship with:

Grace: the understanding that players don't achieve great things on their own; they need others to work with whom they trust and respect; and players build empathy and loyalty with their colleagues, stakeholders, customers and audiences through personal generosity and warmth. Grace inspires, influences and animates play.

Craft: the ability to apply a novel idea and mould an answer to a problem when the climate is complex and uncertain. Craft combines and balances the playfulness of experiment and intuition with the seriousness of expectation and intent. Craft frames, shapes and fashions play.

Fortitude: the resilience players develop against the inevitable knocks they receive when they're trying to change things, and the patience, energy and tenacity they have to maintain when things get difficult. Fortitude maintains, sustains and

15

upholds the playful capacity to adapt and learn and provides the ability to negotiate turbulence at work.

Ambition: the efforts to meet the expectations people have of themselves, including to achieve particular productive aims, such as solving a problem, building a product or a company, satiating their curiosity or contributing to the society of which they are a part. Ambition involves the appreciation that making money for money's sake is shallow and true rewards come when players combine personal advancement with improvements in their communities. Players are passionate about giving back and leaving a proud legacy. Ambition motivates, encourages and adds meaning to play.

The terms we use emerged from our research and were discussed with the scores of people interviewed. There was the occasional difference in language, but the sentiment behind the terms rang true with them all. The people we interviewed work in all sorts of areas; they are women and men of all ages from around the world. There is no age or gender bias when it comes to playful work, no innate differences between men and women, young and old. As George Bernard Shaw put it: we don't stop playing because we get old; we get old because we stop playing. Few of the subjects display all the behaviours described, but all show one or more in abundance. Some are primarily character-ized by their perseverance, resilience and grit, others by their concern for their employees or in working collaboratively. Some expend extraordinary energy giving to others, while others display exceptional skills in shaping solutions to complex prob-lems. All have generosity of spirit, intellectual curiosity, passion for learning and a desire to express their individuality and inde-pendence. We tell the stories of these players throughout this book, and lessons unfold as their work is explored. They are at the core of the book, and there is much to learn from them. Readers can expect a developing narrative of the importance of play and its supportive noble behaviours, interspersed with and based upon studies of a diverse range of remarkable people and organizations.[11] The studies comprise a series of shorter cases and a number of longer characteristic cases, especially revealing of the behaviour in question.

A brief history of work and play

Our interest lies with the nature and implications of playful work today and in the future, but there is much to learn from the past. Many attitudes to work have long histories, and although we are experiencing a period of massive change, the assumption that everything is so new and different that only new and different answers will do for the problems we face has to be questioned. Historical cases are included because they amply demonstrate one or more noble behaviours that helped deal with and gain advantage from turbulence and uncertainty at work. As Winston Churchill put it: 'The farther back you can look, the farther forward you are likely to see.'

Imagine a conversation among a group of people who want to understand the world in order to change it. The talk in the room might jump between the consequences of failed financial markets and inadequate national infrastructure to threats to personal security and the dangers of pandemics. Caring about the state of the world might involve discussion about current social and religious upheaval and international political turmoil, continuing government incompetence and the behaviour of the unruly Tea Party in America. Emphasizing the point that we should learn from the past, this conversation might easily have been held by a number of entrepreneurs who really did change the world, in Birmingham, England, in the latter part of the eighteenth century.

Such as exchange could conceivably have occurred among a group known as the Lunar Society.[12] Its members were scientists, engineers, industrialists, poets – people difficult to categorize because they were all these things and more. Beginning in the 1760s, they met as a group to talk about ideas and their application. The diverse interests of industrialist members, such as Matthew Boulton, James Watt and Josiah Wedgwood, extended into science, politics and the arts. Joseph Priestley was a scientist, preacher and polemicist; Erasmus Darwin was a doctor and a poet; Benjamin Franklin was interested in virtually everything. Knowledge had no boundaries and its possibilities were endless. The objective of the Lunar Society was to embrace the challenges of the world by first understanding them and then shaping them to their will. These were players in a most profound sense. The polymaths of the Lunar Society celebrated the optimism of the age, exploring how the possibilities of science, technology and the arts could build their personal wealth and at the same time construct a better society.

The problems the Lunar Society debated remain eerily current. We often hear the view that we live in an era of such extraordinary complexity and uncertainty that individuals and groups, and even large companies and governments, can do little to influence the directions of future developments. But consider the circumstances of Lunar Society meetings. The Industrial Revolution was underway, with profound new understanding of physics and chemistry and its rapid application in emerging manufacturing industries. There were massive social upheavals as the population, which doubled in England in the eighteenth century, moved from farm to factory. The populations of large new cities – Birmingham, Manchester, Sheffield – were exploding, with chaotic implications for transport, housing and sanitation, as well as for social cohesion.

The Lunar Society was so called because it met during the full moon, as travel otherwise was too dangerous, with the ever present fear of robbery and assault. Adam Smith's recently published views were affecting the conduct of commerce and the way work was organized. Business collapses in the South Sea Bubble and in the powerful East India Company continued to question faith in the financial system. Politically, the conditions were being laid for Jacobite insurrection in France, and the fledgling United States was fighting for independence, both of which profoundly disturbed political and social hierarchies headed by unstable royal families. The emerging working class was beginning to get organized. Religious rivalries led to violence on the streets: nearly 300 people were killed in London in the anti-Catholic Gordon Riots. New markets and novel goods were responding to and creating unprecedented levels of demand. The growth of consumerism moved demand from primitive needs to sophisticated wants. Samuel Johnson, author of the first comprehensive English dictionary, gloomily proclaimed at the time that the age was running mad for innovation. If an optimistic new world could be conceived and planned in such circumstances, there is no reason why there can't be similar ambitions today.

The work ethic

Attitudes to work can have long and deep antecedents. This is shown in the writings of the great German thinker, Max Weber (1864–1920), who produced a canon of work that has profoundly influenced modern Western thought. In common with many other geniuses his personal life was unusual to say the least: he was a depressive insomniac whose attempts to enter politics verged on the bizarre, and his marriage of twenty-seven years was reputedly unconsummated. Personal problems aside, his writings are immensely insightful, not least those concerned with work.

Early industry was anything but playful for those working in it. In 1904 Weber wrote a book called *The Protestant Ethic and the Spirit of Capitalism*,[13] in which he argued that after the Reformation, Protestantism endowed spiritual significance to hard work, self-sacrifice and denial of worldly pleasures. This religious and moral movement, Weber argued, provided the basis for the development of capitalism, especially in the form found in Northern Europe. At their most extreme, Protestant behaviours – often associated with Puritanism – extend from earnestness and prudery to an aversion to celebration. Early Puritans in New England, for example, banned Christmas festivities and discouraged children from playing with toys, while John Wesley wasn't keen on laughter, music or luxury of any kind. Oliver Cromwell's rule in Britain saw a clamping down on the celebration of Christmas and saints' days. The idea that joyless work is spiritually rewarding was not objectionable to early industrialists, as they created their new factories with repetitive, often dangerous and unpleasant jobs.

Pat Kane, journalist and broadcaster, member of the 1980s band Hue and Cry and previously Rector of Glasgow University, has written a book, *The Play Ethic*, in which he discusses the persistence of attitudes to work. 'The work ethic has been a cornerstone of industrial modernity for over 250 years – and in many ways, is its most powerful and enduring ideology', he writes. 'Its essence is simply stated: that work, no matter how alienating or ill-suited to temperament, is noble in and of itself. And work is good for the soul.'[14]

One of the most profound changes industrialization brought was a new meaning of time. As the historian E.P. Thompson shows, in peasant and rural societies time was associated with the rhythms of nature, with, for example, tasks linked to the seasons and tides. As the factory system developed, employers paying wages saw time as *theirs*. It became currency – not passed but spent – and employers became concerned with punctuality and time thrift. As time is valuable it needs to be harnessed, and as work became increasingly specialized it required greater synchronization. Josiah Wedgwood (of whom more later) was a pioneer of the Industrial Revolution, and one of the first things he did in his new, state-of-the-art factory was to introduce a bell to be rung at the precise time that work was to start, and workers were to 'clock in'.

Thompson explains how the first generation of factory workers were taught the importance of time by their masters, the second fought for a ten-hour day, and the third for overtime and time-and-a-half. In his words, workers had accepted the categories of their employers and learned the lesson that time is money.[15] Time, of course, or more precisely lack of it, is an issue that still continues to affect modern work. We live our lives in fear of time getting away from us, and we never seem to have time to get away from immediate and pressing demands so that we can think.

Despite the emergence of this work ethic – of grim, joyless and disciplined labour – and of a worldview in which there is no place for being joyful or playful at work, there was no denying the place of these elevated feelings in the human spirit. At the same time that William Blake was writing about the enslavement to 'dark, satanic mills' during the Industrial Revolution, Friedrich Schiller was writing his poem 'Ode to Joy' about humankind's intrinsic need for joy and play, a view further promoted by use of the poem in Beethoven's Ninth Symphony. Schiller also wrote about the aesthetics and beauty of what he called the 'play impulse'. In *On the Aesthetic Education of Man*, he says, 'man only plays when he is in the fullest sense of the word a human being, and he is only fully a human being when he plays.'[16] And, echoing Rousseau's Emile, François-René de Chateaubriand, the nineteenth-century French writer, politician and historian, held that 'A master in the art of living draws no sharp distinction between his mind and his play.'[17] Play may have been relegated in the prevailing work ethic, but it remained an important human aspiration.

Work and technology

There has been a long historical debate about the impact of technology on work, with its role celebrated as liberating on the one hand and denounced as repressive on the other. It was always clear that technology has a deep impact on work. Charles Babbage, inventor of the first mechanical computer, the 'difference machine', wrote in his 1832 book *On the Economy of Machinery and Manufactures* that 'At each increase of knowledge, as well as on the contrivance of every new tool, human labour becomes abridged.'[18] His intention was to point out the effects and advantages that arise from machines and tools and trace the consequences of 'applying machinery to supersede the skill and power of the human arm'. The most common and valuable

21

contribution of machines, he argued, is to produce economies of time, that is to produce not only more consistently but more quickly. Babbage's concerns lay with the efficiency of production rather than the nature of work, but as the pioneer of computing he clearly outlined the massive impact machinery could have on work through the application of scientific principles.

For some, technological advance was positively linked with social progress. David Hume, the eighteenth-century Scottish philosopher, economist and historian, author of a six-volume, million-word *History of England* and a contemporary of Rousseau, argued in 1742 how in progressive societies '*industry, knowledge,* and *humanity,* are linked together by an indissoluble chain'. In 'luxurious' societies, as he put it, knowledge flows between and mutually supports the arts and sciences.

> Another advantage of industry and of refinements in the mechanical arts, is, that they commonly produce some refinements in the liberal; nor can one be carried to perfection, without being accompanied, in some degree, with the other ... The spirit of the age affects all the arts; and the minds of men, being once roused from their lethargy, and put into a fermentation, turn themselves on all sides, and carry improvements into every art and science. Profound ignorance is totally banished, and men enjoy the privilege of rational creatures, to think as well as to act, to cultivate the pleasures of the mind as well as those of the body.[19]

Such optimism became rarer as the reality of work in mechanized industry became clearer over time. The nineteenth-century Scottish philosopher, essayist and historian, Thomas Carlyle, gloomily complained about the impact of industrialization by saying: 'Men are grown mechanical in head and in heart, as well as in hand ... Their whole efforts, attachments, opinions, turn on mechanism, and are of a mechanical character.'[20]

According to Richard Sennett in his book *The Craftsman*,[21] this domination of men by machines resulted because of the way technology comes to rather than from workers. It reflects a view that technology is something that is imposed and is inevitably detrimental. What it does not allow for is the ambiguous nature of technology. This is most elegantly captured in Joseph Schumpeter's dictum that innovation is a process of creative destruction, with both positive and negative impacts. Ever since the Industrial Revolution, successive generations have experienced both the creative and destructive consequences of new technology. Much of the British railway network, for example, was built during a ten-year period of 'railway mania' in the middle of the nineteenth century. In 1845–47, the British Parliament authorized 8,000 miles of railway lines to be built at a staggering cost equivalent to the country's entire gross domestic product. This investment totally transformed the nation's economy and society, allowing progress in trade and urban development and extending people's freedom to travel and explore. By 1860 the railways employed 100,000 people. But it was also a time of fear and trepidation for many people worried about the psychological consequences of travelling at speed, and of disruption to their traditional parochial ways of life and doing business.

The electrification of cities, including private homes at the beginning of the twentieth century, also happened at pace, with large numbers of houses receiving electric power in a ten-year period. Despite its benefits, many people felt threatened, struggling to understand the consequences of such novelty. Initially each home had just one socket, because users and suppliers of equipment could not conceive of requirements for more. Only a few electrical goods were available to be plugged in. Blanking plates that covered sockets were sold to those who, mistrusting advice about the new technology, feared that electricity could spill onto the floor, resulting in electric shock. Progress was accompanied by a sense of anxiety.

Records of workers breaking new machines in industries such as agriculture and mining go right back to the beginning of the Industrial Revolution. Fear of the impact of technology led to the Luddite movement in early nineteenth-century England. The Luddites are probably history's most notorious social movement associated with opposition to technology. In contemporary times a parent resisting the use of a function or app on their mobile device is likely to be called a Luddite by their children. This is a misunderstanding: the Luddites weren't opposed to technology *per se*, but wished to protect their way of working and its rewards as mechanization advanced in large-scale factories.

The Luddites mainly comprised skilled artisans in the wool and cotton industries which had blossomed in the late eighteenth century in the Midlands and Northern England. They sent threatening letters to factory owners and in organized groups sabotaged numerous machines, such as the new steam-driven looms. Government reaction to this movement was extreme: 12,000 troops were sent to control any insurgence, breaking machines was made a capital offence, and 17 men were hanged, with many others deported to Australia (a much less agreeable destination at the time).

The Luddites railed at the way the machines were used to break up tradition and custom, to deskill artisans and to lower wages. The historian Eric Hobsbawm suggests Luddism was concerned with protecting freedom and dignity as well as wages. Where machines did not disadvantage workers, he argues, they were generally accepted. He also contends there was overwhelming sympathy for machine-wreckers in all parts of the population fearful of the disruptive effects of technology on society.[22] There was a concern from the beginning of industrialization, in other words, for technology to fit with social expectations, for society to dictate the terms by which technology is used.

Work, craft and skills

Traditional craft skills combine knowledge of materials, understanding of the tasks to be done and the manual dexterity for performing them. Possession of a craft has historically been deeply meaningful, personally and socially. Craftsmen often made their own tools and skills were handed down from parent to child.[23] The basic unit of production was the family, operating from a workshop. Master craftsmen, who employed journeymen and managed their own apprentices and labourers, carried out the coordination of the various stages of production. They organized their activities in guilds linked to specific trades. The arrival of mechanization threatened the meaning and structures of this form of organization as well as craft skills. This deskilling was accentuated by the implementation of Adam Smith's analysis of the division of labour, showing how dividing tasks and deploying machines could achieve productivity gains.

The denigration of craft in industrial mass production led to the Arts and Crafts movement of the late nineteenth century. With leaders such as William Morris and John Ruskin, the movement called for a reinstatement of craft, and it had a profound influence internationally (especially in Japan and the US) on all areas of design, from architecture to the decorative arts. The movement emphasized that the exercise of craft is one of the greatest pleasures of work, and the removal of craft is dispiriting and destructive of self-esteem. A major concern of the Arts and Crafts movement was the disconnection of the design of products from their manufacture, which its proponents believed led to unsatisfying work and unpleasant, shoddy products. The way things were made had become divorced from an appreciation of the materials from which they were made. Craft, it was argued, connected intellectual and manual acts, bringing dignity to the worker with aesthetically pleasing results.

William Morris (1834–96) was a polymath with an astonishing range of talents. He was an artist, designer, poet, polemicist, social and education reformer, environmentalist and active socialist, who ran decorating, manufacturing and retail businesses. By all accounts a strange man, not readily sociable, he laboured prodigiously and work was a major part of his life and interests; as he said, 'give me love and work – these two only'. As

Morris's wife is reputed to have had affairs with two of his friends, it is perhaps no surprise that much of his attention turned to the nature of work and its results. One of his leading biographers, Fiona MacCarthy, says Morris's major concern in life was 'proper human occupation, whether going under the name of work or play'. His thoughts on work are encapsulated in the view that: 'Nothing should be made by man's labour which is not worth making, or which must be made by labour degrading to the makers.'[24]

Morris's writings were preoccupied with making work and workplaces more attractive: 'It is right and necessary that all men should have work to do which shall be worth doing, and be of itself pleasant to do; and which should be done under such conditions as would make it neither over-wearisome nor over-anxious.'[25] With immense foresight, in an essay on 'A Factory as It Might Be', he argued factories 'must make no sordid litter, befoul no water, nor poison the air with smoke'. Foretelling the sort of modern playful workplaces described later in this book, his factories of the future are agreeable buildings, with dining halls, libraries and places for study of various kinds.[26]

Morris argued there are two kinds of work, one good, the other bad: 'one not far removed from a blessing, a lightening of life; the other a mere curse, a burden to life'.[27] Good work is undertaken to provide time for leisure and rest, to make something useful, and for pleasure. 'We must begin to build up the ornamental part of life – its pleasure, bodily and mental, scientific and artistic, social and individual – on the basis of work undertaken willingly and cheerfully, with the consciousness of benefiting ourselves and our neighbours by it.'[28] He was especially interested in promoting the beauty of the results of work, to which end he invested significantly in his own skills as a maker. MacCarthy writes: 'With an almost manic industriousness Morris set out to rediscover lost techniques for fabricating, in succession: embroidery; stained glass; illumination and calligraphy; textile dyeing, printing and weaving; high-warp tapestry.'[29]

This passion for meaningful work was shared by John Ruskin, who stressed the importance of skills that unify experience, intellect and passion and whose use in work helps define who people are.

Frederick (F.W.) Taylor (1856–1915) is the person most associated with applying scientific principles to destroy the meaningful and playful work espoused by people such as Morris and Ruskin. Taylor was a man of privileged upbringing who won the US tennis doubles title and competed at golf in the Olympics, but despite being offered a place at Harvard he chose to work on a shop floor and learned engineering through night study at an institute of technology. Taylor's obsessive mission in life was to combat slackness at work and improve output. Working in large companies, such as Bethlehem Steel, he developed a series of principles that became known as 'scientific management'. They included: replacing casual work methods with those based on scientific study; formal training methods; detailed instructions to workers on the performance of each task; and the separation of planning by managers from performance by workers. While Taylor's contribution to improving industrial productivity through systematic planning is widely acknowledged, his views on the nature and importance of work for the worker led to some questionable behaviour and distorted views. He told a congressional committee that 'the science of handling pig-iron is so great that the man who is ... physically able to handle pig-iron and is sufficiently phlegmatic and stupid to choose this for his occupation is rarely able to comprehend the science of handling pig-iron'.[30] Taylor was much enamoured with a worker he called Schmidt, whose 'ox-like' strength and capacity for hard work set the benchmark for possible performance.[31] There is some doubt about whether Schmidt existed, as Taylor continually changed his account of his capacities.[32] Taylor was eventually fired from Bethlehem Steel for fomenting discord among fellow managers, and became one of the world's first management consultants.

Taylorism became the dominant approach to organizing work and, by the 1920s, industry remained largely play-free and unpleasant to work in. Mass production emerged under the guidance of Henry Ford, a man not averse to spying on his employees for evidence of gambling and drinking, and who could include Hitler among his admirers. Ford's Tayloristic 'time and motion' studies of assembly lines ensured that no period at work was wasted and no movement superfluous in maximizing the output determined by central management control units. Taylor and his scientific management successors aroused considerable opposition and for many affirmed Marx's view that machines were weapons employed by capitalists to 'quell the revolt of specialized labour'. Taylorism confirmed to a great deal of Marxists the systematic tendency in capitalism to deskill and create unsatisfying work.

Marx wrote that the attractiveness of work results from the free play of physical and mental powers, but his message did not reach another Taylor enthusiast, Vladimir Lenin. It is ironic that, under his successor Joseph Stalin, the nadir of a lack of play at work was reached with the Stakhanovite movement in the USSR in the 1930s, in a regime describing itself as Marxist. This movement was based on the example of the Russian hero, Aleksei Stakhanov, who reputedly mined over a hundred tons of coal in his shift, more than ten times his quota. Such was his fame that he was awarded two Orders of Lenin, and graced the front cover of *Time* magazine. The obsession with raw output became core Communist Party policy, and saw numbers of Bolshevik stalwarts recognized for their hard labour. They included Pasha Angelina, fêted somewhat ridiculously for being one of the first women to drive a tractor. Illustrating the power of those who make the rules, it was later revealed that Stakhanov might have had some help from fellow workers during his monumental shift. The Soviet government, needing a hero to figurehead the drive for production, could possibly have chosen another of his colleagues.

Essentially the Soviet industrial system was designed to remove creativity, self-expression and variety from work. As everything was planned and predetermined, the only requirement of the workforce was compliance. Playfulness and entrepreneurship in the USSR were tickets to the Gulag. Soviet-style command-and-control forms of organization assume ordered and predictable circumstances. Unfortunately for them, the world has never been so structured, and the inability to experiment and respond to changes and unforeseen circumstances helps explain the inefficiencies and poor productivity of Soviet industry.

Work could also be very challenging in completely different industrial systems. The stresses at work in Japan led in the late 1960s to the phenomenon of *karōshi*, or death by overwork, where workers suffered strokes or heart attacks brought on by too much overtime and excessive and conflicting demands. In the car industry, the Japanese variant of 'lean production', which in contrast to Ford's approach gave workers more say over how tasks are performed, was preoccupied with increasing speed on production lines. During the early 1970s, the Japanese journalist Satoshi Kamata got a job on Toyota's production line and kept a daily diary about his experiences. In his book, *Japan in the Passing Lane*, he wrote of the real physical danger of the work and its monotonous senselessness.[33] Once everyone was settled into working as fast and efficiently as they could, the line speed was increased, adding to the stress of the workforce. In 1973, Huw Beynon wrote a book, *Working for Ford*, based on his experiences of a Ford factory in Liverpool, in which he vividly portrays the brutality of life on the shop floor and the battles of trade unions to challenge managerial control.[34]

The view that the deskilling of work was an inevitable consequence of capitalist industry was most forcefully argued by Harry Braverman in his influential 1974 book, *Labor and Monopoly Capital: The Degradation of Work in the Twentieth Century*. Braverman, a Marxist activist and editor with a background of manual labour in the shipbuilding industry, argued capitalism is characterized by the 'incessant drive to enlarge and perfect machinery on the one hand, and to diminish the worker on the other'.[35] Braverman contended that modern work was characterized by managers' control over knowledge and the separation of 'conception' from 'execution' at work. Contemporary work, he argued, was epitomized by Taylorist deskilling and the destruction of craft. His book became hugely significant among social scientists at the time, leading to the popular term Bravermania.

Not every observer was convinced about the inevitability of deskilling in modern industry. Alternative views were developed in the 1950s and 1960s by some of the leading social scientists of the day. Clark Kerr and colleagues, working on a large project on industrialization, management and wage earners, argued industrialism can bring about a better existence for workers, and may lead to a new bohemianism and search for individuality.[36] They argued new technology needed upgraded skills, where workers take increased responsibility for the performance of assigned tasks. In this view, one of the roles of managers is to incentivize and energize workers. Kerr eventually became one of the most influential academics in America following his appointment as president of the University of California.

A Quality of Working Life movement emerged in the early 1970s, consisting initially of a group of academics later joined by some trade union officials and personnel management professionals. It argued that workers should have work satisfaction and that this would be achieved by workers designing their own jobs and working in autonomous groups without regular supervision. Experiments were undertaken in a number of car factories, such as Volvo in Kalmar, Sweden, to give workers more freedom to plan their own tasks and increase their skills. Because these approaches have been combined with other practices, such as 'total quality management' and 'quality circles', the direct impact of these efforts is unclear. These experiments did, however, contribute to greater discussion of issues such as 'empowerment', and this has been a feature of many advanced human resource management practices ever since. In most modern factories, for example, quality management is 'pushed down' to the responsible worker, opportunities are afforded for workplace discussions on continual improvements and it is more common to find job rotation or organization in self-directed work units, providing for skills improvements and the reduction of repetitive tasks.

The relationship between technology and skills became the central question for both authors of this book early in our research careers. In the early 1980s, Mark was working in a small company making loudspeakers for bands such as Pink Floyd. He was bored (not many invitations to concerts), saw in the newspaper that Imperial College was advertising PhD places in its social science department and thought he might apply. His previous excursion into a Master's degree followed three years as a lorry driver where he became interested in the industrial relations consequences of the introduction of the tachograph, known in Braverman style as the 'spy in the cab'. Remembering his Braverman and that the factory next door had just bought a new piece of equipment called a computer numerical controlled (CNC) machine tool, Mark phoned Imperial and asked if they'd be interested in a PhD on CNC and deskilling. They said yes, come in for an interview tomorrow. Not knowing the first thing about CNC, he rushed around to the nearby factory to find out about it, then blinded the interview panel the next day with his extensive knowledge of the technology and was immediately offered a scholarship (things were much easier and more relaxed in those days).

Delighted to be off the factory floor as a worker, but completely in the dark about how to go about doing a PhD, Mark decided it would be best to return to factories as a researcher and talk to as many companies with CNC machines as possible, asking them how the machines deskilled their workers. His reading of Braverman had told him that the clever computer bit of the machine – 'conception' – would be separated from the dumb, manual work – 'execution' – and previously highly skilled machinists would have their work degraded. After a year visiting fifty companies in some of the ugliest industrial estates in the UK, he found that rather than a universal, capitalist tendency to deskill, a wide range of choices were available on how the machines were used. In fact, many companies chose to increase the skills and range of tasks of machine workers, such that people with mechanical skills began programming computers. This, they found, was not only rewarding to the workers concerned, who appeared unperturbed about learning completely new skills, but also improved the performance of the machines. The lesson he learnt was that technology does not deskill, but people's choices about the design and use of technology can. There are choices to be made by organizations, entrepreneurs and workers on how technology is developed and used.

On learning from history

The philosopher Alain de Botton, in his book *The Pleasures and Sorrows of Work*,[37] says that the observation of work can be as stimulating as anything on a stage or chapel wall, and there is a long history of people studying and thinking about the nature of work and changes in its practice from which we can learn. There are deep roots behind the ways we work, found for example in the Protestant work ethic. Particular approaches to work, such as Taylorism, can have considerable impact, attracting, as it did, enthusiastic proponents as diverse as Ford and Lenin. History also tells us about alternative voices, seen in the continual reference to the importance of play, craft and skills in meaningful working lives and society's concern since early industrialization for technology to be subservient to its needs. Technology can be a creative or destructive force, but there is no inevitability – no capitalist imperative – to the way it is used. Choices can be made.

Technology is not something that happens to us, but something we can influence and shape. The degree to which it disrupts work or not lies to a significant extent in our hands, and our choices rest ultimately with our will and desires. In the 1990s, the popular British band Blur brought out an album called *Modern Life is Rubbish*, which one band member memorably described as being about 'how the whole world is shit, except for us'. Amusing, but the point is not to moan about the state of the world, but to change it.

History shows the power of optimistic, purposeful effort. The Lunar Society worked in a time of extraordinary uncertainty and turbulence, but was not distracted from attempting to understand the world and actually succeeded in changing it. The Arts and Crafts movement demonstrated the value of reinstating craft and meaningful work. From an initially small start, the Quality of Working Life movement introduced practices aimed at increasing work satisfaction and productivity that have become engrained in many modern workplaces. These examples show the value of getting away from fatalism in the way problems are approached ('it is all too complicated') and abrogation of responsibility ('there's nothing we can do about it'; 'it's someone else's fault'). If the world comprises people who make things happen, watch what happens and wonder what happened, then it is time to accentuate and celebrate the former.

This short history of work frames many of the issues experienced in its modern manifestation. Technological change is ubiquitous and disruptive. Contemporary examples include the increasing use of automated processes in the delivery of services, for instance the application of AI and machine-learning algorithms in industries such as banking and insurance, and in jobs such as making travel bookings and answering calls on helplines. AI learns from patterns in data and develops its own rules for how to interpret new information so it can solve problems and learn with very little human input. Many professionals – accountants, lawyers, consultants, surgeons, university professors, border guards – are concerned about changes in their work. Machines, for example, have become better than people at determining someone's identity at border crossings, and AI is being used to replace insurance workers when assessing claims. Robots are rapidly taking the place of people in manufacturing: for example, Foxconn, the Taiwanese maker of the iPhone, replaced half its workforce with robots in a two-year period. In the medical profession, AI is being used to improve diagnoses and robots are used in surgery.

Uber – the digital platform for booking taxi services – epitomizes the current debate about the disruptions to employment caused by new technologies. In cities from New York to London to Tokyo, hundreds of thousands of regulated taxi-cab drivers with expectations of secure work and pay are threatened by new private-hire drivers working for Uber in what is dubbed the 'gig economy'. Yet Uber also has plans to reduce the number of jobs through the development of driverless vehicles. Uber points to the flexibility it provides drivers who want to work in their own time, but is castigated for exploiting them through low wages and lack of employment protection, and this has led to it being banned in some cities. The case again reveals what history teaches us: innovation is a process that continually creates and destroys at the same time.

Although turbulence at work has always been a feature of industrial history, present circumstances are particularly volatile. The combined effects of technological innovation, the need to compete in global markets by improving efficiency and the pace of change where entrepreneurs can build multi-billion dollar businesses in a few years with a handful of employees have never been experienced in quite this manner before. In their book *Team of Teams*, General Stanley McChrystal and his colleagues introduce the military acronym VUCA (volatility, uncertainty, complexity and ambiguity), arguing that these unsettling conditions affect many contemporary workplaces.[38] All these disruptions have profound consequences for work, and the story of one modern woman's experiences illustrates its pressures and anxieties.

Emily's story

Emily is a manager in a large consultancy company. Her mornings start early, and she hasn't slept well because she's been fretting about work, and particularly about the attitude her client took at their previous meeting: 'It isn't a criticism, but we wondered whether you are still as committed to our project as you once were.' She felt like telling them about all the fourteen-hour days and weekends she's put in over the past four months, and then reminding them that they are only one of her clients. What she really wanted to do was to tell them they are spineless and stupid, and she's fed up with them changing their minds every day and sickened by their preoccupation with looking good to their corporate office rather than doing the right thing and pushing back on some of its idiotic instructions.

Emily drops by the office before her first client meeting. Simon, her direct boss, isn't in yet. He's been avoiding her in any case, and hasn't answered her last three emails. There is a meeting in the diary later in the day though. Emily is anxious about how to address the issue of her bonus, since she raised the vast majority of money for her department last year, and is managing most of the projects. Yet, mysteriously, her bonus is minimal while Simon's is rumoured to be very generous. She gets the distinct feeling, shared by her female colleagues, that despite the company's lofty rhetoric about equality, women get a bad deal.

In spite of her seniority, Emily has no allocated workspace and enthusiastic young interns and recent hires have already taken all the hot desks. Don't they ever sleep? Not that they could sleep in the narrow and uncomfortable spaces available: more like places for battery hens, she's often thought. She checks her diary; another three meetings have been inserted since she looked at her schedule at 6 a.m. Two, in her opinion, are completely unnecessary and one means her presence is demanded in two different places at the same time – nothing new there. She bumps into Derek, her people manager, in the corridor who says that Bob, the head of department, has been talking to him about her annual review and perhaps they should all have a nice chat. How pleasant it would be, she thinks, if just for once, Derek's behaviour towards her were supportive, rather than passive-aggressive!

It's not only people who are letting her down. Her computer has been playing up for weeks and IT Support, when they finally got round to looking at it, seem to have made the problem worse. She finds the documents she sent out to her staff last night are stuck in her outbox.

She wishes she'd had more time to think about today's client presentation. Her client is the central IT services group for a number of diverse businesses and her job is to get substantial reductions in their IT costs by the end of the financial year, along with significant increases in performance. Emily has done this before in other jobs, but knows that during the meeting it will dawn on the general managers of the businesses that some will suffer drastic cuts. She dreads the reaction of the 'losers', knowing her client will pass the blame onto her, while taking all the credit with the 'winners'.

Walking into the meeting she looks down and finds she's laddered her tights and then learns the overhead projector isn't working. She's printed out copies of her presentation and circulates them; two men snatch them with the attitude that this is evidence of her incompetence (it isn't her office or projector!). If this were a one-off, she'd put it down to bad manners, but it's not; this whole project seems to be run on intimidation rather than argument and evidence.

The situation is complex because several of the businesses are already, or are prospective, clients of her employer; she has been reminded on several occasions by the vendor of the new equipment and software needed for the project that it is also a major client of her firm. So all parties in the meeting will in some sense be clients, and they all have contradictory demands and will be pulling Emily in different directions. On top of this Emily knows that the package being so actively promoted by central IT and the vendor of the software and equipment will cause problems going forward, and she feels awkward knowing that sorting it out will mean another contract for her company. Great for profits, but it makes her feel uncomfortable. There will be job losses in the short term, but the client will recognize it can't do without many of these people further down the line. It is all so wasteful and avoidable.

The meeting becomes unpleasant: even the 'winners' are complaining about the time it will take them to get new equipment and software up and running, and demanding more staff to make it happen. The 'losers' are beside themselves, facing substantial job losses and diminished responsibility. As Emily expected, her client fields the easy questions and passes the vexatious ones onto her, and she keeps trying to bring the discussion back to the reasons for the investment and rationalization, with so much unnecessary duplication in their various systems and so many opportunities in the future. She explains why the decisions were made, using all the evidence her team has carefully prepared, but people are angry, and evidence counts for little. She's getting flushed, and she angrily reflects that Simon, who took so much credit when she won this contract, has not attended any of these types of meeting.

Somehow she manages to get through the morning, but only by promising to return to yet another meeting with even more data supporting her case – data, she reflects, that will be hidden or subverted as soon as the 'losers' get back to their offices. Returning to the office she finds that Simon has cancelled their meeting, and can't be contacted to rearrange it. Two of her favourite colleagues tell her they are leaving. One is going to work for a competitor; the other has a long-term stress-related sick note. They are both key members of her team, and she worries about how to replace them and how she's ever going to collect more data to back up her case for the client. Since the recent round of cuts, there simply aren't enough people to draw on. She bumps into Vikram, head of finance, who unsmilingly says he wants to talk to her about last quarter's figures. Dammit, there's no one left in this organization she *likes* any more!

Late afternoon Emily makes it to her annual health check, one of the benefits of working for her company. Blood pressure high, cholesterol worrying: the doctor says she needs to reduce stress, sleep more, drink less and take a holiday. If only, she thinks ...

Sitting in the waiting room, the first time she's sat still all day, she considers how much she regrets having no time to think any more. There's never a moment to work through issues, to consider things from different angles, to ponder consequences. She can't remember the last time she had time to talk with colleagues whose work she relies upon. She knows that better decisions could be made and mistakes could be avoided, if only she wasn't so rushed and pressured.

There are two children playing in the doctor's reception, and she smiles at them, thinking of her own children. How different their behaviour is from what is expected of her at work. They are so uninhibited and in touch with their essential humanity. They are restlessly curious and energetic, chasing each other, falling down, picking themselves up, dusting themselves off, crying unashamedly when they're hurt, laughing uncontrollably when they're happy. Meeting other children is always an opportunity to have some fun.

How have things come to this? Emily's always been a glass-half-full person, looking for the best in circumstances and people. She was so excited to get this job. It had responsibility, was well paid and gave her status with her family and friends. She could use all her IT and project management skills, and relished opportunities to work through problems with others and shape answers that satisfied them all. She was proud of her ability to communicate with people from all walks of life and to get things done. Nowadays, Emily feels her job is nothing but drudgery, and when miraculously her projects are implemented, her contributions are never recognized or appreciated. Her early hopes of promotion – who knows, even to become a partner in the company – seem unlikely. All the enjoyment and optimism of her early years has disappeared.

She makes it back to the office where she sees Nigel, her department's accountant, in reception and he says in front of everyone he has a question about her last expenses claim, and can she come and see him. Why did he need to do that? Why this continual hostility? Could it be the stress he's under, knowing the pressures to deliver on the company's totally unrealistic profit projections? More likely a reflection of Bob's bullying leadership style. There's nothing Bob likes more, it seems, than humiliating people, preferably in front of his acolytes like Nigel and Simon. In a company that so publicly promotes its commitment to diversity, and invests so much in management training, there are an awful lot of Bobs at the top.

Last week Emily got a phone call from Amy, a well-known headhunter, and agreed to meet her for dinner. She was perplexed about why Amy contacted her. Had she heard anything? Was it widely known that she was dissatisfied with her job? Had someone told her she was going to be fired?

Emily arrives late for the dinner and, apologizing profusely, she notices Bob glaring at them from a nearby table. She has known Amy for years, but isn't too impressed with her commenting on how tired she looks. Amy explains that a job that has come up: it seems made for her, a smaller consulting organization, the same sort of work but a very prestigious leadership role. It would use all her skills, is closer to home and fewer hours. Emily is attracted to the idea. She'd have a lot more autonomy and freedom while doing the same sort of job. Then she learns about the salary – a considerable pay cut. She quickly calculates mortgage repayments, and the loan on the car. Can't be done: she's the main family breadwinner and the sums don't add up. Waving weakly to Bob, who looks at her thunderously, she trudges off home.

Before collapsing into bed Emily checks her email. There are dozens to process. One from the client jumps out. There was a lot of dissatisfaction about today's meeting that has got back to head office. A meeting has been arranged to discuss events at headquarters, some 50 miles away, for 8 a.m. tomorrow. There is no message from Simon.

Emily's story, or parts of it at least, will ring true for many people.[39] The challenges and disappointments of work, its pace, complexity and uncertainty will seem familiar to those in a wide range of jobs and in all stages of their careers. But things do not need to be like this. The message of this book is that while things look bleak for Emily at the moment, there are alternatives: the work she does can be energizing, fulfilling and fun. The stories of a wide range of innovators and entrepreneurs told in this book provide insights about working lives such as hers, and how work can become better and more rewarding. They show she has choices in what she does and how she does it, and by relating to the behaviours of playful innovators and entrepreneurs she can put herself in a much better position to thrive in the modern world of work.

2

Play

Action, activity, operation, working; often implying the ideas of rapid change, variety.

Freedom or room for movement; the space in or through which anything can or does move.

In contrast to Emily's experiences, and to illustrate the character and virtues of a playful life, we will now tell the stories of two playful people, beginning with a truly exceptional woman, who to our minds is quintessentially noble.

Steve Shirley

Among the hustle and bustle of Liverpool Street, one of London's busiest railway stations, it is always rewarding to spend some time looking at its bronze statue of five children. The children carry small suitcases; one holds a violin case, another a teddy bear. They look contented, even determined, yet the numbered labels on their clothes reveals a story of amazing fortitude in the most appalling of circumstances. The statue is one of four sculptures created by Frank Meisler – the others being in Gdansk, Berlin and the Hook of Holland – placed along the route of the Kindertransport, the extraordinary exodus of 10,000 mainly Jewish unaccompanied children sent overseas by their parents to escape Nazi persecution. Steve Shirley's earliest memory of England was arriving at Liverpool Street station in 1939. She had her label and a little yellow star sewn on her coat, spoke no English and was five years old.

In the autobiography telling the story of her extraordinary life as an entrepreneur and philanthropist, Steve says that after this start it took her several years to appreciate the effort so many people had put into saving her life. Once she had, 'a simple resolution took root deep in my heart: I had to make sure that mine was a life worth saving'. She explains that being a survivor of the Nazi Holocaust left her with very strong values, learning early on 'never to expect tomorrow to be the same as today', and says 'that has served in making me, I believe, more open to new ways of doing things'.

Her working life began in a relatively menial job in the technologically world-leading Post Office Research Centre. With an interest and natural ability in mathematics, she gradually accumulated qualifications at night school, gained incremental promotions and was exposed to powerfully entrenched sexism. Women's pay was lower and their aspirations were an affront to the male-dominated workplace: women simply were not expected to be promoted. Steve learned a lot at the time. She had the opportunity to work with Tommy Flowers, one of the great figures in the history of computing, who taught her the value of gathering suggestions from teams. At this time she also, in her own words, 'learnt – mainly by trial and error – how to use information, how to prioritise, how to manage money, how to impose structure, how to manage time; and, not least, how to get on with colleagues'.

Steve moved into the private sector, an exciting and enjoyable period of using her mathematic skills working with computers, but after a while, dismayed at the continuing obstacles to her progressive ideas, she decided, aged twenty-nine, to create a software company. It is hard to appreciate the extent of the ambition involved: Steve had no experience of running a company, no customers, no money (actually £6: the initial start-up investment), no staff and, in 1962, very few companies understood the importance of software or the principle of paying for it. The company's name was 'freelance programmers', self-mockingly kept in lower case as the company had no capital. With classic entrepreneurial motivation, she said: 'I ... had a gut feeling that there was a programming industry of some kind waiting to be born, and I liked the idea of being in at its birth.' She said she wasn't seeking wealth, but 'a workplace where I was not hemmed in by prejudice or by other people's preconceived notions of what I could and could not do'. She also came up with the extraordinary idea that she would only employ freelancers working from home, and they would all be women. Steve has described her experiences of hitting the glass ceiling and being aware of the number of talented and skilled women who left work to have children and their difficulties in going back, so she embarked on a campaign to create a company of women for women. As an indication of the difficulties women faced at this time, opening a bank account required a husband's written permission. Getting no response to her marketing efforts under her original name of Stephanie Shirley, she changed her signature to Steve and business picked up; ever since, she has been known as Steve.

The ambition behind the creation of the company was 'to be part of some kind of high-powered creative commune, full of free, kindred spirits, held together not by rules and conventions but by our shared joy in what we did'. More and more highly skilled women programmers joined the company, and the list of customers grew: Tate and Lyle; Mars; British Rail; Rolls Royce; GEC. Steve kept all these customers happy, learning the skills of cash flow and quality control as she went along while all the time caring for her newborn baby. Mistakes were made and learned from: a contract with Castrol went very wrong due to a programming error and cost a fortune to rectify. After this experience, better project and cost controls were put in place. Steve worked very long hours, often writing business proposals deep into the night. Her home was her workplace: the photocopier was in the bathroom and she spent winters stoking up coal fires. Her approach was that if something worked, they'd do more of it and if it didn't, they'd try something else. There were post-mortems after each project to see what could be learned, and it was totally acceptable to ask for help, to offer help and to exchange skills.

Concerned at one stage about the growing administrative load on her shoulders, she considered selling the business until the purchaser questioned the need to have a crèche at the work-place. She refused to have decisions she knew to be right being overturned.

Her company offered profit sharing early in its history, and allowed job sharing. It grew and thrived, mainly through dedicated hard work and cripplingly long hours, conducted during the heartache of discovering her son was severely autistic and the exhaustion of coping with his condition. Then the recession of the early 1970s hit, and work dried up. Worse, a key employee left to start up a competing company using the same business model, addressing the same clients with many of the same workforce. Steve showed extraordinary tenacity to get through this dreadful period for the company and considerable grace in allowing a highly prized employee who had joined her competitor to re-join her firm. Efforts to internationalize the company – now called FI (Flexible Information) Group – had mixed success. The unusual employment contracts attracted undue and time-consuming attention from the tax and employment departments. The introduction of Equal Rights legislation meant the company could not continue its women-only employment policy, and over time the company moved from home working to work centres with flexi-time and flexibility in choice of where to work; offices were located near motorway junctions, making them easy to get to.

In her autobiography, Steve speaks frankly about the appalling stresses of having an autistic child, capable of considerable disruption and violence, compounded by the difficulties of running a complex business in challenging circumstances. Exhausted and totally dispirited, she considered suicide and eventually had a nervous breakdown. Her recovery involved recognition that she was not indestructible or indeed indispensable, and as she recuperated the company did well under the Group managing director Steve had previously appointed. Her return to work was marked by a burning anger that her breakdown was attributed to her being a woman, rather than a combination of relentless and intolerable strain, and a growing realization about where her particular skills lay.

She networked assiduously with the great and the good, sitting on numerous committees and advisory boards, building valuable connections and insights for the business. At this time, much of her thinking was devoted to shifting ownership of her company to its employees because she rationalized that the company was based on trust: trust that the workforce would do a thorough and professional job. Employees had worked under the system where they only got paid when the company was paid, not when their work was completed, so had to trust FI. Such mutual trust had been rewarded by the success of the company, and Steve's next project was to repay that commitment by tackling the administrative difficulties inherent in making the company employee-owned. Over time she progressively transferred her shares to a fund owned by the workforce, so that by November 1991, management, employees and sub-contractors (known as associates) owned 42 per cent of the company's shares. Through the system of double voting, the total workforce was given final say over decisions about FI's future. Nearly three-quarters of employees purchased shares, and in the process she says the company emerged from a cooperative culture to a co-ownership organization, and the future of the company, its focus, its successes, failures and challenges, became more deeply shared.

Steve explains the reasons why trust is so important in business:

All the business about doing better can only be achieved through people. You can throw in money and tools, but it is basically people who must be given the freedom to apply their professional skills and business acumen in a way that keeps the business a step ahead of the competition ...

Effective utilization of discretion – in essence, individuals inducing that better performance from themselves – requires a high level of trust and confidence in others.[1]

She also got the board's agreement that 1 per cent of the company's pre-tax profits should be donated to charity.

The company went from strength to strength, but problems and failures arose in international operations and when a trusted managing director became very ill and had to retire, tensions arose with her successor. The problems took time and considerable emotional energy to resolve, leading to the MD's eventual resignation. Steve confesses that she felt uncomfortable with someone else running her company. Now named F International, the company embarked on a lengthy process of writing its mission statement and articulating its values. Steve acknowledges that she was reconciled to letting go of her company managerially and financially, but she could not bear to let go of its values.

Steve gradually disengaged from the company she created, an often emotionally painful process as she dealt with what she felt was rejection. She admits that surrendering power was her biggest challenge. But while ceding control of an enterprise that really matters to you is painful, she writes, 'the art of surrender is the key to many kinds of success'. Her powerful successor as leader of the company, now renamed Xansa, rapidly built it through acquisitions and by taking advantage of the huge growth experienced in the IT industry. The company's workforce grew to 6,000. It was floated on the Stock Exchange and its stock price rose and rose, leaving Steve with a paper share value of £140 million, making her one of Britain's richest women. Because of the shares she had given to employees, seventy of them became millionaires, and many others did very well financially.

Yet she recognizes the limits of her skills, especially in her financial know-how. 'My talent is for being an entrepreneur . . . I love thinking of new ideas, questioning first principles, sensing new opportunities, starting things, changing things, recruiting new teams, attacking new challenges. That kind of work, for me, is indistinguishable from pleasure.' In line with the philosophy of the company, she also claims: 'If I have a talent it is ... the ability to believe in what others can achieve.' Asked about the best advice she could give someone in business, she says 'take a risk more often'.

Motivated to share her knowledge, Steve continued to sit on numerous committees, and has received many recognitions and awards: for example, becoming president of the British Computer Society. In 2000 she was made a Dame of the British Empire. Appalled at the treatment her son had received, Steve also established a charity that houses and cares for autistic children, including her son until his death aged thirty-five, but her ambitions were much larger. She created the Shirley Foundation to give away her wealth; the sums she donated included £5 million to the Worshipful Company of Information Technologists, and £30 million into a new kind of specialist school for children with autism, to which she also donated significant works of art in belief of their stimulating qualities. Assured of the need for society to better understand the implications of technology, she funded the University of Oxford Internet Institute.

The company Steve founded gradually floundered in difficult commercial circumstances and was acquired by a French firm. The paper value of her wealth halved, but she persisted in her philanthropy, deciding to focus on autism. She has funded numerous research groups, and devotes her energy and wealth to finding a cure. She has given away £65 million, and her foundation has orders to spend the rest of her wealth within five years of her death. The title of her autobiography is *Let IT Go*.[2]

Steve's autobiography is remarkably frank about her personal life. She talks openly about the heartrending circumstances of her son's condition and the pain of his death, suicidal thoughts, marital difficulties and, going right back to her arrival in London, of her 'irrational survivor's guilt' and the sadness and depression it elicits. Her restless energy as a workaholic has helped her to overcome the challenges thrown at her. With no intention of retiring, she has thoughtfully applied her business skills to her philanthropy, saying it is much more than writing a cheque and should be undertaken strategically. Extolling the pleasures of giving, she feels giving her wealth away has been the most rewarding stage of her life: 'the money I have let go has brought me infinitely more joy than the money I have hung on to'.

When you meet Steve Shirley it is impossible to believe she is over eighty years old. She is elegant and courteous, with a ready smile and easy laugh. When she disagrees with you she has a way of pointing it out very politely, and her reasoning makes you seriously consider your position. Her energy is remarkable: she devotes hours to charitable work and public presentations promoting the causes of women and technology. She continues to show that hers was a life most certainly worth saving.

Steve Shirley shows the journey of the entrepreneur may not be smooth, with as many severe downs as ups. Yet, her story also reveals that when that journey is motivated by a passion – in her case to build and benefit from the 'shared joy' of trusting relationships, working together with others and giving back – it can be richly satisfying. She tells us about play and its supportive behaviours: issues that will be further developed in this book. She explains, for example, the importance of always being open to new ways of doing things, and being prepared to experiment. If the experiment worked her company would do more of it, and if it didn't they'd try something else. Steve continually refers to the value of trust in others, and how the cohesion this fosters not only produces sound economic returns but also creates a workplace energized by people with shared objectives. She shows the levels of tenacity, will power and sheer hard work necessary to succeed. With her motivation to live a worthwhile life, she created a work environment that, for much of the time, was enjoyable, fun and playful. She demonstrates that work and pleasure can be indistinguishable and how it is possible to make a positive contribution to her profession and the society of which she is a part.

Personal motivation to make a serious, positive social contribution whilst also finding enjoyment in work is an attribute found in many young entrepreneurs, just starting out in their careers. Since the mid-2000s there has been a growing interest in 'social entrepreneurship': forming enterprises that provide enriching, satisfying and profitable work, with a passion for delivering wider value in communities and across society. Rajeeb Dey provides a good example of someone motivated by these values.

Rajeeb Dey

Rajeeb Dey is a young entrepreneur who has already accumulated many accolades. He has won entrepreneurship awards and been named a Young Global Leader by the World Economic Forum. He was awarded an MBE (Member of the Order of the British Empire) in 2016 for services to entrepreneurship.

Rajeeb has a steady gaze and engaging style, and listens intently and courteously to those with whom he is conversing. His father and sister are both doctors, and he attributes a great deal of his self-confidence to his parents, who, he says, are very supportive even though they don't really understand what he does.

His career as an entrepreneur began, without him realizing, when he was seventeen. He became aware of an Irish national school organization, and was conscious of the way pupils in Britain had no equivalent. He formed the English Secondary Students' Association to give students a voice. Not even eighteen years of age, he was speaking to the Minister for Schools and at political party conferences.

The young entrepreneur's personal journey began at school when he received a £5,000 grant from UnLtd – an association of some 10,000 social entrepreneurs – to 'begin to make things happen'. He didn't have a plan, and he says he was playing with the way he tried things. He made mistakes, but was motivated to make a difference and passionate about giving people opportunities. As a student at the University of Oxford he became involved with Oxford Entrepreneurs, a group which encourages entrepreneurship among the student body and runs training and networking events. It is one of Europe's largest networks of student entrepreneurs and Rajeeb became its president.

Rajeeb graduated in 2008 with First Class Honours in Economics and Management at the height of the economic crisis. He'd had internships at the Bank of England and Boston Consulting Group (BCG), and was offered jobs at both, but wanted independence. BCG even offered to defer his employment for a couple of years. Instead, Rajeeb decided to do something his friends thought was 'stupid': he started his own company.

Realizing that while large companies had processes in place to attract interns, small companies and entrepreneurs didn't have any brand that would attract students. Rajeeb founded Enternships.com in 2009. It began as a simple listing site, and it took two years of trial and error to learn what to do. The business became a formalized portal connecting students and graduates to paid work placements in entrepreneurial start-ups and small firms, and by 2016 Enternships.com had worked with 6,500 companies. Rajeeb says the company's intent is to expose graduates to start-up workplaces to help develop their entrepreneurial skills and flair, and expose them to these companies' challenges and excitement. It gives young companies an opportunity to 'look before they buy', and in many cases the 'enterns' become indispensable, creating their own jobs. He says his aim is to encourage entrepreneurship as a career path. As well as his direct business interests, Rajeeb supports entrepreneurship as an advisor on a number of public bodies, such as being a founder of StartUp Britain, described as a campaign by entrepreneurs for entrepreneurs, and which uses a bus to travel around the country offering free advice.

The image of entrepreneurs is changing, according to Rajeeb. Young entrepreneurs are not interested in making money at any cost, but in balancing it with social good. He refers to the author Daniel Pink's view on GenY and Millennials and how they seek opportunity and purpose, and Rajeeb says that these age groups possess an innate and broad entrepreneurialism. He encourages young entrepreneurs to put their 'heart and soul' into their ideas; while many ideas won't make it, and there is always an element of luck, you need to try with conviction because you never know what will happen and what exciting opportunities might unfold. Everyone should have the chance to pursue an entrepreneurial path, he argues, and this means letting go of the overly structured approach to thinking about careers and being risk averse, worrying about everything that can go wrong. Pursue this path, he contends, and you have freedom and autonomy to do your own thing and make a difference: to take a vision and make it a reality.

He doesn't sign up to the school of thought that you must trample over people in order to succeed. Like us, he is uncomfortable with the aggressive, combative style of business portrayed in the television show *Dragons' Den*, where people seeking investments for their businesses make pitches to sceptical investors. While making good TV, he says, it is not a true and fair representation of being an entrepreneur. The technology start-up world, he argues, is far more collaborative and open than many businesses of the past, as can be seen, for example, in their use of open mailing lists. Business is not a zero-sum game: 'if you can help someone why wouldn't you?' He says a genuine generosity of spirit with no expectation of returns usually pays off. Good things normally come back full circle, so giving people opportunities through your connections brings opportunities back to you. 'If you try and be a nice person, people will want to help you.' As Rousseau told Emile: 'love others and they will love you; serve them and they will serve you'.

There have been challenges along the way. In 2011 Rajeeb had to buy out shareholders who had a large chunk of the company's equity – 'my sweat capital'. Being grown-up about it wasn't as difficult as he thought it would be, but he has to balance the way that in the 'talent business' it is easy to be led by the heart rather than the head. He's driven by the desire to help people find their passion, but along the way he has had to take hard decisions that have required fortitude in changing the company's direction and have involved considerable upheaval. One of the characteristics of the entrepreneur, he says, is being comfortable with uncertainty.

He talks excitedly about a new service he launched in the summer of 2016, Learnerbly, an online learning platform connecting communities to improve the ways people shape and extend their own learning journeys throughout their employment. Companies have their own training and induction processes, but in Rajeeb's opinion they tend to reflect old corporate thinking that doesn't teach you how to do new things. He explains the principles behind his new business. Small firms usually don't know how to 'do' learning. By building peer-to-peer learning people can gain lessons of direct relevance to themselves, unfiltered by human resources and training departments. You tag what people are interested in, therefore providing learning sources. It is an open-source approach to learning and recruitment, and insights will show whether you are in the right job or not and what you need to learn to succeed. The idea is to create the obverse of LinkedIn: it is not who you know, but what you know that matters. Rajeeb relates how product development is a continuing process, and its name has already changed three times. There is a process of continual reflection on how the company itself learns. This experimentation and focus on learning are key elements of playfulness.

For Rajeeb, ambition is limited by imagination. Fear of failure often holds people back, but Rajeeb wouldn't have regrets even if his company failed tomorrow. He would be content, as he has helped people get to where they want to be. Unembarrassed, he says: 'you need love and happiness in what you do'.

Although they come from very different generations, and the circumstances in which they have worked are poles apart, Steve Shirley and Rajeeb Dey both show how to confront uncertainty and what it is to be playful in the sense of combining hard work, social responsibility and care and commitment to others. Steve and Rajeeb have a passion for innovation: for doing new things and managing their associated risks. Both decided to pursue their personal objectives outside the constraints of working in (impressive) large organizations. They have an experimental approach to new initiatives, being open to new ideas and directions provided these comply with their strong motivation to work with others in efforts that are socially beneficial. Both entrepreneurs are respectful, open and speak enthusiastically about their beliefs. Their work has been a central element of their lives and it has focused on expressing their freedom; despite all the challenges that have confronted them, there is no doubt they go to work each day with a spring in their step and a twinkle in their eye. They have behaviours from which everyone can learn.

Playful businesses

Businesses and organizations as well as individuals can be playful, and this is explained in large part by the way the circumstances in which they operate are unpredictable and uncertain, and their need to be flexible and responsive to change and opportunity. The Danish company Lego has created a business separate from its toy company that trains people to think innovatively by playing with its plastic bricks. The US author Michael Schrage wrote a book called *Serious Play* that shows the value for business of simulating and prototyping ideas to make their application better, quicker and cheaper. We always enjoy our regular conversations with Michael, an innovative thinker associated with MIT's Media Lab. His most recent book, *The Innovator's Hypothesis*, highlights the importance of cheap experiments and develops what he calls the 5x5 framework: giving diverse teams of 5 people up to 5 days to come up with portfolios of 5 business experiments costing no more than $5,000 each and taking no longer than 5 weeks to run.[3] Experiments are a form of play. Roman Krznaric suggests that we should experiment with our careers: 'there is compelling evidence that we are much more likely to find fulfilling work by conducting career experiments in the real world'. When it comes to choosing our careers, he says we must enter a more playful and experimental way of being, where we *do then think*, not *think then do*.[4]

Even the largest companies play. Some are easy to imagine being playful. Google's Project Loon is both highly playful and very serious. It aims to provide internet access to all, including across remote regions of the world, by using a network of balloons in the stratosphere connecting wireless internet services. IBM, on the other hand, has a more formal reputation, yet during one of our studies of the company we came across an occasion where a female staff member insisted in turning up to meetings as a rabbit. A male colleague, bearded and middle-aged, appeared in similar meetings as a young woman, glamorous and statuesque. These people were experimenting with avatars in virtual world technology in a company driven by profit and efficiency but also prepared to be playful. Playfulness at IBM encouraged ideas to bubble up from below and created methods for supporting them from the top.[5] Walter Isaacson says of Steve Jobs in his career at Apple that he was 'passionate and super-serious about design, but at the same time there's a sense of play'. Where there are rules of behaviour, for example in ensuring respectfulness, work can be playful even in the most serious of modern companies. As well as providing a more stimulating place to work, such play also inoculates the organization from external changes and shocks by immersing it in experiments that test the future. Many organizations see the encouragement of play as a means of making work more attractive, improving the engagement and commitment of existing staff, and a winning strategy in the 'war for talent' among skilled and mobile employees.

This is certainly the case with IDEO, a company that is playful to its core. IDEO, headquartered in Palo Alto and with offices around the globe, is one of the world's most highly regarded design companies. It shows us how to play by encouraging freedom and fun.

IDEO

The Tuesday staff meeting begins with a Latin American dance class. Afterwards some people sit around tables, some stand, others recline on a tiered arena of steps leading up to the ceiling; nice food is provided, the day is sometimes called Souper Tuesday. Pet dogs are patted as people listen to the colourful presentations; one person tells of her wedding planning; another explains a new approach to a client project; another describes what he's learned from visiting local robotics companies. Everyone is invited to attend and contribute; the emphasis is on intimacy and sharing. We are in IDEO, the iconic design company.

The company has gone through a major transition, with a turnover of staff and many new employees joining. IDEO is keen to maintain the playful culture that has served it so well in the past and its refurbished building is designed to help. Upon entering IDEO's offices in Palo Alto one of the first things you see is a large glass box full of advanced 3D printing machines. But above this statement of serious technological intent is a gigantic white plastic flower whose sensors open and close it in response to motion throughout the day, with changing coloured lighting. Around the case of the box are small, high fidelity 3D printed models of all the staff in the company. There's David Kelley, IDEO's founder, with his distinctive moustache. There's Dave Webster, erstwhile leader of IDEO Palo Alto and resident Scotsman, in his kilt and *Braveheart* pose.

To the left is a magnificent coffee machine, with no shortage of people keen to display their barista skills. Following the path down to the left, past displays of earlier design projects – a school chair, better approaches to spinal surgery, a new ATM, the Faraday electric bike – leads to an open area with an abundance of always available tempting food. Turn to the right and you hit a burst of project team activity. Groups work in hives of visual stimuli: cascades of colourful Post-it notes, a wooden replica van, vast posters curating ideas on client needs. Between buildings there's a tree house and a classic Airstream aluminium caravan available to be towed to clients for meetings at their sites. There are quiet spaces to reflect and write, and a bar for central IT support. The office is open plan and group working is the norm, but many wear noise-cancelling headphones when working alone.

IDEO's ability to innovate has been celebrated in numerous books, articles and television programmes, but to illustrate its fun culture there is the case of the Sand Hill Challenge, as told to us by Dave Webster. In past years Silicon Valley had a go-cart race down the lengthy and steep Sand Hill Road. Hyper-competitive venture capitalists contested enthusiastically, drawing on their connections with Lockheed and NASA to design the fastest, most aerodynamic cart. IDEO decided to enter and, after a great deal of testing and prototyping, designed an arrow-shaped cart. The driver was a petite Asian woman, and the cart was designed around her to minimize the width of the vehicle. The race allows the cart to be pushed for the first 50 feet. IDEO used two pro football line-backers to give their go-cart the start. IDEO won the race.

The next year IDEO entered again, and the competition consisted of a series of replica arrow-shaped carts. IDEO, however, entered a wide vehicle, relatively high off the ground, and its advantage lay in the design of particular tyres and wheels that had minimal contact with the road. To improve the push at the start, IDEO recruited the US bobsleigh team. IDEO won the race.

By the third year, IDEO staff became less enamoured of the excessive competitiveness of the event and entered three welded-together Honda off-road motorbikes topped by a large Chinese dragon. It was especially slow and not particularly safe, and having made its point about the danger of taking things too seriously IDEO never entered again. There's little incentive to play when the fun diminishes.

This example emphasizes the importance of prototyping ideas in IDEO. As Tom Kelley, brother of Dave and previous general manager of the company, says in his book *The Art of Innovation*, success came from quick prototyping, and from play and adventure imitating work. As he puts it, childlike curiosity and enthusiasm is second nature at IDEO, and 'a playful, itera-tive approach to problems is one of the foundations of our culture of prototyping'.[6]

There is continual effort to foster the playful culture at IDEO. Katie Gorman is an 'experience specialist', whose job is to help people feel happy. She organizes events for IDEO staff and for clients. She provides imaginative gifts for birthdays, births, long service or recognition for exceptionally demanding periods at work. Recent events include a fitness class called sexitude, where participants in spandex and wigs have to assume poses that are intended with various degrees of success to be sexy or display attitude. Recent parties have been themed around outer space, along with fortune-telling aliens, and surrealism, where local academics visited beforehand to provide some art history context. There's been a Hawaiian day, with shirts and music, and the company's works built a device for roasting a pig. A superhero meeting had presenters in masks and capes: Captain America was a big hit. Gorman really likes that once a week, one project group starts the day with a very loud thirty-second blast of music which has them all up and boogying. Serious meetings are also arranged, for example, for local thought leaders influential in the health sector. Her job includes encouraging quiet people to contribute to meetings and moderating the overly enthusiastic.

IDEO's organization is fluid and evolving, so its strategy is sometimes difficult for outsiders to grasp. Even allowing for California-speak, when one of its leaders refers to 'setting up delicious tensions and paradoxes that need continual resolution and reinventing ourselves every day', it requires some disentanglement. Essentially, IDEO's work processes emerge and develop with different clients. The chairman and CEO have identifiable offices, but are often seen working in the open spaces. Visitors regularly use their offices. An informal approach is encouraged: an elite athlete takes time off during the day to train, people walk across the road to the gym during working hours. As Dave Webster puts it: 'we want to create a sustainable lifestyle. If you want to work killing hours, go and work for a start-up.' Paul Bennett, in his piece on 'a loosely designed organization' in *The Little Book of IDEO*, describes IDEO's work spaces as 'warm, embracing, fun, human, serious, businesslike and playful', while David Kelley in the same publication says: 'What we do is a way of life, not really a job, and it feels good.'[7]

Organization, it is admitted in the *Little Book*, 'does not come easily to us'.

The views of some of the younger designers on working there are illuminating. A number of features about them jump out. They are smart, and have very diverse backgrounds: an installation artist with a degree in classics and chemistry; people with PhDs in behavioural economics and synthetic biology; an English major. They are not well paid by Silicon Valley standards; one mentioned he'd been offered a salary four-and-a-half times larger elsewhere. They refer to the attractions and compensations of working at IDEO and the importance of the quality of the work they do.

One talks of the special, inspiring people he works with, the creative people who actually make things. He says he has incredible access to senior people in client companies, meeting their CEOs and boards and getting to understand their systems. He has immense freedom and autonomy in selecting his projects and choosing the people he wants to work with. Another employee talks of the attraction of the selflessness of the place and he likes the emphasis on improving the design processes of clients so they improve at making better products, experiences and systems. Design studios, he argues, are usually strictly organized around projects or around charismatic leaders, but IDEO is different and 'radical free thinkers' work productively with 'doers' in a very organic sense. Both these designers have opportunities to teach at nearby Stanford University. One spends his Fridays working with local start-ups, helping them bring design into their plans. The other spends one day a week talking with a biologist, helping to develop common understanding and language. One says the company needs more systematic career management, the other says he thrives in its ambiguity.

One of the designers helps clients create business models and has devised a game-like system of colourful tiles that can be attached to white boards. These tiles are designed to represent the company's ecosystem for creating, delivering and capturing value; they are put up to represent all the company's key stakeholders, assets and channels, and how money and products flow between them. It is very simple, but the ability to visualize the ecosystem is powerful in understanding how the business makes money.

IDEO enjoys close connections with Stanford University. Its founder David Kelley was and remains a professor in the Engineering School. While IDEO has links with both Stanford's engineering and business schools, its key touch point is with its Institute of Design, the d.school, which David helped to establish and which provides much of the focus of creative design work at the university. According to David, Stanford wants to make 'design' a key skill for all its students so they are better able to cope with unpredictability. The two-way flow of ideas between the company and the university is encouraged in a number of ways. IDEO staff regularly teach courses, some staff have taken time off to study Stanford's MBA and at any one time there are a couple of surgical registrars based at IDEO improving their design skills. The enthusiasm of IDEO staff in searching out cutting-edge new ideas is seen in the celebration of staff as great 'technology sniffers'.

As an indicator of a company at the cutting edge of play, IDEO runs a Toy Lab, led by the toy designer Brendan Boyle. It is a different sort of business to the rest of IDEO: it designs toys and then sells them to toy companies for royalties. Ten people work in the Toy Lab, surrounded by toys of all descriptions and banks of containers with thousands of parts such as motors, springs and clips. There are great vats of foam rockets and in the corner three people are taking turns to jump on what looks like a mini-skateboard to see if it breaks. Boyle says the Toy Lab is very good at making things; it has great spaces for design, all sorts of machine tools, and a photo studio, all used for early prototyping of ideas. When they are between projects, IDEO designers may come and work in the Toy Lab for a while, and the Lab is often visited by IDEO clients to see tangible results from the company's design strengths.

Much of the Lab's activities focus on digital toys, and it designed the most popular app for children under five, using

Sesame Street's Elmo to call and remind them to do things, such as clean their teeth. Around 250 million calls have been made using this app. Boyle is also a great advocate of physical toys, especially those that help children build tangible things. He says physical, manipulative play that develops spatial dexterity is crucially important for development. Rousseau had plans to employ Emile in a workshop, where 'his hands work for the development of his mind'.

Brendan Boyle is a wholehearted advocate for play. He is on the board of the National Institute for Play and is Consulting Professor in the Mechanical Engineering Department of Stanford University, where he teaches a course on play and innovation. Boyle's course is based on design thinking, with three stages: *inspiration*, where there's a lot of role-playing, *ideation*, with exploratory play and brainstorming, and *implementation*, with constructive play. Students from a wide range of degree programmes choose this option, working on projects for corporate partners. Brendan also runs an annual boot camp on design thinking for high school students. He says IDEO is a strong believer in craft; designers think with their hands as well as their brain, and manual tinkering with things is crucial in design. Using the analogy of 'I'-shaped and 'T'-shaped people, where the former is depth and knowledge and experience, and the latter is its breadth, he says craft is the 'I': the depth of what you can do and build.

Indicative of play for a purpose is understanding the markets you wish to address. Boyle says the mind of the child is fundamentally curious. People in the Lab spend a lot of time observing children and talking with parents. It is crucial to understand exactly what a three-year-old can do, and a three-and-a-half-year-old: six months means a lot at that age. If you are ten years old you have enough life experience to understand what is going on, but not yet enough awareness that some things cannot work.

As an aside, two Dutch academics, Roland and Rogier van Kralingen, argue that getting in the mind of a child is important not only for understanding how they play, but also because their values are becoming more important in work. They emphasize the importance at work of childlike values such as 'freedom, boundlessness, fantasy, innocence, authenticity, energy, creativity, cheerfulness, simplicity, transformation and magic'.[8]

Brendan encourages humour and a failsafe environment at work, remembering his first job in a major corporation where the main preoccupation was the size of your office. To get brilliant ideas, he says, you have to be comfortable with ridiculous ones. He co-authored a book with John Cassidy called the *Klutz Book of Inventions* which includes hundreds of wacky ideas, from scratch 'n' sniff menus to bug zapper earrings, a screen shaver that combines an iPhone and electric razor, and scratch-off parking tickets where you can take a chance on doubling the fine, being let off the fine or being paid the fine.[9]

His advice for getting more play into a stuffy organization: 'try experiments over in the corner somewhere, get a story to tell, and then propagate'.

IDEO epitomizes the playful organization. It has evolved to support players who have fun with their work and have wide degrees of freedom coupled with serious intent.

The workplace environment and playful culture found at IDEO has been much admired and sometimes imitated in other innovative organizations. As well as spending time at IDEO, we have also enjoyed visits to Airbnb in San Francisco, which starkly reminded us of how workplaces have changed during our lifetimes. During our careers we have visited a great many workplaces for our research, and indeed have worked in a wide variety of them ourselves. A typical office in the past would have masses of small, enclosed cubicles for clerical and secretarial staff, and offices for managers that grow in size – and proximity to windows – according to their seniority. Such workspaces might have the odd family photograph or the occasional pot plant to add individuality (although we know of one major company that banned photographs as the CEO believed they made desks look cluttered). In the past, large corporations often had different levels of catering, representing the hierarchical structure of their organizations: for example, silver service for senior managers, a restaurant for middle managers and professionals, and a canteen for shop-floor workers. It is hard to imagine a greater difference than between these traditional arrangements and Airbnb's playful offices. Airbnb, which was founded in 2008, has become the world's largest website for short-term rented lodgings. Although the company is not without controversy, for the ways in which it disrupts the existing accommodation industry and poses challenges for governments in tax collection and regulatory matters, it has been phenomenally successful.

You enter Airbnb's building, passing a large, pink truck selling sushi, through a massive atrium into which dangles a large cloud sculpture. On one side is the US's largest living wall, where plants are reconfigured in different patterns every day. The various floors of the building are hives of activity and each separate area seems to offer a different form of international cuisine and drink. A bar with nine beers on tap and six kinds of wine is open 24/7, and an ice cream cart cycles around tempting people away from their healthy Californian diets – all free, of course. At the start of the day, people arrive for breakfast – we enjoyed a fabulous choice of healthy and not so healthy fare. Staff bring their dogs to work and they have their own special play areas.

The emphasis is on meeting spaces. There are dozens of rooms that are direct replicas of actual spaces available to rent through Airbnb: Shanghai, Copenhagen, a tree house in Vermont and the original room which sparked the idea of renting available accommodation spaces in the sharing economy. Some have pull-down curtains for some privacy, and there's a large mushroom-shaped house and an Airstream caravan. There are images everywhere: the history of the company's progress on one long wall; its awards on another; replicas of the cornflake boxes printed with Barack Obama's face that the founders filled with $2 product and sold for $40, demonstrating their entrepreneurial flair to the company's initial investors.

Each of the 1,400 employees, whose average age according to one senior member of staff is in the mid-twenties, has shares in the company, from the most senior programmer to the cleaners. There's a large Apple Genius Bar where staff can take the computer given to them on their first day at work to be upgraded. The atmosphere is relaxed and enjoyable, but purposeful. Growth rates on the scale of Airbnb are impossible without serious intent.

IDEO and Airbnb are playful organizations, and we now turn to the reasons why they and other organizations play, beginning with the need to deal with the high levels of uncertainty surrounding them.

Play and uncertainty

When he was US Secretary of Defense, Donald Rumsfeld was castigated for his reference to 'unknown unknowns'. He was accused of abstract philosophising and nonsensical management-speak, but he was right and the phrase has entered our everyday language: the world in which we live is full of the unforeseeable and inconceivable. Unexpected things happen that can't be predicted by ascertaining the probability of their occurrence. The military saying that 'no plan survives the first contact with the enemy' has its counterpart in the observation of the boxer Mike Tyson that 'everyone has a plan till they get punched in the mouth'.

All of us are confronted by uncertainty at work. Unpredictability is a feature of modern life, in complex technical systems such as the internet, and biological systems such as the brain. Such complex systems, say in economies or the environment, evolve and adapt over time, and can be deeply affected by unforeseen events, such as financial crises or tsunamis. In 1977, the economist J.K. Galbraith wrote a book called *The Age of Uncertainty*, but the instability in economic and political systems he referred to at the time seem positively benign compared to present-day circumstances. Sociologist Zygmunt Bauman captures the extent of the uncertainty facing the world by referring to our 'liquid times' of capricious and untameable volatilities.[10] These circumstances bring great turbulence for organizations and work, placing a premium on awareness and adaptability, experimentation and learning.

Because the world is so changeable, it is a rare decision that can be made with absolute confidence, or plan that turns out completely as expected. Comedian Spike Milligan comforted us with the reassuring but unrealistic alternative that 'we haven't got a plan so nothing can go wrong'. The organizations creating and affected by new technologies are especially dynamic, surrounded by instability because of rapidly evolving market opportunities and threats. In business, for example, it is hard to predict where new competitors will emerge from. Billion-dollar companies are created from nothing in a few years, and long-established companies with worldwide presence disappear almost overnight. Who could have predicted that a major threat to the photographic film industry would come from companies selling telephones? Who would believe that an idea dreamt up in a Harvard dormitory for letting students connect with one another would lead to the creation of a company that within ten years would be worth more money than the Bank of America? The average tenure of a company in the Fortune 500 list has shrunk from forty to fifteen years, so it is harder to stay at the top. Bill Gates once said the greatest threat to the might of Microsoft was probably a couple of guys working in a Californian garage. In some senses he was right, and reflected his experience of where competitors, such as Apple, had emerged. But his words also reveal some of the unknown unknowns, as he failed to appreciate the unexpected threat from massive Korean companies such as Samsung or Chinese companies such as Huawei.

The speed of change in the economy and amount of churn at work have increased as intangible services rather than tangible goods have become a more important part of modern economies. Services – broadly, actions that were traditionally provided by one person for another – currently account for 70–80 per cent of economic activity in developed nations. The focus in services is on speed and idiosyncrasy, which contrasts with the concerns of traditional manufacturing for scale and repetition. Play is especially important in services as they often focus on delivering new experiences. Nowadays on a long-haul airline flight, for example, you can make phone calls, use the internet, shop, eat a gourmet meal, watch the latest movies, have a massage, and, if you can afford it, enjoy a hot shower. With many services it is not so much a case of doing existing things better, but of doing new things that move the boundaries of what is possible, especially when it comes to enjoyable experiences. Services are more open to playfulness, so cinemas that once displayed films in 2D, for example, now use 3D and some have seats that move and can release smells to accompany the entertainment.

Playing with such opportunities can be liberating. The author Margaret Drabble says that when nothing is sure, everything is possible, and the great German poet J.W. von Goethe said that one never goes so far as when one doesn't know where one is going. However, when confronted with such uncertainty, having options for the future matters and this requires high levels of curiosity, experimentation and learning, adaptability and responsiveness.

This point about uncertainty is well made by Pat Kane in his book *The Play Ethic*, which puts play in the context of the confusing world we live in. People who play, he argues, need to be energetic, imaginative and confident in the face of an unpredictable, contested, and emergent world: 'living as a player is precisely about embracing ambiguity, revelling in paradox, yet feeling energised by that knowledge ... An ethic of play ... makes a virtue, even a passion, out of uncertainty.'[11]

Likewise, in *Play, Playfulness, Creativity and Innovation*, the behavioural psychologists Patrick Bateson and Paul Martin argue that play enables the individual to discover new approaches to dealing with a world of conflicting demands, and it enhances their ability to compete, cooperate and coexist.[12] And as that most creative of humourists, John Cleese, says: 'play is what allows our natural creativity to surface'.[13] Thus play builds resistance to the organizational atrophy that grows as people inevitably become comfortable with, and defensive of, existing ways of doing things. A lovely *New Yorker* cartoon sums this up, with a manager informing a subordinate that 'This really is an innovative approach, but I'm afraid we can't consider it. It's never been done before.'

Isabel Behncke is a Chilean primatologist based at the University of Oxford. She has spent years studying the bonobo ape in the jungles of the Congo, and her observations about their play have great resonance for the understanding of play in humans. She says play is foundational for bonding relationships and fostering tolerance for both apes and humans. It is where we learn to trust, where we learn about the rules of the game and the limits of what can be done. Play, she suggests, increases creativity and resilience, and it is 'playful curiosity that drives us to explore, drives us to interact, and then the unexpected connections we form are the real hotbed for creativity'. She continues:

> Play suspends reality; things that don't normally happen can happen. Play loves risk and uncertainty, when in other circumstances we hate uncertainty ... we need to adapt to an increasingly challenging world through greater creativity and greater cooperation. The secret is that play is the key to these capacities. In other words, play is our adaptive wildcard. In order to adapt successfully to a changing world, we need to play.[14]

The importance of play is also starkly revealed in the work of the physician and psychiatrist Stuart Brown, head of the Institute for Play. He studied mass murderers and found in all cases that highly violent, anti-social men suffered an absence of play in childhood.

Sameness and repetition without a view to improvement is the antithesis of play. People learn to do existing things better, learn to do new things and learn how to learn. While practice makes perfect in doing existing things better, real advances occur when players create novelty, interpretation and variation. Difference is capitalism's great advantage over centrally planned states. The motivation of players – to grow rich, to prove something can be done, to create an enterprise and to give back to the community – is realized when they create something new and compelling, different to what existed before. Play leads to choices and options for innovation, and innovation is the only way of progressing when everything is in a state of flux.

Before further exploration of the value and virtue of play, we offer a story of the devastation that results when you are not playful. The example describes an extraordinarily influential man who was the opposite of playful, and whose approach to life and the way things should be done strangled the freedom and initiative necessary for creativity, innovation and progress.

Robert McNamara

Robert Strange McNamara (yes, that was his middle name), who was born in 1916 and died in 2009, was an exceptional man. He was president of Ford Motor Company, US Secretary of Defense in the Kennedy and Johnson administrations during the Vietnam War, and president of the World Bank. Many of his achievements were admirable. He may well have saved Ford from bankruptcy, and certainly made cars safer. He improved the efficiency of military procurement and helped the world out of the Cuban Missile Crisis. At the World Bank he did much to improve infrastructure, health and food production in developing nations. Yet as his biographer Deborah Shapley says, 'Few Americans of the twentieth century have been so admired – and so despised.'[15]

Few indeed have had to deal with such enormity in the consequences of their decisions, with McNamara responsible for the deaths of 58,000 of his countrymen and perhaps, staggeringly, of over 1 million Vietnamese. Few have had to live with the sight of a man burning himself to death outside their office as a protest at their decisions.

Robert McNamara did an MBA at Harvard Business School in 1939, and he joined the faculty two years later, becoming a founding member of the US Army Air Corps Statistical Control School. In the Second World War he became involved in planning military logistics, and his expertise in statistical control led to his recruitment, along with a number of his colleagues – known collectively as the Whiz Kids – to Ford in 1946.

The most common epithet used for McNamara is 'brilliant'. In David Halberstam's book *The Best and the Brightest*, about the outstanding talent surrounding John Kennedy, McNamara is considered the brightest.[16] The term sometimes had a pejorative connotation. Barry Goldwater called him an 'IBM machine on legs'. Robert Lacey's book on Ford says: 'The programmer who wired up the circuits beneath the slicked-down cranium of Robert S. McNamara might have missed a connection or two when he reached the sense of humour zone.'[17] At a funeral of a friend McNamara was seen sorting out his notes for a speech the following day.

McNamara was a demanding boss who did not tolerate fools gladly. His approach to management and policy was totally focused on efficiency, defined by applying cost–benefit analysis. He used his army statistical control methods to produce huge efficiencies in financial planning at Ford. He managed by numbers, stating 'Numbers are a language to me.' Deborah Shapley says: 'Nobody else used numbers the way McNamara did. They symbolized his supposedly detached, objective approach to policy. He embodied the school of statistics-based management.'

His approach was one of control. Shapley continues, 'Ford's management controls made McNamara's language of numbers universal in the firm and required others use it, too.' This caused problems for designers and creative people. 'He once ordered a new car by specifying the weight, dimensions, proposed price, and so on. But what do you want the car to be? The designers asked. How should it feel? He had no answer.' In his book *The Reckoning*, David Halberstam describes how Ford engineers

gradually [came] to doubt themselves. Repeatedly beaten on certain kinds of request for their plant over the years, they came to realize that some items would not go through, no matter how legitimate, and so they began to practice a form of self-censorship. They would think of something they needed, realize they could not get it through, and cut the request down so severely that the original purpose was sacrificed.[18]

Shortly after McNamara became president of Ford, he was invited to become John Kennedy's Secretary of Defense. From being one of the world's best paid executives, with a salary of $800,000 – an astronomical sum in 1960 – he moved to a salary of $25,000. His involvement in the profound events of the time has been extensively analysed, as has his role in the escalation and conduct of the Vietnam War.

According to a scathing book about McNamara's methods, H.R. McMaster's *Dereliction of Duty*, the Defense Secretary ignored the collection and analysis of information based on military experience and diplomatic expertise because it was too subjective.[19] McMaster – who in 2017 became the US's National Security Advisor – writes that McNamara viewed the war as another business problem that, he assumed, would ultimately succumb to his reasoned judgement and others' rational calculations. He and his assistants thought that they could predict with great precision what levels of force applied in Vietnam would achieve the results they desired, and they believed they could control that force with great precision from halfway around the world. He 'used line charts to depict change over time in the counter-insurgency effort . . . He tracked the numbers of people killed on both sides, the rate of Viet Cong activity, weapons captured, number of aircraft sorties, North Vietnamese naval activity, the percent of South Vietnamese boats on patrol . . . He used his team of systems analysts to help him determine the meaning of this data.'

McNamara would optimistically report that the body count in a couple of months was 7,000 enemy and 3,000 US casualties: his main statistical control was the ratio of enemy killed in relation to the number of friendly deaths. McMaster further reports how McNamara, his notebook full of statistics, assured a reporter in Vietnam that 'every quantitative measure we have shows that we are winning this war'.

He was, of course, measuring the wrong things and using the wrong assumptions. David Halberstam's book about Vietnam, *The Quagmire*, says the statistics used were very much those that McNamara wanted to hear.[20] And they were misleading. He put great store, for example, on bombing fixed installations, when the North Vietnamese were mobile forces for whom infrastructure was of secondary importance. Halberstam praises McNamara's phenomenal intellect and energy, but reports that one of his most fervent admirers admitted that McNamara was interested in everything 'but men and ideas'. The war, notes Halberstam, unfortunately was about little else.

McNamara could be callous and despicable. Deborah Shapley tells how the military came to loathe him when it became clear that, just at the time he was spouting statistics and sending more troops to Vietnam, he had lost confidence in the US's ability to win the war. He sent soldiers to go and fight for a cause he no longer believed in.

Later in life he came to realize – particularly after reflecting on Vietnam, and especially over the Cuban Missile Crisis – that 'rationality will not save us'. Rationality is necessary, but as a philosophy – like the shortcomings of management by numbers – is insufficient to guide the behaviour of organizations in the complex and confusing world of today. He admits to a terrifying naïveté about Vietnam: 'How were we to know, when we were moving in an alien environment, alongside a people whose language and culture we did not understand and whose history, values, and political traditions differed profoundly from our own?' And to a frightening rigidity and narrowness: 'Eager to get moving, we never stopped to explore fully whether there were other routes to our destination.'[21] It was only later, after harsh experience, that he began to appreciate the importance of differences in culture, history, values and traditions.

McNamara's character was at its finest when he began to reflect on his decisions and mistakes. He published a book on Vietnam in 1995, which has some of the bravest, and most honest and chilling lines imaginable. He writes: 'We of the Kennedy and Johnson administrations who participated in the decisions on Vietnam acted according to what we thought were the principles and values of the nation ... Yet we were wrong, terribly wrong.'[22]

When asked whether he might, as head of defense, visit troops called up during the Berlin crisis of 1961, McNamara replied that he could serve the nation better by spending the same time at his desk. To paraphrase David Halberstam, organizational life is all about people and ideas. To immerse oneself in numbers is to avoid real leadership. It is impossible to imagine what would have resulted from McNamara being more playful in our sense, and having the grace to recognize the views and opinions of others. Being attuned to the people around him rather than the data in front of him could have had profound implications.

Underlying McNamara's approach was a blind belief in rationality and the relegation in decision-making of anything that is emotional, subjective or playful. Albert Einstein said: 'The intuitive mind is a sacred gift and rational mind is a faithful servant. We have created a society that honors the servant and has forgotten the gift.' Rationality, reason and logic are critically important for organizational life – and easily replicated by machines – but rationality celebrates the conventional, is bounded by what is known and is tied to established institutions and power structures. It seldom generates radical, creative and intuitive ideas and innovations. The esteemed organization scholar and poet, James March, says releasing the focus on rationality and consistency can help 'to develop the unusual combination of attitudes and behaviors that describe the interesting people, interesting organizations, and interesting societies of the world.'[23] Rationality is also hopeless in highly uncertain and complex situations, as seen in the debacle of centralized planning in the Soviet Union. It completely ignores the messiness, inconsistency and contradictions of people and ideas, and the way the most effective decisions emerge when ideas are questioned and tested following consultation, collaboration and negotiation: that is, when they are played with.

Play and the medical profession

A lack of playfulness can be devastating not only through the actions of individuals such as McNamara but also through the behaviour of groups of people and professions. Work practices can be dangerously detrimental when they become totally engrained, intolerant of play and impervious to change. This is seen in the contrast between the search for treatments for cancer and AIDS.

As Siddhartha Mukherjee puts it in his marvellous book, *The Emperor of All Maladies*, the history of cancer is full of conflict within the medical profession about treatment options, with deep rifts between groups pursuing different approaches.[24] For centuries a central tenet of cancer treatment was the mistaken belief that cancer radiated from an original location in the body. This underlay the practice of increasingly radical surgery, excising more and more of the patient to prevent cancer's spread. At its most extreme, for example, Mukherjee describes radical mastectomies involving 'the removal of the breast, the pectoral muscles, the axillary nodes, the chest wall, and occasionally the ribs, parts of the sternum, the clavicle, and the lymph nodes inside the chest'. The development of chemotherapy provided an alternative, if similarly brutal, treatment, and communities of surgeons and chemotherapists spent years unproductively arguing over the efficacy of their different approaches. Mukherjee refers to the 'virtually insurmountable segregation between cancer therapy and cancer science ... as if a sealed divider had been constructed through the middle of the world of cancer, with "cause" on one side and "cure" on the other. Few scientists or clinical oncologists crossed between the two isolated worlds.'

Eventually, after ten years of collecting evidence on breast cancer, it was proved that a small local excision along with radiotherapy had exactly the same effect on women's survival rates as radical surgery. As Mukherjee puts it, however, this finding had to confront 'the hierarchical practice of medicine, its internal culture [and] its rituals of practice [... which] were ideally arranged to resist change and to perpetuate orthodoxy'. He tells of careers ruined as scientists attempting to work in a broad and interdisciplinary way chafed against orthodoxy and disciplinary boundaries. His view of cancer research in the 1970s is scathing: 'Pumped up with self-confidence, bristling with conceit, and hypnotised by the potency of medicine, oncologists pushed their patients – and their discipline – to the brink of disaster.'

Further decades of research were conducted before the genetic basis of cancer was discovered, and the recognition grew that cancer is not one, but many different diseases. Breast cancer, for example, is estimated to have twenty different forms. It took decades for the medical approach to change from focusing on the problem as *cancer* rather than on *people* with cancer. It wasn't until the 1960s in Britain and 1970s in the US that research seriously addressed the issue of palliative medicine: pain and anxiety relief and anti-nausea drugs to deal with the side-effects of chemotherapy. Also crucially, in the frantic push to find a *cure* for cancer, little effort focused on its *prevention*, especially, for example, through public health campaigns about the dangers of smoking (Mukherjee notes that medical journals in the 1950s routinely carried cigarette advertisements). It also took powerful external forces – for example the women's movement, appalled by the fact that by 1981 half a million women had suffered radical mastectomies in the one hundred years of this practice, including Audrey Dodgson, Mark's mother, who built a vocal and collective opposition to such surgical practices.

The comparatively rapid and effective search for treatment for the HIV/AIDS epidemic to a large extent circumvented the problems of insular and conflicting working practices found in the history of cancer treatment, and recognized the value of openness and public awareness along with expert opinion. The ultimate pharmacological 'cure' for HIV/AIDS would be a vaccine to prevent the disease, but this does not exist. At present combinations of drugs restrict its progress. Actual prevention is assisted, but not entirely assured, by safe sex and safe drug use practices. While AIDS remains one of the main causes of death, especially in poorer countries, and although the incidence of new AIDS cases dropped from 1.7 million deaths in 2011 to 1.1 million in 2015, it remains a public health disaster of massive proportions, with a death toll equivalent to the 9/11 disaster every single day for the last thirty years. Despite this continuing high incidence, there have been many successes in the campaign against the disease, and these have depended on the contributions of multiple, diverse people, working together. They have also depended on the goodwill of civic, media and religious leaders, active lobby groups and charities, and the central role of companies experimenting with novel business strategies. In contrast to the long history of cancer, the AIDS epidemic relatively quickly led to effective collaboration between scientists, clinicians, government, business and patients, prepared to play together to develop treatment.

In a sense, the comparison between cancer and AIDS is unfair as cancer is very much more complex, with hundreds of different manifestations, involving a combination of genetic, environmental and lifestyle factors, but it nevertheless reveals stark differences in approach. Medical researchers have made a seminal contribution to understanding and managing HIV/AIDS, but so too have a wide and diverse range of people and organizations that have worked in new and collaborative ways and built important consensus about the problem and the ways it is addressed. Scientists have themselves relatively rapidly built mechanisms for communication and coordination. Firms have collaborated with each other and with universities, governments and charities in new ways. Lobby groups have coordinated disparate voices, giving notice about the needs of otherwise marginalized groups such as intravenous drug users. International agencies and governments have attempted coordinated policy development. Playfulness of approach, in the sense of being open to experimenting and learning, has been seen broadly, even, as we shall see later in the case in the UK, in the very conduct of government.

By way of sharp contrast to the above discussion about war and disease, we now turn to the decidedly more cheerful matter of fun.

Play and fun

As John Cleese has shown in his series of management training videos, important matters at work can be addressed using levity.[25] For example, on the issue of meetings – the curse of many a working life – he offers this sketch:

> *Wife (lying in bed alongside Cleese's character, who is reading a report)*: Why can't you do your work while you are at work?
> *Cleese*: There isn't time. I have to go to meetings.
> *Wife*: Do you think it would make things easier if I came and slept at the office?
> *Cleese*: Why don't you come and sleep at the meetings? Everyone else does.

Cleese addresses a serious matter, using humour.

Educationalists have long understood how play is a crucial formative experience and how children learn more when they're having fun. Emile's creator, Jean-Jacques Rousseau (1712–88) argued that play is instinctive and essential to everyone's growth and development, and that learning happens best when it is pleasurable. Similarly, the German educationalist Friedrich Froebel (1782–1852), who developed the first kindergartens, emphasized the importance of creative play. In contrast, everyone can recall the tedium of the classroom lesson or PowerPoint lecture that is dry in delivery and purpose, and completely dispiriting in its lack of engagement. Learning is so much more effective when it is stimulating and fun.

Susanna Millar, in her book *The Psychology of Play*, suggests that play is about throwing off constraint,[26] taking us away from the everyday stresses of life. It is rewarding and self-fulfilling and provides opportunities for learning and personal development. It allows intelligent participation in shared activities at your own discretion. Used appropriately, it encourages a light-hearted spirit, jocularity, amusement and humour. Generally, everyone warms to those who are fun and make us laugh. Humorous sharing of life's absurdities enhances our ability to deal with them.

Johan Huizinga, a Dutch historian, was the greatest cultural analyst of play.[27] A brilliant and erudite scholar, he was delightfully grumpy, railing against the puerility of the world. He was also courageous. Huizinga's criticisms of the Nazi forces occupying his homeland led to his being arrested and detained between 1942 and his death in 1945. Play, for Huizinga, is beautiful. It casts a spell over us, and is 'enchanting' and 'captivating'; its essence, he wrote, is fun. Huizinga also notes the competitive sources and purposes of play that appear 'when trade begins to create fields of activity within which each must try to surpass and outwit his neighbour' and how 'some of the great business concerns deliberately instil the play-spirit into their workers so as to step up production'. Playing, testing or toying with material or ideas can be highly productive.

This is even seen at the highest levels of science. Enthusiastic proponents of play include a number of winners of the Nobel Prize in Physics. Commenting on the award of the 2010 prize given to Andre Geim and Konstantin Novoselov for their work on graphene, the Nobel Committee said: 'Playfulness is one of their hallmarks, one always learns something in the process and, who knows, you may even hit the jackpot.'[28] Frank Wilczek, another Nobel Prize winner, who works in theoretical physics, says his work is more like imaginative play than anything else.[29] Theirs is play in the process of discovery.

Nobel Laureate Richard Feynman could be very playful. He was an expert bongo player, practised safe-cracking, and was known to sketch his ideas in shady bars. His autobiography is entitled *Surely You're Joking Mr. Feynman,* and a collection of his letters was brought together in a book called *Don't You Have Time to Think?*[30] Feynman was one of the greatest physicists of the last century, and one of the dicipline's finest communicators, owing to this playfulness. Many thousands have been drawn to the internet to watch his fun and enthusiastic lectures. During the fraught inquiry into the causes of NASA's Space Shuttle Challenger disaster, technical explanations became highly complex and contested, but Feynman still managed to communicate his point brilliantly and playfully. He dropped a rubber band into a glass of cold water. For those present and watching on live television, desperate for an answer, he showed clearly and simply what went wrong with the notorious O-rings that caused the accident.

In his book *The Undoing Project: A Friendship That Changed the World,* Michael Lewis writes about the relationship between Amos Tversky and Daniel Kahneman, two psychologists with very different personalities whose work together won the Nobel Prize in Economic Sciences. He writes that work for Tversky had always been play, and if it wasn't fun he simply didn't see the point in doing it. Over time, he says work also became play for Kahneman, and in the face of all the complexities and uncertainties in their field, they said: 'Screw it, we're going to play with all this stuff.'[31]

Patrick Bateman and Paul Martin have written about 'playful play', where a positive mood induces individuals to behave and think in a spontaneous and flexible way. The stimuli to such creative play range from the colour schemes of workplaces to the use of psychoactive drugs. They suggest that humour is strongly associated with playful play, and provide some heartening evidence that creativity can be stimulated by alcohol (in moderation).

Having discussed some theories of fun, we now turn to its practice with an example of a player who, despite some exceptionally demanding jobs, really knows how to have fun.

Paul Drayson

Visiting Goodwood, a sports venue in southern England, and admiring a fast race between classic motorcars, it was somewhat surprising to see the incumbent British Minister of State for Science and Universities shooting past in a 1952 open-top Jaguar. Sometime later in one of our offices, he displayed some discomfort when explaining that he'd recently broken his back racing at Monaco. Lord Drayson is not your usual politician.

Paul is actually first and foremost an entrepreneur, showing that you can succeed at the highest levels in a number of areas of work. With a PhD in robotics, he gained early experience as a product developer at Rover cars before becoming managing director of two companies. With this background, in 1993, along with his wife Elspeth and her father, a University of Oxford professor, he co-founded PowderJect Pharmaceuticals, a business that subsequently became the world's sixth-largest vaccine-producing company. Elspeth, who has degrees in physics, medical electronics and management, spotted the commercial potential of the technology behind PowderJect, developed by her father: a needle-free injection system, which fires powder through the skin at supersonic speeds. Paul was CEO of PowderJect for ten years until an American biotechnology company bought it for £542 million.

The firm's history is a combination of scientific entrepreneurialism and pragmatic business development. The company had a change of strategy and pivoted from being a technology platform company that licensed to others, to one that develops and produces vaccines directly. A number of acquisitions underlie the strategy, which it took some time to persuade investors in the City to support. At one stage PowderJect was facing competition from an American company and the decision was made to acquire it, except PowderJect didn't have the money to pay for it. Testament to its entrepreneurial drive (some would say chutzpah), PowderJect persuaded the company's ultimate owner to lend it the money to buy its American competitor. The debt was repaid. The depth of Elspeth's commitment to the company is seen in a photograph taken of her after the birth of their first child, sitting in the maternity ward doing the PowderJect payroll on her bed. This is hardly playful, but shows a determination not to let her employees down under any circumstances.

Paul's political career began when he joined the UK Parliament's House of Lords in May 2004. He was appointed as Minister for Defence Procurement, and as Government Spokesman for Defence in the House of Lords in May 2005. In October 2008 he was appointed Minister of State for Science and Innovation, with responsibility for the UK's science research budget, defence science and technology budget, innovation policy and space programme. He left politics in 2010.

Paul now spends much of his time as CEO of Drayson Racing Technologies, which researches and manufactures electric vehicles. The company, again started with Elspeth, runs the Drayson Racing Team, which focuses on electric racing cars. In the Beijing Formula E (electric) car race in 2014, Drayson Racing Technologies provided the chargers. The cars runs on cellulosic bioethanol, a fuel that is not derived from crops, avoiding arguments against valuable food being used as fuel. In 2013, a car made by his company and driven by Paul himself broke the world land speed record for a lightweight electric car, hitting a top speed of 204 miles per hour (328 kilometres per hour) at a racetrack in Yorkshire. The company is also researching the transfer of power over distance using wireless technology.

Paul has raced cars all through his career, including the demanding Le Mans twenty-four-hour race. Born without vision in one eye, a condition that would usually preclude racing, he built up a performance record that persuaded the international racing federation to make an exception and allow him to compete.

Paul pushes the boundaries and takes risks. He recognises the value of advances in science and research – his coat of arms includes a DNA double helix, reflecting his biotechnology background, and his family motto is 'seek knowledge' – and he also gives back. In 1999, shaken by the poor state of the facilities where Elspeth gave birth to their third child, he gave £1.2 million to the John Radcliffe Hospital in Oxford. And, as shown in his love of racing, he knows how to enjoy himself. As a reward for his work in business and politics, his passion for racing is now directed towards the production of environmentally friendly cars. Players have fun while doing good.

Play and freedom

Jean-Jacques Rousseau's Emile enjoyed the charm of freedom in combining play and work, and Rousseau provides a number of insights into the relationship between play and freedom. His philosophy has been hugely influential – his ideas played an important part in the French Revolution – and he somehow found time to write seven operas and numerous other pieces of music. He displayed many playful behaviours but, as an illustration of the complexity of some of the people whose stories we tell, he was also a hypochondriac with delicate mental health whose forceful opinions and blatant hypocrisy turned some of his closest friends into sworn enemies. He fell out with David Hume, for example, and Voltaire thought him a knave. He treated the many women in his life appallingly, and at one stage was involved in a lengthy *ménage-a-trois*. His memoirs reveal his enthusiasm for being spanked. It isn't too hard to relate these problems to his upbringing. Rousseau's mother died shortly after his birth. His father spent most of his inheritance, and Rousseau's childhood was spent hopping between various relatives. He moved between different countries and religions throughout his life. His ideas polarised opinions: his books, including *Emile*, were publicly burnt – one for making the point that, provided they encourage virtue, all religions are the same.

While Rousseau's writings on education are controversial, with his views on the education of girls being especially regressive, they are also influential and are reflected to some extent in today's school curricula, such as those following the educational philosophy of Maria Montessori. Essentially Rousseau didn't believe so much in teaching facts and theories, but in developing a child's character and morality through experience. He contended that attention is greater when it is self-directed and self-motivated, and play is rewarding in and of itself. Although he might not have practised what he preached – he is reputed to have given away four or five of his own children to a local hospital, rather than pay for their upkeep – his views on the importance of play remain particularly insightful. Montessori's emphasis on experimentation, freedom and fun in the education of children also holds lessons for those working in modern organizations. Rousseau's personality and many of his views were distasteful, but he himself freely admitted he would not obstinately defend his ideas, thinking only that it was his duty to put them forward. He says in *Emile* that 'even if my own ideas are mistaken, my time will not have been wasted if I stir up others to form right ideas'.

Johan Huizinga also argued that freedom is the main characteristic of play. Freedom to play includes the ability to decide whether or not to play, and the choice of whether to play within or outside the rules or conventions of behaviour. Rules are important for players, but people play in very different ways within them. Consider artists: some may sketch and test beforehand to see whether things suit their purpose, while others may have a clear vision from the start of what they aim to create. Some may be content with their first go and allow ideas to emerge, moving from chaos to structure. Many experiment and test with various canvasses, trying things out. The painter Francis Bacon, who produced one of the world's most expensive paintings sold at auction, reaching $142 million in 2013, said he saw himself as a medium for accident and chance. In contrast, the Old Masters of the seventeenth century, such as Vermeer, were schooled in a structured method of production that could be replicated. So it is with players: some are more contentedly random, others more happily ordered.

To illustrate how such freedom can work, the film director, Julien Temple, has made a complicated but very compelling documentary on London using old and new film clips. He explains his creative process:

> With films like this you shouldn't have any kind of plan when you start out, just dive into the archive and drown. Let the images hypnotise you and speak for themselves. After that chance and accident take over and if anything does start to work it works from that moment when consciously you don't know what you are doing. You're thinking of nothing but how hopeless and impossible this thing is to achieve. Then suddenly your instinct seizes upon something that seems to offer a way forward. In the end I want a very ordered set of images, but I want them to have come about by chaos and chance.[32]

Other players may like boundaries and parameters and the opportunities to explore within them and test their limits. Jazz musicians, for example, often play with a structure or motif and improvise and experiment within it. For jazz pianist and composer Dave Brubeck, 'There's a way of playing safe, there's a way of using tricks and there's the way I like to play, which is dangerously, where you're going to take a chance on making mistakes in order to create something you haven't created before.' The sense of adventure he describes and the preparedness to confront the fear of failure are all characteristic of the player. Another aspect of freedom is the opportunity to pursue interests outside recognized core areas of expertise – like Paul Drayson, an entrepreneur, politician and sportsman. Take the example of rock guitarists – literally 'players' – who have diverse interests outside of their music. Brian May from Queen, who has a PhD in astrophysics, is an active animal rights advocate and vice-president of the Royal Society for the Prevention of Cruelty to Animals, and has been recognized for his expertise on Victorian stereophotography. Jimmy Page, from Led

Zeppelin, is an expert collector of Pre-Raphaelite art, and Ronnie Wood, of the Rolling Stones, is an exhibited artist. Frank Zappa succinctly summed up his approach to music and life when he said progress is not possible without deviation.

Finding the balance

The first part of the old adage 'All work and no play makes Jack a dull boy' is usually well remembered; the second part, 'All play and no work makes Jack a mere toy', probably less so. Hilary Duff makes the same observation about too much play in one of her songs: 'No work, all play, what a mistake.' Play can be inappropriate and constant fun, freedom and jocularity can be tiresome. Fans of the UK TV series *The Office* will understand the horrible implications of this quote from David Brent, the office manager: 'I suppose I've created an atmosphere here where I'm a friend first, boss second, and probably an entertainer third.' As the series brilliantly reminds us, play can take the form of idleness, triviality, boisterousness and puerility – which, of course, while not being particularly productive, can be wonderfully funny.

The alternative to playful exploration is seen in Charles Dickens's *Hard Times*. 'Fact, fact, fact!' drives headmaster Thomas Gradgrind's approach to life. His pupils are vessels to be filled full of facts. 'Now, what I want is Facts,' says Gradgrind. 'Teach these boys and girls nothing but Facts. Facts alone are wanted in life. Plant nothing else, and root out everything else. You can only form the minds of reasoning animals upon Facts; nothing else will ever be of any service to them.' Finding the balance of when and when not to play is a constant process of exploration and testing between the extreme philosophies of Robert McNamara or Gradgrind's schoolroom and Brent's office, but the point is that play and seriousness at work are not mutually exclusive and a balance can be achieved.

Thomas Edison balanced seriousness and playfulness, founding great companies, such as General Electric, and registering over a thousand patents. His name will always be associated with innovations that changed the world such as the light bulb and phonograph. Work at Edison's 'innovation factory' was extremely demanding: he was a hard taskmaster and you wouldn't last long there if you didn't fit in with his punishing schedule. Employees worked very long hours, yet falling asleep at work was considered disgraceful, and if you were caught you could be exposed to the 'corpse reviver', a terrifying noise released beside the ear, and the 'resurrector of the dead', which apparently involved setting sleepers alight with a small exploding substance. As well as being deadly serious about work, Edison could be playful as well. His whole invention system was based on experiment and learning. He socialized with staff with snacks and cigars at the end of the day, sharing bawdy jokes and tales, dancing and singing around the giant organ that dominated one end of the laboratory, along with an electric toy railroad to play with and a pet bear. Workers acknowledged the costs to family life of the punishing schedule, but said they wouldn't like to work elsewhere because the work was so stimulating and rewarding. One of Edison's assistants said that there was 'a little community of kindred spirits, all in young manhood, enthusiastic about their work, expectant of great results', for whom work and play were indistinguishable.[33]

Even when players are at their most freethinking, their play is often framed and ordered within agreed rule boundaries. They display signals, for example, for when they are playing and when not. Edison had a time and place for jocularity and if you worked for him it was as well to know when he was being playful and when he was not. Signals of what is and what is not play can be subtle. Apes display very similar behaviours when they are playing and fighting, yet manage to convey to others which of the two they are doing. Players similarly can use gestures, facial expressions and intonations to signal when they are playful and when they are not, displaying empathy with those around them or, on the other hand, signalling that now is perhaps not the best time to ask for that raise.

Rules frame how play is undertaken. Before eleven gentlemen wrote down the rules of football in a London pub in 1863, the game was played in a wide variety of ways. Confusion ensued, so that in some games the ball couldn't be caught in the first half, and in the second it could. Melvyn Bragg includes *The Rule Book of Association Football* on his list of twelve (British) books that changed the world.[34] Without it, he argues, the global game – the World Cup can attract 1 billion television viewers – would not have come into existence. Thirteen rules were determined in 1863, including not carrying the ball and no tripping, hacking or pushing; they even disallowed the wearing of protruding nails on boots.

Play can also be framed by time rules. Football games last 90 minutes. Children's playtime can be a distinctive set time at school or home, as can play at work: companies allocate employees a certain number of days or hours a week to work on their own projects, or this time can be 'bootlegged' in a semi-sanctioned manner.[35] Patrick Bateman and Paul Martin argue that play can have an immediate benefit, such as solving a problem, or it can bring no instant practical good but instead deliver improved physical, cognitive or social skills, even many years later.

Rules shape behaviour beyond simple prescription and instruction. According to Sir Bobby Charlton, the English football legend, *The Rule Book of Association Football* not only made it possible to play the game but also embodied the spirit of the game. Here lies the stricture that you can wholeheartedly play to win, but cheating is unacceptable; moving outside of the spirit of the game is frowned upon and may involve being ostracised from a community of which you wish or need to be a part.

In contrast to this noble spirit, some popular TV shows seem keen to pander to our lower instincts, celebrating aggression towards others, relishing humiliation and rewarding those for whom civil behaviour is an inconvenience. These programmes promote hyper-competitive playing in the pejorative sense, where denigrating other people is a victory. Such programmes aren't promoting playfulness, but something that is instead sociopathic.

Players in our sense play within broadly defined rules of acceptable behaviour.[36] Those who operate outside these rules can also be known as crooks. Alan Bond was a famous British-Australian entrepreneur with an international profile. After making his fortune he bought what was then the most expensive painting in the world, Vincent van Gogh's *Irises*. He built a beautiful new university with his name on it, and he bankrolled the team that won the America's Cup, the world's most prestigious sailing competition. Then he went to jail for four years for fraud. His whole corporate edifice was built on lies and he ended his career in disgrace. Bond was a consummate player in the pejorative sense, and the price he paid for his dishonesty resulted from a lack of nobility in the way he played.

Reflections

Play remains a difficult subject to study, although there are many 'play theorists', who devote their career to understanding it. One of the leading thinkers in the field, Brian Sutton-Smith, says the question 'what is play?' is notoriously hard to answer: we all recognize play when we see or engage in it, but it's a domain of life that is remarkably hard to conceptualize.[37] Our intent is to explore play at work and the behaviours that support it. Through the stories of individuals and organizations, our aim is to contradict the view of people such as Jean-Paul Sartre, who argued meaning is found only in creativity and play, while meaninglessness is found in the order and discipline of work. Emile's gift shows the fatuousness of this distinction.

Innovators and entrepreneurs find great purpose and meaning in play at work in ways that can be ordered and disciplined. Entrepreneurs such as Edison are expert at finding the balance between exploring new innovations within broadly defined rules for play. They channel uncertain opportunities into practical, deliverable results; they are open to exploring novelty with a mind to pragmatic application. Balance is a feature in Paul Drayson's career: he has had hugely demanding jobs in both business and in politics, and has also thrived in the highly competitive world of motor racing, providing him with a source of continual fun, motivation and insight.

Play is a crucial element of work as we push the boundaries and express our freedom by trying out new ideas and artefacts, often in concert with others, and enjoy ourselves while we're doing it. Play instils a spirit of adventure. Workplaces such as IDEO and Airbnb are designed to produce environments for productive play, but play is also important for large organizations, such as IBM. The primary reason why play is considered important in the world of work is that it gives us options for dealing with uncertainty. The consequences of not having options and the failure to develop alternatives are summarized in the chilling words of Robert McNamara: 'we never stopped to explore fully whether there were other routes to our destination'. Play, in the words of Isabel Behncke, gives us the 'adaptive wildcard' to help us survive and thrive in an uncertain world, and its contribution to progress is immense. As the writer Philip Pullman puts it:

It's when we do this foolish, time-consuming, romantic, quixotic, childlike, thing called play that we are most practical, most useful, and most firmly grounded in reality, because the world itself is the most unlikely of places, and it works in the oddest of ways, and we won't make any sense of it by doing what everybody else has done before us. It's when we fool about with the stuff the world is made of that we make the most valuable discoveries, we create the most lasting beauty, we discover the most profound truths. The youngest children can do it, and the greatest artists, the greatest scientists do it all the time.

This view also extends to the worlds of the innovator and entrepreneur and through their experiences to all those at work trying to survive and thrive in a turbulent and uncertain world.

The work of innovators and entrepreneurs raises questions we can ask of ourselves about whether we have the capacity – either self-determined or sanctioned by our employers – to play, by:

- expressing our freedom by having discretion over what work we do and how we do it;
- having fun working, no matter how hard it is, by feeling it is enjoyable and rewarding;
- being prepared to explore and experiment, to take some risks by trying and testing new things, without fear of damaging our reputations and careers if they don't work out as expected; and
- improving our learning about ourselves and the world, allowing us to deal better with uncertain and turbulent circumstances that confront us at work.

We now turn to the behaviours that encourage and guide play at work.

PART 2

Noble behaviours

3

Grace

Favourable or kindly regard, goodwill, goodness, sense of duty or propriety, decency; to show respect.
Pleasing or attractive quality; attractively elegant, refined, or accomplished mode of behaviour.
The ability to maintain or display composure in a difficult situation; even-tempered.

In his poem 'If—', Rudyard Kipling tells us the earth and everything in it belongs to those that can keep their heads when all around are losing theirs, walk with kings without losing the common touch, and talk with crowds whilst keeping their virtue. While writing in a very different era, for a very different purpose, he could have been referring to elements of grace in play.

If asked to identify the behaviours of someone with grace, you'd probably produce a long list. U2's song 'Grace' has the lyric 'grace finds beauty in everything'. Marilynne Robinson in *Lila* says that 'Grace is not so poor a thing that it cannot present itself in any number of ways.' The behaviours it presents might include optimism, agreeableness, courtesy, generosity, loyalty, patience, forgiveness, gentleness, humility, modesty and kindness. Kindness was a key virtue Rousseau wanted to bestow in Emile: 'be kind to your fellow-men; this is your first duty, kind

91

to every age and station, kind to all that is not foreign to humanity. What wisdom can you find that is greater than kindness?'

The list of graceful attributes might also include equanimity, the calm acceptance of life's vicissitudes: its ups and downs. Grace involves an absence of hubris and deep-seated belief that you don't possess all the answers, and that when you trust people as much as Steve Shirley and Rajeeb Dey do, they deliver much more than when they are treated with suspicion and doubt. Possessing all the various aspects of grace would make you an angel or a saint, but when writing about grace we are not referring to anything spiritual, but to a behaviour whose implications are practical and pragmatic. The long list of graceful behaviours is unlikely to be found in one individual, but there are good reasons why players would wish to possess as many of them as possible. We now turn to someone who was exceptionally graceful.

Gerard Fairtlough

Gerard Fairtlough (1930–2007) was a great British entrepreneur whose story illustrates what is meant by being playful, noble and graceful. Our first contact with Gerard was a phone call, out of the blue: 'Hello. My name is Gerard Fairtlough, and I'd like you to write the history of Celltech.' Celltech was Britain's first biotechnology company and it had a profound influence on the development of the sector.[1] Intrigued and flattered, Mark arranged a visit to Celltech at its Slough headquarters, and when Gerard's secretary introduced him, he was found feet on desk, engrossed in reading Jürgen Habermas's *Theory of Communicative Action*, a deep and complex philosophical tract: it became immediately obvious that this was a CEO with a difference.

Gerard was a chemist who over a twenty-five-year career with Shell rose to be managing director of Shell Chemicals UK in the 1970s. He became somewhat disenchanted with big business, and was especially disgusted when he was offered a substantial bribe in the US. He wanted to become more involved in government policymaking and left Shell to become a director of the government's National Enterprise Board (NEB). The NEB at the time was primarily noted for its (usually futile) attempts to rescue declining industries by taking them under government control. Gerard's focus was different: he wanted to build new industries. He saw the potential of biotechnology very early on, and worked to develop a coalition of supporters for the creation of a flagship British biotechnology firm, similar to a number of US firms being established at the time. When the decision was made to form Celltech, the challenge of leading it proved so attractive that Gerard applied for and was offered the job.

Gerard displayed all the behavioural attributes of play, and the circumstances in which he worked explain why play can be such a valuable strategy. At the cusp of a scientific revolution, involving considerable turbulence and risk, new experiments were taking place in technology and in ways of organizing and working. A novel type of organization – the biotechnology firm – was being created to commercialize the new technology and to operate as an intermediary between scientists in universities and large, well-established pharmaceutical firms. Play comes into its own when things are so disruptive and uncertain, and players are the people who thrive in such circumstances and get things done.

After a decade at Celltech, Gerard left and became a business angel, advising and investing in a wide range of small start-ups. He actively supported a range of humanitarian, arts and environmental organizations. He wrote two books: *Creative Compartments* (1994) and *The Three Ways of Getting Things Done* (2007), using his experiences of the organizations in which he had worked to describe a new way of thinking about organizational structures and management.[2] He advocated a cell-like analogy for organizations, where the cells that construct an organism have independent identities but porous boundaries to enable flow and communication between them.

The extraordinary stresses of running Celltech placed particular demands on Gerard's fortitude. Along with the power of his intellect, however, the most notable of his traits was grace. As his obituary in the *Independent* newspaper said: 'he was endlessly kind and his wisdom cast light on many diverse lives'. Great pressure was put on Celltech from the start. It had been given exclusive rights to all biotechnology discoveries in all British universities and research laboratories, and was pressured by researchers who, with this restricted option for commercializing their ideas, demanded quick and substantial returns. At the same time, Celltech was privately owned and shareholders, with unrealistic expectations about quick returns in the information technology industry, insisted on a significant return on their investment in this new and risky technology. Gerard found himself trapped between discontented and naïve scientists with little or no experience of commercializing research and corporate investors with no understanding of the technology and the length of time it would take to get products to market. Margaret Thatcher's government at the time was also intently interested in the policy experiment of Celltech. Mrs Thatcher had been furious at what she believed was a previous botched attempt to commercialize British bioscience; she was deeply sceptical of anything that emerged from the NEB (a Labour Party initiative), and was naturally suspicious of any state-led monopoly. The fact that Gerard survived a decade in these conditions and built Celltech into a substantial concern with around 600 employees is testament to his exceptional ability to craft ways to progress in the face of great uncertainty and turbulence. Celltech was eventually sold to a Belgian company in 2004 for £1.5 billion.

One of the major ways Gerard displayed grace was in the openness of his management style and his belief everyone has something to contribute. His office door was always open, he lunched at the staff's canteen and ensured Celltech's building was designed to maximize opportunities for discussions and chance encounters with colleagues. He also made board minutes available for everyone to read, shocking a traditional board member, who demanded the practice be stopped immediately – Gerard continued it, but in a less obviously visible way. Despite significant difficulties on the board – often resulting from the tensions between the company's scientific and business objectives – Gerard never personalized conflicts, respecting people's diverse institutional agendas.

The greatest of Gerard's skills, according to the company chairman at the time, was 'his ability to get his staff to love him'. He was always warm-hearted, forever ready to engage in ideas and he inspired those around him to work in challenging circumstances through his great integrity and clarity of vision for the future.

Grace at work has many manifestations and motivations, as the following cases illustrate.

Alexsis de Raadt St James

Alexsis de Raadt St James is a very successful businesswoman. She has worked for Shell International, as a senior executive in a software company and has held a wide variety of advisory roles in banking and non-profit organizations. In 2001, in the course of a year, her father, father-in-law and a close friend died of heart attacks and disease. Then, aged forty-four with two small children, she received a phone call out of the blue to tell her of her husband's death, aged forty-eight, on the other side of the world, also of a heart attack.

This sequence of shocking events in her personal life led her to think about how better to inform people of the death of a relative. Her grace lay in her desire to help others facing the devastating circumstances that she had confronted, to use her energy and resources to gain some benefit from adversity. Her family had experienced the emotionally draining role of informing bereaved people. Her father delivered death notifications as a telegram boy in the Second World War and then had the job of a death notifier in the US Army. He explained he had no training in delivering such shattering news and was haunted by the reactions he experienced.

Alexsis decided to do something about improving the moment of notification and the emotional shock associated with it. She donated $2 million to the Department of Psychiatry at the University of California, San Francisco, to help develop the Death Notification and Stress Management Program (DNP). Based on research on post-traumatic stress in the department, the DNP is an online education and training programme. Grounded on an understanding of the psychological and physiological impact of shocking news, it was designed to provide practical help for notifiers and those bereaved. The US Army implemented DNP in 2004, improving awareness of how to deliver news of deaths. Previously, horrendous examples had emerged of relatives learning of the deaths of loved ones on the radio or being misinformed, and of notifiers reading pre-printed scripts from cards. Using DNP, news of death is delivered accurately and compassionately, and it is now also used by the UK's Ministry of Defence and Metropolitan Police Service.

In 2003, Alexsis established The Althea Foundation, a social-venture fund in San Francisco, of which she is chair. The Althea Foundation funds, partners and mentors new initiatives and established non-profit organizations. It says of its work: 'We fund people, ideas and initiatives that inspire us with their ingenuity, humanity and social impact.' Initiatives supported include Creativity Explored, which uses art as a tool for communication and self-expression among people with developmental disabilities, giving them an opportunity to play. It supports research into rare diseases, autism and integrative medicine. It promotes career development for vulnerable young people around the world, and the redevelopment of agriculture in Afghanistan.

Alexsis is an enthusiastic promoter of women entrepreneurs. The Althea Foundation supports Astia, an organization of over 5,000 experts committed to the success of women-led, high-growth start-ups in areas such as healthcare, finance and information technology. Althea directly supports the organization's work with women-led companies in Europe. Alexsis is also the founder and managing partner of Merian Ventures, a US and UK venture-investment firm that partners with female entrepreneurs aiming to build companies by pioneering innovation in a range of technologies. Merian states its focus on women entrepreneurs is more than a social statement, but has a clear objective to find and fund the rise in women-led innovation that has been largely overlooked by the investment community. Alexsis provides opportunities for women entrepreneurs to play.

We now turn to a man whose playfulness traversed the worlds of advertising and music.

Richard Wheatly

Richard Wheatly (1946–2015), as one of his best friends put it, 'could lunch for England', and having shared many of them with him we couldn't agree more. An urbane man of wit and humour, Richard was chairman of a major advertising agency before leaving to pursue his passion for jazz music by running a radio station. His undoubted business skills lay lightly on his shoulders; he took some great financial risks and reaped substantial rewards. One of his talents was the way he invoked great loyalty among those who worked with him.

Richard was deeply conscious of the contributions and shortcomings of the advertising industry. One of his favourite anecdotes concerned the CEO of the agency he worked for as a young man. The CEO asked Richard to accompany him to a campaign presentation for a new product launch in a major international car company. Richard asked the CEO whether he was aware that no work had been done on the campaign at all, despite a significant financial advance. 'Don't you worry about that,' the head of his company replied. The two advertising executives arrived at a very intimidating boardroom where the client's senior management team had assembled. At this stage Richard began to sweat. His boss placed a briefcase in front of him, and when asked how planning for the campaign was progressing he pointed to it. Before asking for the advertising ideas to be presented, the client's CEO took it upon himself to remind the visitors how marvellous his company was and how brilliant its products were. Richard at this stage was squirming in his seat, and his boss looked uncomfortable. When asked to speak, the head of the advertising agency replied that he had been labouring under a misapprehension. He had failed to properly understand the wonder of the new car, as its style and performance was completely beyond anyone's experience. Pointing dismissively at his briefcase, he said in the light of this revelation all the work they'd done so far was useless, and would be thrown away. He pleaded for some extra time and money to complete a campaign that could justify such a brilliant new product. Pleased at this affirmation of its genius, the client agreed to the new terms. On the return train journey, Richard apologised to his boss, saying he wasn't aware that so much work had already been done on the campaign. With a wink his boss opened a completely empty briefcase.

Richard saw this occasion as amusing and indicative of the wiles of the advertising industry. With his natural playfulness, manifested in his ease with people and wry humour, by contrast he was a man who instilled confidence in those around him based on substance rather than affectation. Richard moved from the advertising world to running a radio station and was CEO of Jazz FM between 1995 and 2002. As well as managing the station he also presented his own programme, and the company successfully grew until he sold it, enjoying what he called a substantial 'liquidity event' that paid for an enviable life of travel and fishing. He still worked as executive chairman of the Local Radio Company, which runs twenty-five radio stations across the UK. The radio station he left behind reduced the amount of jazz it played and floundered. Showing again his deep love of music and ambition to share it, as well as his preparedness to take a risk, Richard bought it back in 2009 for £1.

Apart from his pleasure in playing jazz records – and the station has over half a million listeners a week, claiming to be the largest jazz radio station in the world – Richard gave back to the jazz community. He launched the Jazz FM Awards, and the Love Supreme Jazz Festival. He was chairman of the National Youth Jazz Collective and actively involved in a programme that sends jazz musicians and dancers into fifty schools a year, often in deprived areas, to run one- or two-day courses. The children then present concerts for the school and parents. Richard once showed us an app on his iPad that displayed where in the world people were listening to his station. His delight was palpable when he indicated the number of people listening in Japan and Korea.

Richard's obituary in *Campaign* magazine said: 'He was driven by an entrepreneurial passion and a deep love of jazz music. The people who worked alongside him over his long career will testify that he was a decent man who brought something different to our industry and was always a calm presence in the room offering sage advice.' Richard's grace was more than that of a well-mannered person with a concern for others: it lay in the risks he took, not primarily for financial advantage, but to realize his desire to make the pleasure of jazz music available to a broader audience.

Being ungracious

One of the most important consequences of grace in someone we work with or for is that it develops affection for that person. Gracious people inspire respect, affection and loyalty from those around them. Success, on its own, gains admiration, but rarely warmth, fondness or love. One can admire Thomas Edison, but by many accounts he wasn't the most loveable of people. Edison treated fellow inventor and one-time employee Nikola Tesla abominably, and his chief assistant lost an arm and most of a hand during one of his experiments for which he received scant compensation. The great inventor excoriated 'pinheads' and 'lunkheads'. In 1903, Edison electrocuted an unfortunate elephant, Topsy, in Lunar Park. He did this to demonstrate the dangers of Tesla's competing alternating current method of electricity generation and distribution. The execution was filmed by Edison then widely distributed in his chain of cinemas for further publicity value.

The way such entrepreneurs can push things to the edge is also seen in the case of Alfred Nobel, the inventor of dynamite. One of his experiments went wrong, killing three assistants and his younger brother. Even Jonas Salk, the man who contributed so much by developing a polio vaccine, could display a notable lack of grace. Upon receiving the first public recognition for his successes, he failed to mention in his speech of thanks any of his co-workers, some of whom were seen to leave the room in tears. It wasn't until fifty years later that his son acknowledged that the work undertaken was a team effort.

Does success compensate for a lack of grace? Certainly it helps if that success is non-financial. Salk laudably helped to eradicate a foul disease and did not seek to benefit from it financially. When asked who owned the polio vaccine, he gracefully replied: 'why, the people, I would say'. There are those who venerate wealth and celebrity, but perhaps we could defer to the wise Victorian author and reformer Samuel Smiles when he says in his popular book *Thrift*: 'riches do not constitute any claim to distinction. It is only the vulgar who admire riches as riches.'[3] It is also our experience that those who take themselves too seriously do so because no one else does. There is no suggestion that you always have to be nice to succeed, and Jon Ronson suggests in his book *The Psychopath Test* that quite a few people who climb to the top of the organizational ladder have psychopathic tendencies.[4] It is also possible to appear nice and agreeable and be quite the opposite, as the following extreme example shows.

As a young man, one of the authors (Mark) had occasion to spend the evening in Entebbe, Uganda, at the house of an Israeli colonel who was showing film he had taken of military action during the Six-Day War. We were joined by a very jolly army colonel (the Ugandan armed forces were being trained by the

Israelis at the time), who spent the whole evening uproariously enjoying himself, being solicitous to his hosts, telling jokes and entertaining everyone there. Mark was completely charmed by his warmth and humour. The fact that he was so intensely interested in the film showing the destruction of Arab tanks and fortresses should have been a giveaway, however: he was Idi Amin, soon to become one of Africa's most despotic heads of state. The irony of the evening was remarkable given his subsequent conversion to Islam and events surrounding the Entebbe Raid – in which Israeli commandos rescued over a hundred hostages from a hijacked aeroplane, with the deaths of twenty Ugandan soldiers and Yonatan Netanyahu, brother of the future Israeli prime minister. Amin's bizarre personality is captured in the book and film *The Last King of Scotland*, and in his declaration to be 'Lord of All the Beasts of the Earth and Fishes of the Seas and Conqueror of the British Empire'. The reality of Amin's period in power involved the slaughter of several hundred thousand people, including several of Mark's school friends.

In contrast, the other author (David) had a memorable encounter as a boy, when a guest and his family came to stay at his home at Newbury Rectory. In the early 1970s David's father was team rector for the parish of Newbury and his uncle worked as chaplain in the then University of Botswana, Lesotho and Swaziland. His uncle's friend and colleague, Desmond Tutu, with his wife and daughters, were to visit England and were invited to stay at the rectory. David vividly remembers a larger-than-life character, full of fun, with a huge, loud laugh. Tutu is an unforgettably charismatic person with an open friendliness and sense of inner calm and confidence. This was the man who fought to end the apartheid regime in South Africa and went on to lead the country's Truth and Reconciliation Commission. He campaigns for women's and homosexual rights and AIDS sufferers, and works with the United Nations on climate change. He was awarded the Nobel Peace Prize in 1984 for his role as a unifying figure in ending apartheid in South Africa. Archbishop Tutu's formal spoken title is 'Your Grace', which he personifies.

These two examples demonstrate how grace lies not with ephemeral charm or bonhomie, but with consistent behaviour over time. The graceless can succeed in their aims, but the point is that real grace is munificent in the way it helps players and the people around them work and play more happily and productively, and that is an important key to success when circumstances are challenging and robust. Resolving the terrible injustice of apartheid required very special capabilities, of which grace and humility are perhaps the most important. People generally prefer to work for people they love and respect rather than admire and fear. After meetings with the former, people feel energized and motivated; the latter leave them apprehensive and hesitant.

The question remains: why work with graceless people, the sort that plagued Emily's work? There are stories of those with terrible reputations yet who are said to be extremely loyal to those close to them, whilst there are others who deserve nothing but opprobrium. Fred Goodwin exemplifies an extreme lack of grace. He became CEO of the Royal Bank of Scotland (RBS) and oversaw the largest loss in British corporate history. Known for his aggressive style, and with the moniker 'Fred the Shred', we learned first hand of his enthusiasm for instilling fear in even the most senior of his colleagues. Following the collapse of RBS and its takeover by the British government, information emerged about Goodwin's reckless decision-making and lavish lifestyle. Consequently, the knighthood awarded to him in 2004 was annulled in 2012: a very rare event in the British honours system.

Another famously unpleasant businessman in recent times is Al 'Chainsaw' Dunlap, a man who made his reputation by cutting thousands of jobs, effectively destroying the companies he led. Following a series of accounting scandals, he was eventually barred by the US Securities and Exchange Commission from ever serving in a public corporation. The journalist John Byrne says in *Fast Company*: 'In all my years of reporting, I had never come across an executive as manipulative, ruthless, and destructive as Al Dunlap ... Dunlap sucked the very life and soul out of companies and people. He stole dignity, purpose, and sense out of organizations and replaced those ideals with fear and intimidation.'[5]

The economist Albert Hirschman wrote that when the benefit of working for an organization declines, you have two options: exit or voice. That is, you register your concerns and discuss them in the hope of changing conditions, or you leave. When confronted with such perverse people as Goodwin or Dunlap, the likelihood of successful voice is so small the only option in such circumstances is exit.

Fortunately, there are counterpoints to the shredders and chainsaws of work. As shown by the numerous innovators and entrepreneurs whose stories are told in this book, there are many benefits to being graceful and providing opportunities for voice. The great economist Joseph Schumpeter realized the entrepreneur knows how to 'woo support' among colleagues, 'handle men [sic] with consummate skills' and 'give others ample credit for the organization's achievements'. Walter Isaacson, in his book *The Innovators*, says: 'Even Steve Jobs and Bill Gates, with all of their prickly intensity, knew how to build strong teams around them and inspire loyalty.'[6]

There are, of course, cases of the most brutal and unsympathetic people reforming. John Newton (1725–1807) was a slave trader who later became an ordained priest and active abolitionist. His extraordinary life, which included being flogged, sold as a slave himself and nearly losing his life in a shipwreck, was a journey of gradual realization about and atonement for the evil of slave trading. His story was a gradual process of accumulating grace, captured in the famous hymn he wrote, 'Amazing Grace', which includes the verse:

Through many dangers, toils and snares,
I have already come;
'Tis grace hath brought me safe thus far,
And grace will lead me home.

Being graceful

We have met some truly awful people in our careers – quite a statement when the point of reference is Idi Amin – but thankfully we have met many more like the people above, who possess the extraordinary grace that compensates for the evil of which some are capable. We have been fortunate to meet people who exude kindness, dignity and a convivial feeling of wellbeing. It is these people that we always wish we could spend more time with.

Grace lies in accepting your failings. Richard Dawkins in *The God Delusion* writes about a respected older scholar of the Zoology Department at Oxford when Dawkins was an undergraduate.[7] The professor had taught for years, and fervently believed that there was no such thing as a Golgi apparatus (a microscopic feature inside some cells). During a regular weekly departmental seminar a visiting American biologist presented conclusive evidence that the Golgi apparatus was real. After the lecture, and in front of the whole department, the scientist strode to the front of the hall, shook the American by the hand and loudly admitted: 'My dear fellow, I wish to thank you. I have been wrong these fifteen years.' Dawkins reports applause erupting from those at the seminar.

Grace also lies in the immersion in worthwhile work. Shakespeare, in *Troilus and Cressida*, observes that 'things won are done; joy's soul lies in the doing': that is, the outcome might be highly satisfactory, but the journey has the capacity to be even more pleasurable. Applying this maxim, when Josiah Wedgwood, a great pioneer of the Industrial Revolution, became treasurer for the construction of the Trent and Mersey Canal, a substantial engineering achievement at the time, his major challenge lay in the deeply political difficulties of building a diverse coalition of interests: Staffordshire potters, West Midlands iron manufacturers, Cheshire salt miners, Liverpool merchants, landowners in three counties and a number of influential aristocrats. He had to compete against rival companies with alternative plans, convince mill owners they would not lose the water that their businesses depended upon, raise the money for the project and determine the corporate structure for the endeavour. He relished the challenge: 'There was something "joyful," to use Wedgwood's own word, about the way he attacked every aspect of his life at this time. As he said of the canal, his "heart was in it": arguments and actions came easily and his spirits soared as his different interests meshed effortlessly together.'[8] His efforts resulted from what the psychologist Mihaly Csikszentmihalyi would call 'flow' – when you're in the zone, immersed and absorbed in a task[9] – and can be associated with grace at work.

Modesty is a core element of grace. Kathleen Schulz brings a psychological perspective to bear on the importance of recognizing our errors and misconceptions.[10] She argues that a lot of us go through life assuming we are basically right, all the time, about basically everything. She introduces the marvellous concept of 'fractal wrongness', where someone is wrong about absolutely everything, all of the time. Yet our capacity to err, she suggests, is inextricable from our most humane and honourable qualities: empathy, optimism, imagination, conviction and courage. Being wrong makes us more compassionate, and modesty can be a great source of, and means to impart, learning.

Ove Arup

The value of modesty is seen in the life of Sir Ove Arup (1895–1988), founder of the eponymous company that has become one of the world's leading design and engineering consulting companies. Ove Arup emphasized how grace can be found in the pleasure of work. In 1970, Arup gave what came to be called his 'key speech',[11] since read by every recruit into the firm and outlining what have become core values in the organization. He says:

There are two ways of looking at the work you do to earn a living: One is the way propounded by the late Henry Ford:

Work is a necessary evil, but modern technology will reduce it to a minimum. Your life is your leisure lived in your 'free' time. The other is: To make your work interesting and rewarding. You enjoy both your work and your leisure. We opt uncompromisingly for the second way.

Arup knew that working with pleasure brings immense satisfaction. Grace lies with the joy of doing things well, and it lies in the capacity to be modest and thereby improve our capacity to cooperate effectively with others. As he further notes in his speech: 'no man is an island . . . our lives are inextricably mixed up with those of our fellow human beings, and . . . there can be no happiness in isolation. Which leads to an attitude which would accord to others the rights claimed for oneself.'

Revealing his attractive modesty, Arup was self-effacing about the ideas in his speech, suggesting they should be called the 'musings of an old gentleman in a garden'. The principles he outlined were humanitarian. He wanted prosperity for all members of the company, but only as a result of doing socially useful work and joining hands with others 'fighting for the same values'. He wanted pleasant working environments and conditions 'where every member is treated not only as a link in a chain of command, not only as a wheel in a bureaucratic machine, but as a human being whose happiness is the concern of all, who is treated not only as a means but as an end'. Other principles include to 'act honourably in our dealings with our own and other people', and 'eschew nepotism or discrimination on the basis of nationality, religion, race, colour or sex'.

Arup's were all profound and laudable principles, yet in his speech to the people working in the company he built he asked, 'who am I to tell you and the firm what you should think and feel in the future when I am gone – or before that, for that matter? It wouldn't be any good my trying to lay down the law, and I haven't the slightest inclination to do so.' His humility explains a great deal about why his principles are so important to the company four decades later. His grace gives permission to play.

From a design company to a design engineer: Professor Peter Childs is an academic with an unconventional career. He started his working life as a locksmith, and has run jewellery and knitwear businesses. The meeting room in his office is notable for the large number of colourful hats suspended from the ceiling. As head of the Dyson School of Design Engineering at Imperial College, he is a world authority on design. He places great importance on play and talks about the 'benefits of the collective mind'. Peter is an enthusiast for the role of clubs, such as the eighteenth-century coffee houses that fostered so much valuable debate, and he belongs to one that meets six times a year and has a diverse membership with the single objective to talk about imaginative ideas. When asked about the importance of grace he surprised us with the significance he places on it. Grace is going to be incredibly important in the future, he argues, because this and the last generation have squandered opportunities for peace and wealth, and it will take grace in future generations to sort things out.

Responsibility rests easily on people with grace, such as Ove Arup, but it is not easily developed and achieved. Yet, as shown in the next two examples of players, it is even possible to find it in the cut and thrust of the technology sector in California – renowned for its aggressive acquisitiveness – in people working in extremely competitive circumstances.

Don Strickland

There can be few parts of the world with a greater preoccupation with the intricacies of business stock options than California. The Silicon Valley experience of producing overnight millionaires makes people there obsess about the financial options and rights associated with their jobs. Don Strickland was CEO of a Californian technology start-up that was acquired by another company. The new owner wanted to keep Don, who is an experienced technology company leader, with previous senior positions at Apple and Kodak. He offered him 5 million shares as stock options. Don was aware of the volatility surrounding the company and informed the board that he would accept 1 million shares and offer the remainder to the staff.

A short time later the difficult situation facing the company became clear. Don had to inform the staff and the market that the company's position was so perilous that in two weeks' time it would be unable to fulfil the payroll obligation and in a month it could not pay the rent. Don says the fact that employees stayed in such circumstances is due to the company's honesty about its position and commitment to them, seen in the example of the stock options. Employees did well out of the stock options, as within five years the company had a stock market valuation of $1.6 billion. Asking Don why he gave up 4 million shares – rather rare behaviour in California – he jokes: 'Well, perhaps it was because I was dropped on my head at eighteen months!' Seriously though, he says, 'it felt right'. It was a graceful decision.

Don's views on the grace of the entrepreneur are captured in the following:

> Entrepreneurs know they can do something better than others. They can do something better because they have people around them that they care about and who care for them. Grace and empathy is what gets people on board and gives them the confidence and trust that things can be done.
>
> The good entrepreneur starts with the company doing things better than others – it is not about 'me, the entrepreneur', but 'the company' that matters. You need the ability to attract key people, sincerely care about them, understand what they want, give them credit for their contributions, and want to make them better off than they were.

Don is a big, friendly man: an ex-boxer who enjoys his time on the golf course, and a superb communicator. He has had a diverse career, beginning as an engineer and then employed in manufacturing, sales, marketing, business development and general management. He has worked in the US, Asia and Europe. During the difficulties with the company, Don came to the conclusion that despite his wealth of experience, he didn't have the answer to the problem it faced. So he called the staff together, told them about the situation and asked them what he should do. A solution emerged from this process of collaborative engagement. Modesty is grace's close companion.

Sean Bowen

Sean Bowen is CEO of Push Technology, a rapidly growing fifty-person company based in London and San Jose, California. His playfulness is seen in his self-confessed stubbornness in expressing his freedom, and the lessons he has learnt from his experience as a high-standard sportsman in appreciating the value of teamwork. He is a player proud to celebrate the quality and contributions of the people around him.

Raised in straitened circumstances in a poor area of London, Sean says he 'threw his schooling away'. He joined the Royal Air Force against the advice of his parents – 'I can't be told what I can't do' – where he developed some technical skills before leaving in 2000. He moved into the finance sector and went to night school to learn about information technology, travelling four to five hours a day for his first job. Working at a time when the internet and mobile communications were beginning to have an effect on business, with classic entrepreneurial flair Sean saw the opportunity for real-time dashboards to display data. He estimates, however, that he was probably six years ahead of banks' ability to appreciate their value. He became interested in the way large amounts of data could be distributed to people using a wide range of devices. Although he coded some early demonstration products, he laughs that his engineers today would be very unimpressed with his level of programming skill.

The first market Push Technology addressed was online gaming, followed closely by finance. As Sean puts it: 'You can decide on which sector is more ethical: gambling or finance.' At the time, not all betting companies understood the internet and the challenges it would bring to in-play betting, but some knew they had to embrace it. Many were struggling with the scale and speed of data that needed to be transferred over the internet so quite often during peak events, such as the Grand National, the UK's iconic horse race, major company systems broke down in the hours before they started. Push Technology not only provided systems to stop these outages but also enabled companies to offer in-play betting on a much wider scale than ever before. Nowadays betting companies are moving data back and forth from millions of customers concurrently. It is possible to bet on almost anything. For example, you can bet on a player winning a single point in tennis, and to do that you need almost real-time betting and results feeds. This requires incredibly fast communications networks and processing power. The growth of online, real-time betting companies has been dramatic. They required a technical infrastructure to handle this new type of growth. Push Technology has developed the means to facilitate these multiple rapid interactions.

Sean explains that he has experience of working in many parts of business management, and that such diversity is good grounding for a CEO needing to adapt to many different circumstances. He also says that his experience of being a high-level rugby and football player has shaped his worldview and skills. He argues that sport teaches teamwork and creates a fantastic work ethic with the added bonus of building a good network of friends. It teaches you how to celebrate successes and deal with losses. He explains how on the rugby field you 'beat the hell out of each other one minute' and then happily join each other in the bar for a drink afterwards, and he uses the same approach in business. Business is hard and sometimes tough discussions need to be had, but you also need to step away afterwards, move on and have a beer.

His intention is to grow and sell the business, and his prime motivation is to ensure his children don't suffer the same deprivations he did. Asked what he'd do when it is successfully sold, he answers, 'Well, I'd start another one, of course.' Having established his business in the gaming industry, he then diversified back into the finance sector. In techspeak, Push Technology has developed what is called a 'reactive data layer which has an event driven architecture that allows optimal delivery of data across unreliable networks to mobile terminals distributed everywhere'. Sean says it has attracted considerable interest from companies such as IBM and Oracle, has an 'amazing' investor list, including one of America's richest families, and has an advisory board that Sean tells us is important for opening doors and for questioning whether the company is going in the right direction. His intention in moving his family to Silicon Valley in 2014 was to expose the technology to large companies and large partners based in the Bay Area. Asked how a relatively small company can negotiate effectively with such powerful companies, he smiles and says, 'We're pretty shrewd.'

Sean's approach to recruitment is to employ people 'better than himself'. He uses the metaphor of Russian dolls: put better people around you and you will have a company that will grow; put lesser people around you and the company shrinks. He takes great pride in the calibre of his engineering team, such as the current chief technology officer who has a PhD from the University of Cambridge.

He has very high energy levels and loves seeing people learn and develop, but says once you see someone doesn't fit you need to move them on quickly, as it is all about the team. He apparently operates a lot on gut feeling, but feels he also has the vision to execute quickly and practically, and enjoys being able to see something and solve it for everyone more efficiently and cost effectively than anyone else.

The notion of play resonates strongly with Sean. Every now and then he gives his engineers a week off, called Demo Week, to 'play with ideas'. He proudly exhibits one major outcome: an app that nicely displays the company's technological prowess. It can simultaneously draw directly onto a computer screen in front of you and, using a mobile device operating through a server, to one on the other side of the world. Sean has thrown himself into Californian life, amused at some of its quirks: 'You wouldn't believe how hard it is to rent a house in a suburb called Los Gatos [The Cats] when you actually have cats.' There is a strong network of expatriate British people, with whom he socializes by holding events including curry evenings in his home ('what could be more British?'). He says sometimes he sits down with his sales director, who started life in London in similar circumstances to his own; they talk about the brilliant people working in the company and they shake their heads in disbelief at how two people from the streets of London got to where they are. This is a display of grace through the proud recognition of the contributions of others in a small company unafraid of giving its employees opportunities to play.

Playing together

Great innovators and entrepreneurs don't succeed by themselves. Josiah Wedgwood is one of history's greatest industrial leaders, innovators, and entrepreneurs,[12] yet scrutiny of his extraordinary achievements shows that rather than being a heroic individual he was deeply dependent on his social networks for success.[13] He belonged to many societies and clubs, and searched widely for new ideas amongst artists, craftsmen, scientists, politicians, aristocrats and other entrepreneurs. As we saw earlier, he was a member of the Lunar Society. Wedgwood's productive relationship with artists – painters, sculptors, furniture makers and architects – resulted from his encouragement 'to sharpen the fancy and skill of the artist by a collision with the talents of others'. He was himself untutored, having started work aged eleven, and was prevented by his non-conformist religion from going to university. He thus relied heavily on his deep friendship with the sophisticated and well-travelled Thomas Bentley to fill in the gaps in his knowledge. Prime Minister William Gladstone celebrated Josiah Wedgwood's ability to create new ideas by crossing boundaries, saying: 'He was the greatest man who ever, in any age or in any country, applied himself to the important work of mixing art with industry.' Wedgwood also relied heavily on his family, who filled many positions in his company, and never made an important decision without getting the approval of his wife.

Few entrepreneurs nowadays fail to understand the importance of building and using personal networks and engaging widely on social media. But, as Wedgwood shows us, it is the breadth and variety of these connections that matter. Not much changes when similar people with similar ideas connect with one another. Playfulness flourishes when there are different ideas to spark off, from dissonant voices, diverse experiences and creative abrasion. The collision of ideas can be uncomfortable, and is something not many seek, but it is at the interface that things get exciting. Most Nobel Prizes are won not by people working at the core of their discipline but rather at the point where it intersects with others.

Enthusiasm for playing together in groups and teams is one thing, but openness to the collision of different experiences and worldviews is quite another. It only occurs when players are committed to being open-minded. They sometimes need to be generous generalists, open and ready to learn from the ideas of others. And it only happens when they have the grace to recognize they can't do everything themselves and that energy should be devoted to motivating those around them. Such collisions are challenging: collaborating with people who have strong ideas, different from your own, poses all sorts of problems, needing effort, patience and fortitude when things do not go well. Even in the most apparently collegial workplaces it is easy to be dismissive and even disparaging of other professions and disciplines. The wise British vice-chancellor, David Watson, said that academics know their own fields of study to be complex and messy, where everything is provisional and ambiguous, whereas they tend to believe what other people do is clear-cut and usually wrong.

The notion of the heroic individual is deeply engrained in the Western psyche, but it is usually collective efforts that deliver most reward. Great innovations commonly result from collaborative efforts, rather than the epic actions of individuals. As Walter Isaacson says in his book *The Innovators*, 'An invention, especially one as complex as the computer, usually comes not from an individual brainstorm but from a collaboratively woven tapestry of creativity.' As collaboration and teamwork become ever more important aspects of work, grace in the sense of being respectful of, and being able to cooperate with, others becomes ever more important. Howard Gardner in his book *Five Minds for the Future* puts it this way:

> The question arises about whether ideas about creativity need to be refashioned to take into account the increasing number of projects and realms where the individual contribution seems less critical, the group mind more crucial. Clearly, the abilities to come to know individuals quickly, to forge a working relationship, to handle issues of conflict and credit, take on added importance. Brainstorming and improvisation come to the fore; personal glory recedes in importance.[14]

The ways in which grace can be fostered collaboratively are seen particularly clearly in the case of the codebreakers of Bletchley Park in the Second World War, consisting of a wide variety of people being playful in their own distinctive manner. The 2014 film *The Imitation Game* related how Bletchley's success was that of a brilliant but difficult individual, Alan Turing, but this runs contrary to the real story. Bletchley is a case of collective grace in the extraordinary personal sacrifices made by many individuals to a great cause.

Bletchley Park

In 1941, Britain was facing a dire situation in the war with the Axis powers. Its supply chain of food and materiel from the US was being destroyed by German U-boats, and there was an urgent need to crack the military codes being used to communicate with the U-boats, so as to locate, avoid or destroy them. The task was given to the government's code-breaking facility at Bletchley Park in central England. The cracking of these codes – especially Enigma – provided an example of the extraordinary persistence and courage in the collective efforts of, and the concentrated application of ideas by, a wide variety of people to solve a challenging problem. The difficulty was immense. The Germans, no doubt reassured by the fact that there were 15^{22} possibilities for each letter encoded, and that a new sequence of codes began at midnight every day, believed these encrypted codes were impregnable.

The creation, construction and use of Bletchley's code-breaking machines involved contributions from brilliant mathematicians, talented and imaginative engineers, effective managers, highly skilled technicians and craftsmen and dedicated machine operators capable of long hours of extended concentration. Although Alan Turing was one of the world's greatest mathematical geniuses and his contribution is now widely recognized, Bletchley's is not a case of individual achievement but a collective story of courage and determination at work. Courage at Bletchley took many forms, from preparedness to explore uncharted intellectual territory, to continuing to operate in intolerable working conditions, to confronting hierarchical barriers and maintaining absolute secrecy. At its peak Bletchley employed 10,000 people, but secrecy was maintained, often at considerable personal cost. Wives could not tell their husbands, nor husbands their wives, what they did in the war, even up to their deaths many decades later. Fathers and headmasters questioned the courage of their sons and students when it appeared they were avoiding active service, since they were unable to explain what they were doing. Reflecting on its importance and incredible achievement of remaining a secret, Winston Churchill described Bletchley Park as the golden goose that never once cackled.

As well as moral courage, the quest to break the Enigma code also involved extraordinary physical courage, such as when three sailors, two of whom drowned, jumped into a sinking U-boat to retrieve a secret codebook. Tommy Brown, the survivor who managed to save the codebooks, was a sixteen-year-old boy who died a year later, trying to save his sister from a house fire.[15]

The geniuses that worked at Bletchley were known for their eccentricity. Max Newman was a brilliant scientist who after the war led the development of British computing. An employee describes seeing Newman standing on Bletchley Park railway station in a shabby coat, holding a rabbit in one hand and looking distressed. She asked if he was all right and he replied he had lost his ticket. She told him not to worry and to explain to the train guard what had happened, but he exclaimed his problem was that without his ticket he could not remember whether he was travelling to Oxford or Cambridge. Turing is reputed to have chained his tea mug to a radiator to prevent others using it and to have arrived for a game of tennis wearing nothing but an overcoat. To avoid hay fever, he used to cycle to work in a gas mask.

Yet, there was method in their madness and in their playfulness there was discipline. The historian Baron Asa Briggs, an analyst at Bletchley, says it 'was a flexible institution capable of adaptation and development which lacked any formal diagram of its organization structure until 1944'. Its vagueness of structure and need for improvisation led to self-government and self-discipline that Hugh Trevor-Roper, later Lord Dacre, who also worked at Bletchley, described as 'friendly informality verging on apparent anarchy'. There was a vibrant social life including amateur dramatics, chess, tennis, visits to the pub (when, circumventing wartime shortages, they actually had any beer), discussions on political, economic, educational and philosophical matters, and a series of seminars organized by the analyst who later founded Amnesty International. It was a strange mixture of military and civilian, with a complicated formal reporting structure to military intelligence and the government's Foreign and Cabinet Offices. Unusually in wartime, however, military rank counted for nothing: military personnel could report to civilians, and junior ranks could oversee their seniors.

Sinclair McKay's book *The Secret Life of Bletchley Park* is subtitled *The WWII Codebreaking Centre and the Men and Women Who Worked There*, and reminds us of the crucial role of women in the operation's success: something that is sometimes overlooked in the desire to celebrate the role of great (male) individuals.[16] McKay tells of the codebreakers Joan Murray and Mavis Batey, the aristocrat Hon. Sarah Baring who ended up working as Bletchley Park's main liaison with the Admiralty and fourteen-year-old Mimi Galilee who worked as a messenger. McKay also writes of the thousands of young women who endured years of freezing weather, appalling food and physically demanding work, and who 'despite the discomforts and privations [... displayed] a general sense of satisfaction, the knowledge that they were fundamentally doing their bit'.

Codebreaker Peter Hilton describes his group as intellectuals 'who couldn't give a damn', meaning they only accepted self-imposed discipline. The open management style was modelled in many ways on that of a Cambridge college from which many cryptologists came. Hilton's section head, Max Newman, was said to have recruited the best and expected the best of them. Despite the urgency of the work, Newman would release two members of his team for two-week research sabbaticals to think about how to improve methods and procedures. A logbook was created where everyone could write down their ideas for improvements, which were discussed at a 4 p.m. tea party every few weeks.

Practical people such as engineers complemented the unworldly scientists at Bletchley. The world's first programmable electronic digital computer – Colossus – that was developed at Bletchley to break the codes relied on a number of key engineers from the British Post Office. Tommy Flowers, Steve Shirley's mentor, was a crucial contributor, whose role, due to the secrecy insisted upon by Churchill, went unacknowledged and unrecognized for decades. It was Flowers who, despite the incredulity of many engineers, realized the potential of using valves as high-speed switches for digital computing, and who essentially brought electronics into the design of Colossus. Flowers's career floundered after the war and he ended up in debt. Had he patented his work he might have become wealthy.

Enigma's coded messages were eventually mechanically converted by Colossus directly into plain language, and once the daily code was broken the whole German communication system became readable to the British. From July 1941, broken Enigma-coded messages to and from German U-boats led to a two-thirds decrease in losses compared with previous months. By 1942 two Enigma messages were being decoded every minute, and by the end of the war it was unusual for German codes not to be broken before breakfast. Bletchley cracked German, Italian, Russian and, eventually, Japanese codes. Messages sent directly from Hitler were decoded. Intelligence from Bletchley informed battles from North Africa to the Russian Front, and was crucial to Eisenhower's plans for D-Day. Of its contribution, General Eisenhower wrote: 'The intelligence . . . from you . . . has been of priceless value. It has saved thousands of British and American lives and, in no small way, contributed to the speed with which the enemy was routed and eventually forced to surrender.'

The risks confronted and opportunities realized among the wide range of people with diverse skills at Bletchley occurred in a working environment that was playful on the one hand, and deadly serious on the other. It was a truly collective effort, showing grace in the combined recognition of the contributions of others, personal sacrifice in the hardship of the working conditions and in suffering the sometimes humiliating consequences of secrecy.

The efforts of the people at Bletchley Park were driven by a noble cause. We now turn to an activity where entrepreneurs show their commitment to their chosen good causes: philanthropy.

Gerald Chan

The great economist J.K. Galbraith observed that 'wealth, in even the most improbable cases, manages to convey the aspect of intelligence'. But in Gerald Chan's case, Galbraith's cynicism does not apply. Gerald's passion for learning and his encouragement of intelligence is demonstrated by one of the largest-ever philanthropic donations to a university. In 2014, his family gave $350 million to Harvard University's School of Public Health.

Gerald Chan began his studies as an engineer, earning two degrees from UCLA before moving to Harvard in the 1970s to study for his PhD. Initially he wanted to research physics, but moved into biology in the School of Public Health. He successfully earned a Master's degree and PhD, publishing in the prestigious journal *Nature*. Rather than remain in science, he returned to his native Hong Kong where he started a venture capital and private equity company with his brother. However, he retained his passion for science. His company, Morningside, was an early investor in Chinese technology and has invested in forty companies, including, among others, biotechnology projects developing membranes for water filtration, solar panels, a mobile app for early detection of autism and cancer-targeting systems. Gerald maintained his connections with Harvard, sitting on advisory boards and endowing a chair, and the Morningside Foundation has made numerous education and science-related philanthropic donations in Hong Kong and China.

Gerald is a director of publicly listed Hang Lung Group Limited, a Hong Kong-based property holding company founded by his father. He sits on the boards of several biotechnology companies in North America and Europe. His desire to give back is demonstrated by his presence on university advisory groups in China, Hong Kong and the US, and he is a member of the Global Advisory Council of the International Society for Stem Cell Research.

Gerald's passion for public health goes back to his experiences of growing up in impoverished China in the 1950s. His mother was a nurse who used to give vaccinations, which weren't generally available in China at the time, to neighbours in the family kitchen. A strong advocate for hygiene, she kept her syringe clean (though not, unfortunately for local children, sharp) by disinfecting it in boiling water. This focus on pragmatism and the public good have infused Gerald's successes. While his businesses have depended on sound pragmatic decisions, his personal philosophy elevates the cerebral. A life is rich when it is rich with ideas, he argues, and a person devoid of ideas will have neither ideals to work towards nor the energy to do so.

The dean of Harvard's School of Public Health says, 'Traditionally in public health we've had two career paths: research and public service, Gerald pioneered a third path of going into entrepreneurship and innovation.'[17] Gerald says the goals of making a profit and doing good works are not mutually exclusive, and that entrepreneurs working in public health will raise money not from donors or benefactors, but from investors. And enterprises run for profit can pursue a mission to deliver benefits to society.

Gerald argues for a new philanthropy in support of public health. He suggests financial capital devoted to the maximization of profits for shareholders hasn't the incentives to support public health, so what is needed is capital where: 1) financial returns are negligible; 2) horizons are long term; 3) tolerance for risk is high; and 4) decisions are made by scientists with product development experience. He calls such resources philanthropic capital.

Giving such large amounts for a good cause is graceful, but it is even more graceful when the donation will be entirely under the control of the recipient. It is common for philanthropists who donate large sums to universities to demand a say in how their money is to be spent, or at least to keep an eye on whether it is being spent well. One major UK business school received a substantial donation to fund its new building and its leaders were shocked when at its ceremonial opening the donor asked where his office was located. The Chan donation was unrestricted: that is, the money is to be spent in the way the university thinks best. Research in the Chan School of Public Health will focus on pandemics, humanitarian crises, failing health systems and social and environmental threats to health. The money will also support junior researchers in areas that don't qualify for government funding, as well as advanced classrooms and computer resources.

Gerald's philosophy extols the virtue of learning that strives towards ambitious aims, and he is all too aware of the challenges that threaten such purpose. His views are eloquently captured in his Commencement Speech at Harvard in 2012.

> Being flooded with minutiae of everyday life subverts our intellectual life by luring us into, and holding us captive in the present, in what is, such that we have no time and no energy left to consider what might be, or what can be, or what should be. The peril we face in today's society is that we unwittingly become mere pragmatists, and soon, exhausted realists.
>
> Today, whether a person can be considered a learned person hinges on what he does with the knowledge he has. A beautiful mind is not beautiful by virtue of its storage capacity, nor even what has been stored in it. A beautiful mind is a mind with beautiful ideas.

Gerald's nobility lies in his support for beautiful ideas, providing conditions for the freedom to push back boundaries. He has used his wealth to provide the means for scientists to pursue their ambitions to explore and learn, and help make their lives and the organization for which they work rich with ideas.

Luck

One of the signs of grace is attributing a significant amount of success to luck. A recurrent theme in Daniel Kahneman's book

Thinking, Fast and Slow is that luck plays a large role in every story of success.[18] A psychologist who won the Nobel Prize in Economic Sciences, Kahneman argues it is almost always easy to identify a small change in the story that would have turned a remarkable achievement into a mediocre outcome. The quality that Napoleon most desired in his generals was luck. Not every successful person is prepared, however, to say luck mattered as much as their talent or ambition. The *Financial Times* magazine has a section called 'The Inventory', where a series of famous people are asked questions about their lives. These people come from the arts, business, sport and politics. All are highly successful in their fields. They are asked the question: 'Ambition or talent: which matters more to success?' Out of fifty interviews, fourteen people elevated talent over ambition; nine elevated ambition over talent; and eight thought both equally important. Hard work and perseverance were cited by fourteen people, and luck by seven. Other characteristics mentioned include inspiration, curiosity, passion, knowing yourself and intuition. One person ducked the question and one pronounced ambition and talent to be modernist nonsense.

This piece of casual empiricism reveals there's no consensus among successful people about the causes of success. It shows that most agree you do well through possessing talent and/or ambition and working hard and only a few attribute success to luck, maybe pointing to the value of reflecting on the findings of Daniel Kahneman's research. Sometimes luck plays a role in providing the conditions in which you can play.

As a startling example about how small, chance events have the capacity for massive influence, Eric Beinhocker in his book *The Origin of Wealth* tells the story of Annie Oakley, touring Europe in the late 1800s with Buffalo Bill's Wild West Show (as an illustration of just how quickly the world has changed, the show was seen by one author's – Mark's – grandfather).[19] Annie's act as a rifle sharpshooter included shooting a cigarette out of someone's mouth. She asked for volunteers in the audience and when, understandably, no one responded, her husband, planted among the onlookers, came forward and she demonstrated her skill on him. Except one night, someone did respond: a young man called Frederick. Deeply shaken, Oakley continued with her act and despite her nervousness succeeded in her remarkable demonstration. Frederick was Prince of Prussia, soon to be Kaiser Wilhelm II, the man who led Germany into the First World War and its loss of 17 million lives. If Annie had missed by an inch or two, who knows what the history of the twentieth century might have been. Grace lies with those who remember Marx's dictum that men (as he put it) make their own history, but not in circumstances of their own making, and also, as this example shows, that those circumstances have the potential to be profoundly affected by the most trivial and random events.

Reflections

Grace appears in many ways, and it enthuses, influences and animates play. The grace of innovators and entrepreneurs such as Gerard Fairtlough, Alexsis de Raadt St James, Richard Wheatly and Ove Arup influences the way they work and inspires those around them, encouraging others and giving them the confidence to experiment, explore and pursue worthy objectives. The grace of such leaders, and philanthropists such as Gerald Chan, animate those seeking to follow Gerald's dictum that a life is rich when it is rich with ideas.

As seen in the examples of Don Strickland and Sean Bowen, grace is a feature of those leading in the most profit-orientated and uncertain circumstances, where open-mindedness and collective intelligence are needed to innovate new products and services, ways of organizing and business models. Modesty and the preparedness to trust others and give them credit for their achievements are behaviours that deliver benefits in even the most competitive – not to say cut-throat – of circumstances. As Thomas Watson Sr, the founder of IBM put it: 'Really big people are, above everything else, courteous, considerate, and generous – not just to some people in some circumstances – but to everyone all the time.' Being ungracious is a sure way of killing all those behaviours needed to survive and thrive in a changing and unpredictable world. Grace, as shown in the achievements of the men and women at Bletchley Park, can be a collective behaviour – a 'collaboratively woven tapestry of creativity' – and as seen in the story of John Newton, the writer of the hymn 'Amazing Grace', it is something that individuals can learn and accumulate over a lifetime.

The grace of innovators and entrepreneurs gives us the opportunity to reflect on our own behaviours at work, and of those around us, by asking whether we:

+ are respectful, trusting, encouraging and collaborative;
+ stress modesty and avoid hubris;
+ accept constructive criticism;
+ recognize personal shortcomings and celebrate the abilities of others; and
+ credit success to joint efforts, but take responsibility for failure.

4

Craft

Ability in planning or performing, ingenuity in constructing.
Trade, or profession, requiring special skill and knowledge.
A skilful contrivance or expedient.

The exercise of craft is intrinsically pleasing and rewarding, and historically groups such as the Luddites and Arts and Craft movement have enthusiastically defended its practice at work. The latter placed great emphasis on the dignity to be found in merging intellectual and manual tasks. For Rousseau, engaging with materials is a core element of Emile's education:

> He wants to touch and handle everything; do not check these movements which teach him invaluable lessons. Thus he learns to perceive the heat, cold, hardness, softness, weight, or lightness of bodies, to judge their size and shape and all their physical properties, by looking, feeling.

The modern application of craft extends far beyond its traditional association with material and manual skills, and importantly includes crafting digital media and designing services. Glenn Adamson, formerly the director of New York's Museum of Art and Design, has written several books about craft, and he says it is a process or activity, rather than a category, and it exists even in the most high-tech situation.[1]

Craft, in our sense, involves knowledgeable and insightful people shaping simple, useful and elegant ideas and solutions that create new opportunities or solve complex problems. It often realizes opportunities and solves problems in the face of the uncertainty of imperfect and even contradictory information and circumstances. True craft can be an immense source of personal satisfaction, but it can also be found in making products and delivering services that give pleasure to others. It combines intellect, reason, skill, understanding, judgement and intuition.

We shall explore how craft contributed to the design of a 'seed cathedral' made of acrylic rods, and helps explain how we might become more accustomed to the sign 'in case of fire, please use the lift'.

Joseph Schumpeter saw innovation as the result of new combinations. Innovation combines old and new knowledge, various techniques and technologies, different professions and skills, and the creativity that leads to a practical outcome. Josiah Wedgwood's great strengths as an innovator and entrepreneur lay in his efforts at combining the worlds of business, science and the arts. The new combinations that produce novel products, services and ways of doing things often require the merging of the previously separate through shared acts of curiosity. Craft shapes and fashions action. As Michael Nielsen says in his book *Reinventing Discovery*:

> in creative work it's often the unplanned and unexpected insights and connections that matter the most. In many cases, what makes a creative insight important is precisely the fact that it combines ideas that previously were thought to be unrelated. The more unrelated, the more important the connection.[2]

Craft is needed in many situations where there are conflicting possible solutions to complex problems on offer. The most extreme form of these problems has been described as 'wicked'.[3] These are big, societal problems that have no clear resolution and have proponents answering them with wildly different and fiercely contested views. They include reducing carbon emissions, controlling illegal immigration, preventing crime, improving education standards and designing financial systems that don't collapse. Because it is unlikely that there are universal answers to these problems that are sufficiently widely acceptable, the only way to answer to them is through a playful process of continual experimentation, trying and testing solutions and learning quickly about what is possible and what works best. Similarly at work, there are times when circumstances are so uncertain, and problems are so 'wicked', that there is value in answers emerging through a process of trial and error involving many interested parties. As Nicholas Negroponte of MIT's Media Lab says, iteration is learning. That process of iteration and learning can be crafted.

Solving a problem often draws on a vast body of existing knowledge about how things work, and then, through considerable intellectual effort, extending this knowledge to progress what is known. Take designers, who commonly need to combine the existing, routine and well established with experiments in the largely unknown. Designers often work in teams, relying heavily on close, personal interaction and conversations to solve problems, to develop ideas and to assess the quality of their work. Designers develop and use their craft by sketching and using digital tools to communicate, direct and stimulate thought, visualize – either in reality, virtually or the mind's eye – and use language or cultural references as an informal vocabulary to communicate ideas. So, for example, a vague reference to 'Gehryesque' would immediately convey meaning to those knowledgeable about the work of the architect Frank Gehry.[4]

Craft is an enduring, basic human impulse to do a job well for its own sake. Everyone appreciates simple things that are done expertly, such as well-made, comfortable clothes or a good meal. There is much to admire about well-crafted wine and beer, great tennis players crafting a victory or the craft of an *auteur* director's great film. Experiences can be crafted, as seen in every visit to a theatre, museum or gallery. Those lucky enough to have eaten at Heston Blumenthal's restaurants or at Noma in Copenhagen attest to the quality of an experience that moves beyond the extraordinary taste of the food. Craft lies in what we do, why we do it and how we enjoy it.

The possession of a craft is personally meaningful as a way of expressing our individuality, learning or skills, and demonstrating our expertise and value to others. The development of certain craft skills and their protection has historically been jealously guarded.[5] In London since the twelfth century various guilds – weavers, needle makers, bakers, vintners – have tied apprentices to masters of their craft both to learn and to control the labour market by restricting the number of new entrants. The adherence of machinists to their craft skills during the Industrial Revolution were such that they were known to draw a chalk circle around their machines into which entrance by others was prohibited. The Arts and Crafts movement emerged as a reaction and antidote to the loss of craft.

Craft is still crucial for contemporary business, and its practice brings great pleasure to its beneficiaries. Take the Vespa scooter. One of the authors rides a Vespa into work, and it transforms him (in his mind at least) into Gregory Peck in *Roman Holiday* – on a good day he has Audrey Hepburn on the back. This enjoyable experience isn't incidental. It is crafted: in this case by the great Italian designer, Corradino D'Ascanio. Scooters used to be considered masculine motorcycles, designed for high-speed racing. The engines were in easy reach so mechanics could easily tune them. D'Ascanio redesigned them for simplicity, convenience and enjoyment. He made them unisex, with a footrest so female riders could wear skirts, luggage racks for bags and shopping and leg shields for safety. He rounded their shape and made them available in lively fashionable colours. In essence, he crafted a new meaning for the vehicle.[6]

The Arts and Crafts tradition has a contemporary, although much more eclectic, version in the 'Maker Movement'. In addition to traditional crafts such as metal and woodworking, the

Maker Movement includes electronics and uses tools such as 3D printing and robotics. It is a highly diverse collection of interests that encompasses, for example, people growing their own food and producing their own textiles. Its approach is to transform people into makers as well as consumers by encouraging the creation of small start-up companies. Cheaply available electronic tools and online marketplaces in which to sell products, such as Etsy and eBay, underpin the Movement. Large 'Maker Faires' are held around the world at which people can demonstrate their craft, and which large companies attend in order to pick up ideas. The largest of these, held in California, attracted 120,000 people in 2014. The movement also uses hackathons, events where programmers and designers work intensively together for a period of time on emerging projects, often with the intention of producing computer code that is both functional and elegant.

The cultural movement in engineering and design that emphasized hands-on experimentation and production led, in the mid-2000s, one of the authors (David) to be heavily involved in developing ideas with the Royal College of Art (RCA) in London. It resulted in the formation of a new collaboration between the RCA, Imperial College's Business School and the Engineering Faculty, chaired by Sir James Dyson, inventor of the bagless vacuum cleaner. The 'Design London' Centre was established with hackspaces and studios.

Ideas for the centre channelled the spirit of 1851, applied in London's South Kensington by Prince Albert, Queen Victoria's Consort. The 1851 Great Exhibition in Hyde Park was the world's first Expo, hosting 6 million visitors, equivalent to almost a quarter of the UK's population at the time. Prince Albert collected a penny from anyone using lavatories at the event, leading to the phrase 'spend a penny'. The money raised was used to buy land and endow the South Kensington district to 'bring together arts and sciences for the betterment of humanity for a thousand years'. This vision resulted in a huge uplift in the creative arts and sciences. It produced the Victoria and Albert,

Natural History and Science Museums, Royal Colleges (including the Royal College of Art and City & Guilds, predecessor to Imperial College) and the Royal Albert Hall.

The modern-day incarnation of Design London has grown into Imperial College's Dyson School of Design Engineering, with maker spaces, design studios, craft workshops and rooms to experiment, test ideas and engage with the passing public.

Elegance is an objective of craft. Many owners of Apple products talk about their aesthetic, the simplicity of their designs and the pleasing nature of their shapes. Lovers of fast motorcars will talk endlessly about the beauty of sports cars. Craft is important for the chief designers at Apple and McLaren. Sir Jonathan Ive, chief design officer at Apple and chancellor of the RCA, says: 'I want to know what things are for, how they work, what they can or should be made of, before I even begin to think what they should look like. More and more people do. There is a resurgence of the idea of craft.'[7]

When he is designing, Frank Stephenson, chief designer at McLaren, uses computerized models to help him conceptualize, but he's keen on things that can be brought to life through touch. He talks of the craft of the trained sculptors, masters of their trade, who model car shapes in clay, a process that he describes as a 'labour of love . . . it is almost as if you can design the car blind. You don't have to see it, but by feeling it you can know if it is right.'[8]

These two preeminent designers point to the importance of craft, and something of its nature. For further insight we turn to a graduate of the RCA and someone who epitomizes the spirit of 1851. The craftsman and designer Thomas Heatherwick has become one of Britain's greatest modern 'makers', whose craft epitomizes what is meant by play.

Thomas Heatherwick

In the opening ceremony of the London Olympics in 2012 each competing nation carried a copper petal that was then attached to long pipes joined in a ring at the centre of the arena. At the climax of the ceremony, flames flew from the individual petals, which then converged to create a giant cauldron of flame. This stunning visual centrepiece was designed by Thomas Heatherwick. The director of the opening ceremony, Danny Boyle, says the cauldron was immense and spectacular but also approachable and on a human scale. The lighting of the flame is a hugely important symbol of the Olympics, and Thomas says that his challenge as someone used to designing places and spaces was to design a moment. His approach was for that moment to be created by everyone together, making the whole more than the sum of its parts.

In a sense, the approach Thomas adopted captures his desire for inclusiveness in what he does. Like Morris and Ruskin, he has an enduring concern about the way designing and making have become separated. A designer himself, he has written a book entitled *Making*.[9] He talks about being exposed to making, craft, materials and invention as he grew up, and in an interview for the Victoria and Albert Museum to coincide with an exhibition of his work entitled 'Designing the Extraordinary', Thomas says it is the responsibility of designers to have proximity to making. You get a feeling for the physics of materials from the experience of using them, and that gives you confidence, he argues, making it easier to communicate with building contractors, welders, carpenters and tradespeople of all sorts. This desire to integrate approaches and disciplines is seen in the range of people working at Heatherwick Studio, which includes designers of products, landscapes and theatre stages, architects, engineers and city planners. An article in *Wired* suggests Heatherwick's studio is a tool for making ideas happen that he is still designing: 'You don't know what the outcome will be, but it feels like we're trying to solve a crime. You're eliminating options from your enquiries. Then you're left with something, and it's probably not what you expected.'[10] Stuart Wood, head of innovation at Heatherwick Studio, says that R&D is vision coupled with dogged persistence.

Along with 73 million other people, visiting the imaginative buildings at the Shanghai Expo in 2010 was a wonderful feeling. But no building surpassed the UK pavilion: Heatherwick Studio won the bid to design the UK structure and was given the challenging brief by the government to produce a building that would be voted among the top five by visitors. The British Foreign Office was rather nervous about the idea of Expos, and was only prepared to invest if it was convinced its pavilion would be a remarkable success.

Over 200 countries vied at the Expo to have their economies, technologies and cultures outshine each other, and while the UK pavilion was allocated a site the size of a football pitch, its budget was roughly half that of competitors from other developed nations. Each design team was given a similar brief to showcase its country's attributes, such as leading industries and major tourist attractions.

Heatherwick's team worked backwards from the desire to 'win' in order to develop the design brief, challenging itself to make an exceptional pavilion. The group imagined what it might be like to visit the Expo with so many pavilions competing for visitors' attention: the scale and diversity, let alone the massive crowds, would make a visit to the Expo overwhelming. So the challenge was to produce a pavilion that everyone would remember. The team decided to present one powerful idea with simplicity and clarity that would make people think. As it was clearly impossible for all the visitors to walk inside the pavilion, attention was instead devoted to its exterior. Rather than filling the whole site with what Thomas called 'a mediocre, cheap shed', he decided to make a small building that was the right size to be photographed in one frame.

His inspiration came from a bit of British eccentricity. He was thinking about Victorian collectors and garden designers at the 1851 London 'Expo'. He thought about the value of parks and gardens and why they still make London a great city. Thomas explained that he was walking around the Royal Botanical Gardens at Kew and thought of doing something using plants, before coming up with the idea of a seed and representing the Millennium Seed Bank that saves seeds from around the world. This led to the idea of a Seed Cathedral. He also found inspiration from the film *Jurassic Park* with its story of DNA trapped in amber, and from a toy that extrudes hair from a figure when squeezed. The result was an ingenious concept crafted with deep design and engineering expertise to make a pavilion comprised of 66,000 acrylic rods, each 25 feet long, containing 250,000 plant seeds. After it was dismantled, rods were distributed among Chinese schools, spreading a legacy about the importance of preserving the world's plant life.

The master plan for the rest of the site was left deliberately superficial in order to leave no lasting memory at all. Everyone would concentrate on the Seed Cathedral. A clever thing about the structure is that the outside shows what is inside. It also shows the British flag from almost every angle. It was visited by eight million people in six months and won the top prize, the gold medal for pavilion design.

Thomas himself prefers the term 'making' to craft, but both imply combinations of multiple inputs towards designing and producing special things. He has made a bridge that rolls up, stunning sculptures and a new bus for London. In each case he involves many different people, integrating design ideas from multiple sources, and making sure the techniques of making inform the process of designing. The issues in designing the new Routemaster bus, for example, ranged from the vehicle's structure, format and aesthetics, to the fabrics to be used on seats, to the requirement for 40 per cent greater fuel efficiency. Achieving all these requirements by necessity involved a wide range of people.

These designs take form in Heatherwick Studio, which like IDEO and Airbnb is a very playful place. Interesting and striking objects of all shapes and sizes sit, hang and protrude throughout its considerable space, surrounding the invariably young designers on rows of computer screens. Frank Stephenson at McLaren also talks about being inspired by sculptures, shapes, paintings and things on the street. He surrounds his workplace with toys: 'You'd think we're kids because we're allowed to have these toys in front of us. That's the nature of any designer, you'll find they have a toy shop around them.' Today, as at IDEO, many of these toys are digital.

Digital craft

Digital technology profoundly affects the world in which we work and how we behave, and it has huge consequences for how, as well as why, we play. Whether it is playing with Lego bricks or using computer-aided design tools, craftspeople use their tactile and visual skills to explore, build and demonstrate using instruments. In recent years, new virtualization technologies have enhanced the ability to play with a range of tools that allow skilled people to craft imaginative and innovative new products and services. The tools include multi-dimensional computer-aided design (CAD), 3D printing and virtual and augmented reality. What these tools do is provide a highly sophisticated capacity to collect, visualize, navigate and represent data. The digital imitation of the real world simulated on computer models allows fast and cheap experimentation. One of the major challenges in prototyping ideas and then developing innovations is getting quick feedback at low cost. Stefan Thomke, in his book *Experiments Matter*, refers to the way these new technologies allow companies to create more learning more rapidly, and that knowledge, in turn, can be incorporated in greater numbers of experiments at less expense.[11]

Digital tools can make complex data, information, perspectives and preferences from diverse groups visible and comprehensible. Many of us will have attended meetings where we thought we'd reached agreement about something, only to learn later that our understanding about the whole matter was completely different from others'. In 1983 Richard Feynman gave a BBC lecture entitled 'On Thinking' in which he argues the importance of effective imagery: 'The images people use when we think and converse can be entirely different, which explains why some people have difficulty seeing things that you consider obvious, and vice versa.' Many of the new digital tools are visual, and – as half of the human cerebral cortex is devoted to visualization – where everyone sees the same image, they help us to understand issues better.

The new technologies that provide vast computational power and the ability to visualize can open new opportunities for science, improving the ways discoveries are made. Michael Nielsen says these technologies can actively amplify collective intelligence, and 'new computerized tools can help us find hidden meaning in all that knowledge'. Martin Rees, Astronomer Royal and ex-president of the Royal Society, says of his research that he works and thinks in pictures, not using vast computational capacities, and 'we can predict before we observe'. However, he says that 'without the technology and the symbiosis of science and technology, we wouldn't have got anywhere', and that 'computer simulation of extreme phenomena [provides] a boost of the virtual world of computers to do experiments that are more and more realistic'.[12] Some leaders in the field of AI, such as Demis Hassabis, founder of DeepMind, believe that the technology will significantly increase the rates of scientific discovery.

When designers work with digital technologies they practise a form of craft by manipulating digital symbols and models, navigating within datasets, finding new relationships and recognizing new patterns. They also help communicate with and engage interested parties. Anyone lucky enough to be involved in designing a new home recently won't have had to struggle looking at complicated architectural drawings. They will have a high-fidelity 'fly-through' visualization of the eventual design, getting a good sense of what the building will look and feel like before a brick is laid. This computerized model helps clarify and integrate the expectations of architects, builders and clients, and helps better craft the use of space, allowing for the testing of preferred colours or positioning of favoured furniture or pictures.

As well as involving more people in the way things are designed, these technologies help bring more craft from the designer into the end product. The design of the extraordinary shapes of buildings by the architect Frank Gehry, for example, relies on the use of a variety of technologies. Gehry's buildings, such as the Bilbao Guggenheim Museum and Disney Concert Hall, with their highly expressive bold shapes and innovative materials, involve a great deal of creative input. Gehry says he is as much a sculptor as an architect and it was possible to model and engineer his designs through many iterations using a toolkit including the traditional media of paper, clay and plasticine models as well as digital technologies. This toolkit enhanced Gehry's role, bringing more of his craft to the overall result.

Other technologies, such as web-based systems – blogging, wikis, crowdsourcing, online encyclopaedias and podcasting – are creating an environment in which people develop their ideas in a more horizontal, collaborative way than before. They may provide new ways for firms to relate to markets and to understand highly engaged and active customers expecting to be involved in the development of the products and services they want. Such engagement needs to be crafted.

The work of people such as Frank Gehry and Thomas Heatherwick shows starkly that even with the advance of machines and reliance on algorithms for decision-making, it is important to emphasize the continuing necessity of human intuition and judgement. Humans are brilliantly capable of using the mind's eye to imagine things and connections impossible to see in the digital world. As Marx says, the architect differs from the bee because humans see in their imagination before creating in reality. Brynjolfsson and McAfee say: 'for all their power and speed, today's digital machines have shown little creative ability. They can't compose very good songs, write great novels, or generate good ideas for new businesses'. A US study of the impact of AI and automation for the Executive Office of the President says AI 'still cannot replicate social or general intelligence, creativity, or human judgment', and that in the future 'employment requiring manual dexterity, creativity, social interactions and intelligence, and general knowledge will thrive'.[13] AI, furthermore, draws upon *what is known*; it takes human intelligence and imagination to consider *what could be*.

Yet leading scientists and digital entrepreneurs express concern that developments in AI are moving so rapidly that they envisage the Turing test will be successfully passed – meaning that answers to questions from computers will be indistinguishable from those of humans. Stephen Hawking and Elon Musk have both expressed fears for a world where machine learning becomes so powerful that people will no longer develop ideas as quickly or powerfully as machines.

The Canadian ice hockey player Wayne Gretzky, nicknamed 'The Great One' as he is widely acknowledged as the finest player of all time, was asked about the secret of his success. He said he skated in response to where the puck is going to be, not where it has been. That intuition is not yet machine-replicable. However, predictive modelling is the holy grail of data scientists. An experiment in the LA Police Department, for example, used predictive modelling to determine where a crime may be committed next, based on millions of historic data points. Instead of police officers working their usual beats, they spent a year based in their station, occasionally deploying to a specific address determined by computer analytics. Crime rates dropped by 12 per cent. Driverless cars, drone delivery systems, self-driving trains and jet engine health management systems all have predictive capabilities that are improving at a rapid rate.

Digital technology can be a great stimulator, facilitator and supporter. Working with a wide community of involved parties using these tools to play with and evaluate options has become part of crafting the 'creative conversation'. And, as the following example shows, they can help throw up some radical ideas and then help get them put to use.

In case of fire, please use the lift

Most fatalities in the 9/11 attack on the World Trade Center in New York occurred in the stairwells of the collapsed Twin

Towers. People escaping down the stairs were trapped along with firefighters moving up to save them. This horrific event led to a great deal of research into how best to evacuate people from tall buildings in the case of disasters.[14]

Some of this work took place at the engineering design company Arup, which was involved in the design of the replacement building, the Freedom Tower. As a result of trying to improve understanding of how buildings and people respond to fire and other emergencies, a category of work called 'fire engineering' emerged that uses digital technologies to craft new ideas.[15]

Prior to the use of this technology, the movement of people in buildings on fire was represented, in the words of one engineer, as 'stupid little lines drawn through floor plans'. This particular engineer helped develop a computer program that simulates the movement of people in buildings in normal circumstances and emergencies. Changes can be made in the number, height and girth of the people, and according to whether they are in groups or families and how familiar they are with the building. It also manages to distinguish between people's behaviour in polite societies, such as the Japanese, and other less polite cultures (you know the ones). By using this and other software systems, she and other fire engineers began to play much more completely with how people behave in catastrophes.

It is extremely difficult to get out of a tall building quickly – more so, of course, the higher up you are. Everyone is conditioned not to use the lift if there is a fire, which leaves no option but the stairs. Moving downstairs from high levels can take a long time and can be impossible for some disabled or elderly people. People on the top floors often need to queue for access to the stairs. By using simulation technology, however, it was shown that by using fire protection material, pressurizing lift shafts and blowing the smoke out of them, lifts could be used as a means of escape for more people more quickly than the stairs. By playing with this technology the startling conclusion was reached that in some circumstances the message should be: 'in case of fire, please use the lift'.

Simulation technology is used in Arup by people with a wide range of different professional backgrounds, including project management, architecture, mathematics, physics and structural, electrical and mechanical engineering. The technology is used by widely different organizations: engineers, architects, researchers, regulators, planners, contractors and builders. Simulation technology was one of the means by which all these different people and organizations together crafted this innovative solution to a problem.

Craft here is seen in a couple of senses. First, like many engineering problems, answers needed new combinations of components, materials and technologies to be brought together in novel and productive ways. It involved dialogue, debate and negotiation engaging different organizations, professions and technical specialists to decide what works and is safe. Building designers and local planning and fire authorities can hold widely divergent views on the fire safety implications of new buildings. Traditionally (and understandably) conservative and wary of unproven designs, fire prevention and control staff have to be convinced that new designs are safe for those working and living in buildings and for emergency services personnel who might need to enter them if they're on fire. It is all well and good developing a new approach using a computer, but these people are responsible for putting the lives of others at risk. Getting agreement to apply a radical approach from such a diverse group required craft. Playing with digital technology provided the means to involve all interested parties, air their scepticism, test their ideas and arrive at a converged understanding, so that using the lift to get people safely out of the building is one of the methods being used in the Freedom Tower. In 2017 a devastating fire in Grenfell Tower, a twenty-seven-storey block of flats in London, killed over seventy people. That this occurred in one of the wealthiest areas of one of the richest and most technologically advanced cities in the world highlights the pressing need for better and wider application of solutions to the problems of living and working in high-rise buildings.

Second, use of the technology itself also tells us about its relationship with craft. The developer of the people-movement software said it allowed her 'access to information about people movement at a much more intuitive level'. She tied optimization, a statistical measure, with intuition, a behaviour, combining computer code with craft. Everyone interviewed for this particular study talked about how the use of simulation technology requires good judgement because unsophisticated users can make life-threatening mistakes. Caution is needed because small errors can be amplified and unnoticed: as one engineer put it, 'you may not realize you've made a mistake'. Decisions need to be made on when to use the technology and how to use its results, with judgements founded on basic principles and past experience. Craft combines information and intuition, data and judgement, experience and experiment.

Just as play is a serious modern activity, so is craft. Play and craft are intimately related. Craft disciplines play and gives it shape and direction, planning and order. Craft liberates by being playful, seen, for example, in the way digital technologies allow shared exploration and experiment, occasionally producing totally unexpected and radical innovations. It involves a special skill or knowledge in the way it combines insights and understanding, and that skill is difficult to delegate to machines. Even in the digital age, craft resides in people whose skills depend on their extensive practice and use. Technology is useful, but it is only a tool in the hands of the player, to be used more or less effectively.

This is especially apparent in the case of robotic surgery. Robots are increasingly used in surgical operations, because they are accurate, highly stable (no hand tremors) and capable of bringing additional information to the surgeon's task, for example, through augmented reality where reality is supplemented by computer-generated content. An example of the way technology assists surgeons is through a medical device known as the 'iKnife', which attaches an electronic 'nose' to a scalpel. Led by Professor Zoltan Takacs, a multidisciplinary team of chemists, surgeons, engineers and computer scientists developed the invention. No one discipline on its own would have resulted in the idea; it was through the interaction and crafting of an approach through experimentation that the device was created. It sucks up smoke given off as the blade cauterizes tissue and analyses it in a mass spectrometer. The device uses chemo-profiling to test the chemistry of cells. It can detect almost instantly what kind of tissue the surgeon is cutting through: for example, whether it is cancerous or not. This improves the accuracy of surgery, informing the surgeon whether he or she has excised all the cancerous cells in a tumour. In using these technologies the surgeon remains in control of the operation but has almost real-time intelligence about the quality and performance of the surgery, resulting in much more accurate outcomes. The process creates data about the chemistry of cancer cells every time the iKnife is used. This cumulative database can be analysed and modelled such that the system can begin to predict what type of cancer tumour, primary or secondary, is being operated on.

Robotics coupled with AI are transforming other areas of surgery too, including neurosurgery where highly tuned craft skills are required to avoid damaging delicate vessels. The craft lies in combining the technology and the doctor's judgement, which remains paramount. As one eminent heart surgeon told us: 'you never know what is going to happen once you open them up!' The relationship between craft and technology is symbiotic, or mutually supportive.

We now turn to an entrepreneur who aims to use her science to improve healthcare by means of an app, and who explains her approach as combining play and craft.

Jenna Tregarthen

'You can do a lot with a little,' says Jenna Tregarthen, and her entrepreneurial career shows how it can be done. She has carefully crafted a playful product with a very serious use. Jenna is the founder and CEO of Recovery Record, a company that in a very short period of time has helped nearly 400,000 patients and 10,000 specialists treat eating disorders. By 2015 more than 10 million therapy sessions had been completed using the product. The company's formal goal is to become the gold standard in the delivery of eating disorder treatment and to increase access to care for sufferers. Jenna's own motivation for creating the company is simple: she has personal experience of someone very close to her with an eating disorder and, as she puts it, is 'enraged at the unnecessary suffering caused by the lack of effective treatment'.

Jenna's background is in clinical psychology, and she has worked as a counsellor at Lifeline, a crisis support and suicide prevention service. She was progressing with a PhD in an Australian university when an opportunity arose to attend a course at Stanford University. The six-week course was designed to help scientists develop ideas for a business. She says the course was a revelation and she subsequently became a teaching fellow in innovation and entrepreneurship at the university's business school.

She arrived with an idea for a company to help people with eating disorders, and the structure of the course brought an interdisciplinary team together, including engineers and designers, to work on developing a plan for the business. Initially, there was little excitement about the idea but then the group applied some of the concepts of design thinking,[16] including a brainstorming session, and, in her words, 'let our inhibitions go, coming up with all sorts of dumb ideas and some very good ones, captured in a chaos of coloured Post-it notes'. Then, she said, they had a 'moment': the idea of playing games with therapy.

One of the major challenges of treating eating disorders is recording what and when you have eaten: consistent record-keeping is challenging. The onset of eating disorders usually starts aged fourteen or fifteen; the majority of sufferers are under twenty-five, and 90 per cent are women. Existing pen-and-paper systems are tedious to manage and proper records are difficult to maintain. Yet record-keeping compliance is proven to assist recovery, so Jenna came up with the idea of using cognitive behaviour therapy that rewards patients for keeping accurate records with an app that is fun and easy to use. She says she wants to make the app social, rewarding and engaging. The app records meals and snacks, thoughts and feelings and addresses coping strategies. Jenna says eating disorder recovery is about daily battles and victories, and Recovery Record provides 'micro-interventions' any time of day, no matter where the user is and whatever their situation. Patients learn to see patterns in their behaviour, and see triggers in their environment that they can change to help them recover. Jenna explains that 'girls have critical moments where they have a really extreme urge to binge or purge. We are catching them in that very moment and doing therapy on the spot.' Data can be shared with a team of clinicians and supporters, and photographs of meals can even be loaded and shared. The company is also exploring the possibility of developing a tool for family and friends to empower them to play a proactive part in recovery.

Jenna describes the development of the idea and subsequent progress of the company as a process of play and craft: an innovation process that has brought many 'moments' along the way. She says 'a lot of our biggest breakthroughs have come through play'. This has involved a great deal of personal learning. When she arrived at Stanford she admits her thinking was very linear and structured, but she learned to let go, to 'build your parachute as you are falling'. 'Suddenly the rules disappear and you have to trust yourself to solve problems and come up with solutions.' She was apprehensive about not having years of business experience, and says being a perfectionist she couldn't get used to the idea of 'anything goes'. 'You need to think really hard about a problem, but embracing naïveté and letting go of what is right and wrong is a powerful source of progress in ways that are surprising and delightful.' As for the company and its product, Jenna says the crafting and playing never stops and there is continual development: 'perfection is the enemy of the good enough'. Build a bridge, she says, and you can find a blueprint, but there is no blueprint for a company nowadays where the business model has to be as creative as its product.

Getting feedback from customers is an important part of the company's innovation process, and by 2012 the app's development had already built on over 2,000 feature requests from users. Engaging the community involved crowdsourcing images and quotes that were affirming and inspirational. Recovery Road partners with a number of universities and Jenna still has time to publish academic research.[17]

In line with her motivation for creating the company, the app is publicly available and free. The value proposition in the business model is to work with healthcare providers and intensive day-care and residential services that pay for the use of the product and its data to help them meet their obligations to treat eating disorders. The product's value lies in its use of evidence-based treatment, and by keeping care teams connected with timely clinical data. Jenna says the company's biggest challenge has been to find a business model that reinforced its objectives of treating eating disorders by providing free access to its product. The healthcare system in the US is very complicated and there are often conflicting agendas. No organization has a budget line to support what Recovery Record offers. Jenna also admits to her lack of experience with sales, and feeling discomfort in selling to large corporations. Her approach has been to listen and empathize with customers to craft a value proposition for them. Of the app's users, 30 per cent have never told anyone about their condition and the stigma of the disorder is preventing them from seeking help.

Talking about her personal journey, Jenna says success is hard earned. She has been challenged by all the uncertainties that confront her and by her own high expectations of herself. She attributes her success to date to hard work and resilience: 'surviving is three-quarters of the battle' and the rest is coping, indeed thriving, on uncertainty. As a way of sharing her learning Jenna is a frequent speaker on the topic of women in entrepreneurship, an adviser to several entrepreneurship accelerator programmes and is involved with a number of non-profit organizations.

Jenna is on the board of an organization called Project HEAL which raises money for those suffering with eating disorders and who want to recover but are unable to afford treatment, which according to the project can cost up to $30,000 a month. This desire to bring about change for good in the area of eating disorders motivates her future ambitions for Recovery Record. She realized that pursuing this path through a career in clinical psychology wasn't for her, and she had the experience of working on a report to government in the area that was subsequently ignored. Jenna believes that as 70 per cent of the company's product can be adapted to deal with substance abuse and anxiety, the company has the potential for bringing positive change to other conditions. All future development paths are open, she says, but one thing is non-negotiable: the product has to be freely available to those seeking help.

In an interview with an eating disorder blog, Jenna provides an insight into her motivation: 'I start every day by reading user reviews on the app store or email testimonials and am blown away by Recovery Record's life-transforming impact.'

Players and performing

Like Jenna, many of the entrepreneurs and innovators in this book are gifted communicators who dedicate a great deal of time to publicly sharing their experiences through conferences, advisory bodies and various meetings. They are skilled performers on these platforms. The craft of musicians and actors reveals why and how best to perform and also provides further insights into how distinguishable humans are from machines.

Players perform on one stage or another. They need to perform in front of co-workers, bosses, customers, investors or indeed the general public. Here playful workers in our sense can learn from artistic performers – literally 'players' – not only in determining how the performance is expressed, but its very nature.

In his book *The Craftsman*, Richard Sennett explains the complex and sometimes contradictory objectives that stimulate the commitment needed to achieve the 10,000 hours of practice typically thought to be needed to master a craft. Sennett, a leading sociologist, is also a competent cellist. He knows that craft involves play and practice for the reward of 'price in the work'. There is a desire to do something well for its own sake and to achieve a standard acknowledged by peers to be 'excellent'.

Musicians practice technique so that they can transcend the purely technical limitations of a piece in order to explore its expressive and sensitive qualities. It is impossible to do this if you don't have the technique. Reaching this emotional level is what journalist Alan Rusbridger tried to do in learning to play Chopin's 'Ballade No. 1' – one of the hardest pieces in the repertoire.[18] He was only able to gain enough technique to perfect a technical rendition – never reaching the 'sublime' emotional qualities that the music was composed to express. Rusbridger himself is critical of the modern generation of accomplished technical perfectionists who can rattle off pieces like this note-perfect. He says they lack the emotional intensity and communication intended in the music. They are being driven partly by technical perfection in recording instruments, where there is no hiding place if people make mistakes. Some great pianists play with intense feeling without worrying about making the odd mistake, and most people in the audience never notice. Emotion and feeling transcend perfect replication.

The emotional and intellectual power of stories and how they are told leaves an imprint on the mind and memory that endures. Philip Pullman is one of the most highly regarded and best-selling storytellers in the world, and the winner of numerous awards. Many of his novels have been produced on the stage. Our relationship with Philip is not impartial: he is a brother of one author and the friend of the other. As testament to the power of stories, the former accompanied Philip to the staging of one of his books at the National Theatre in London. The audience largely comprised children, around 1,000 of them, who were completely entranced and sat still for the two three-hour-long performances. There was no whispering or crisp packet rustling – just silence – as the children, most of whom knew the story, were engrossed in its brilliant staging and acting. Good, well-told stories are captivating for everyone and are a key tool in a player's toolbox.

There are choices in how a particular play – or pitch – is offered. Scripts are interpreted widely in stage plays, with different settings and emphases. *Hamlet* can have an Elizabethan or a contemporary staging, or anything in between. There are choices to be made that can respond to audience demand, and also push and challenge it. Rehearsal for a play offers a period for improvisation, reflection, practice or trial and error, as all the contributors – director, actors, costume and set designers – play together to craft something they're happy with. IBM uses avatars to rehearse pitches to clients, making sure mistakes are made virtually rather than in front of potential customers. New ideas may emerge in rehearsal, but they do so on the basis of considerable knowledge and experience. As the actor Christopher Walken says, 'the thing is that you cannot improvise unless you know exactly what you're doing'. The golfer Gary Player tells the story of how after a particular display of his talent, holing three shots in a row from a bunker, a member of the crowd said he'd never seen anything so lucky. Player responded with the aphorism that the more he practised, the luckier he got.

Sir Nicholas Hytner, previously artistic director of the National Theatre in London, has spoken about the roles of rehearsal and that of a play's director,[19] suggesting the adjustments large and small that constantly occur as everyone involved learns about the play and its production. He says rehearsals are about getting actors 'as grounded, as rooted, as imaginatively engaged as they possibly can be with the play and with each other'. Rehearsal is especially important for actors to discover

147

why the words are what they are. 'There's a communal effort as well. Everyone has to tailor their own processes and emotional and intellectual journeys to others' emotional and intellectual journeys.' They learn the play and to play together. As for the role of the director, he says they have to make the final decisions but no one can do it all, and they 'have to be open to the gifts of everybody'.

This collaborative process is much like jazz improvisation, which crafts a relationship between individuals as they collectively explore the unexpected within the confines of accepted styles and structures. Jazz reflects the way that effective improvisation, seen as spontaneous experiment, actually reflects depth of experience and degrees of discipline by its players. In a very different musical form, the experience of a performance at a great artistic institution such as La Scala in Milan or New York's Metropolitan Opera builds on the strength of a well-directed ensemble of many gifted people. The merger of magnificent music, singing and staging in a gorgeous environment crafts an experience that is hugely satisfying. Each element in itself is fantastic, but the elevated experience comes from the way they are crafted together. Players weave together compelling stories that might put one person in the spotlight but reflect the collective efforts of many.

Reflections

Craft frames, shapes and fashions play. It relies on judgement and intuition, but also disciplines and structures behaviour. It helps combine thinking and doing, designing and making. The possession of a craft is deeply personally meaningful, and it manifests itself in a wide variety of ways. Products and solutions to problems are crafted, and so are the businesses and organizations that put them to use. Experiences, moments, and performances are crafted. Craft is a way of exploring by eliminating options and building on what is already known to address problems, even those that are the most vexatious. Digital craft involves the playful use of tools, sometimes described as 'toys', to foster creative conversations and collective intelligence, allowing multiple and diverse partners to work together and remarkably innovative ideas to emerge. Playful craft contributes to Thomas Heatherwick's practical ability to make beautiful structures and experiences. More metaphorically, it adds to Jenna Tregarthen's entrepreneurial ability to build a parachute while falling. Craft is a crucial element of modern work, guiding how and why we devote our efforts. Through mixing our experience, intellect and intuition it differentiates our abilities from AI and machines. As an accompanying virtue to grace, the practice of craft requires recognition of the need for continual improvement in skills and behaviours.

The craft of innovators and entrepreneurs gives us the opportunity to ask ourselves whether at work we can:

* express our creativity and utilize our experience and knowledge towards outcomes that are rewarding for us and pleasing to others;
* have the occasion and tools to combine different abilities and perspectives and utilize and develop our skills;
* engage with problems that interest us and are pleasurable in their solution and meaningful in their results; and
* claim what we do as a source of pride.

5

Fortitude

Moral strength or courage.
Unyielding courage in the endurance of adversity.

Sir Francis Bacon, the sixteenth-century philosopher and statesman, said 'fortitude is the marshal of thought, the armour of the will, and the fort of reason'. Fortitude is very much about strength of mind and will in the face of adversity. Many, if not most, stories of successful people involve periods in their lives when they needed to draw on all their reserves of strength to carry on. They can be motivated by extraordinary self-belief, such as when Steve Jobs was fired from Apple, regrouped and returned triumphant. And they can be driven by a vision that survives exceptional setbacks. Elon Musk continued with his SpaceX project, despite the explosion of one of his rockets. Richard Branson continued his Virgin Galactic project, despite the loss of one his rockets and death of its pilot. In *Emile*, Rousseau writes:

> To be something, to be himself, and always at one with himself, a man must act as he speaks, must know what course he ought to take, and must follow that course with vigour and persistence.

There's an element of stubbornness – freely admitted in the case of Sean Bowen – in innovators and entrepreneurs. This is not arrogant resistance to alternatives but a refusal to give up on an ambition. It is resilience in being able to recover quickly and easily from setbacks. It is being robust in the face of unrelenting challenges and uncertainty. As in the case of Steve Shirley, it is continuing to keep going when everything looks very bleak.

Failure

A major element of fortitude, and indeed of grace, is how people deal with failure. When successful people fail they use that failure to their benefit. While failure is commonly associated with disappointment if not disaster, many – as seen in the diverse backgrounds of those quoted below – associate it with intelligence, wisdom, honour and greatness. Humphry Davy, the famous eighteenth-century chemist and president of the Royal Society, said: 'The most important of my discoveries has been suggested to me by my failures.' Henry Ford put it so: 'Failure is only the opportunity to begin again more intelligently.' Samuel Smiles said: 'We learn wisdom from failure much more than success. We often discover what will do by finding out what will not do and probably he who never made a mistake never made a discovery.' The playwright George Bernard Shaw said: 'A life spent making mistakes is not only more honourable but more useful than a life doing nothing.' And Robert Kennedy said: 'Only those who dare to fail greatly can ever achieve greatly.' In science, business, social activism, playwriting and politics, failure is a passport to success.

So it is with players. Many innovative ideas fail because of the sheer complexity of the science, technology, businesses or markets they emerge from, which is economist Paul Ormerod's explanation in his book *Why Most Things Fail*.[1] He convincingly argues that companies continually fail – and 10 per cent of all the companies in the US disappear each year – because they can never deal completely with the complexity of the real world. There is also the matter of the unpredictability of the future: the unknown unknowns. Consider why Thomas Watson, chairman of IBM, said in 1943, 'I think there is a world market for maybe five computers', or Ken Olson, president and founder of Digital Equipment Corporation, said in 1977: 'There is no reason anyone would want a computer in their home.' No one, not even these great leaders of business, ever knows what is around the corner.

The eminent US scientist Linus Pauling said 'the best way to have a good idea is to have lots of ideas'. Empirical evidence supports this: returns to ideas are highly skewed – there is what physicists and economists call a power law distribution. Only a few company start-ups, products, patents and academic papers are successes. Certainly, in our experience as academics it is only a small number of our research publications that are frequently cited by others (usually recognized as a sign of their quality), despite the others being to our minds equally marvellous. Similarly, the majority of economic returns come from only 10 per cent of innovative investments. In some areas it is even more skewed. At any one time there may be up to 8,000 potential new drugs being researched around the world, but only one or two will make it to market.

The best explanation for the persistent failure of economic and technological ideas is the one cited earlier by Joseph Schumpeter. Schumpeter argued that innovation is characterized by 'creative destruction': failure is inevitable, part of the process of economic development. You can't have creation without destruction, innovation without failure. Schumpeter had some experience of failure. Widely recognized as a brilliant Harvard economist, he was a man who failed during his time as Austrian finance minister and as a banker, while his personal failings included turning a petty squabble with a librarian into a sword duel, and his love life was so complicated he was once married to two women simultaneously. Schumpeter claimed to have three rather immodest ambitions in life: to be the best economist in the world, the most skilful horseman in Austria and the greatest lover in Vienna. On his deathbed he glumly accepted that there was probably one person who'd always been a better horse rider.

What does the scale, indeed inevitability, of failure mean for playful entrepreneurs? Most importantly it entails personal recognition that failure is a valuable opportunity to learn, reflect and develop strength of character. One can approach it as positively as Edison, who said: 'I have never failed. I've just found 10,000 ways that won't work.' Or one can have the attitude of Naveen Jain – a man with a spectacular and often turbulent business career, who is presently building a company to mine the Moon for resources – who told us, 'When you are an entrepreneur you only fail when you give up, everything else is just a pivot.'

Failure can even be used as a badge of honour, as many American entrepreneurs have discovered in their dealings with venture capitalists who prefer backing those who have previously failed, learned their lessons and have the courage to try again. No player sets out to fail or lose, but the more they push boundaries the more likely they are to fail than succeed, so failure had better become accepted and thought of as an opportunity for learning, introspection and keeping egos in check: great methods for continuing to deal with rapid and unpredictable changes at work.

It has been known for a long time that continuously successful enterprises accept the inevitability of failure, tolerate it and always encourage staff to try out new ideas. In the 1920s a young manager at Ford made a large investment that went horribly wrong. With great trepidation he went to the office of the fearsome Henry Ford to hand in his resignation letter. Ford ripped it up, saying he wasn't going to have someone who had learned such an expensive lesson go and work for a competitor.

Players often operate at the limits, as with SpaceX and Virgin Galactic, where failure is more dramatic. Failure stalks such play like a shadow: it comes into starker relief when the sun shines brightest. It could be argued, indeed, that if players are not regularly failing they're not being sufficiently playful. To deal with this level of failure, which could extend to the deepest fear of all – public failure – there is value in mentoring people on the learning it offers and how to deal with it, and many players ensure they do this. The other side of failure is that celebrating our occasional successes is hugely important. Appreciation and recognition of achievement helps us to manage and cope when things don't work out as we hoped.

To succeed, the replication of mistakes must be avoided, but to deal with the challenges of turbulence at work players should never stop adopting new approaches and trying new things for fear of failure. Tim Harford in his book *Adapt* tells the story of Peter Palchinsky, a brilliant, stubborn and courageous engineer who spent years arguing with Imperial Russian and then Soviet Russian politicians and apparatchiks about the foolhardiness of their insane engineering schemes.[2] In 1901 Palchinsky was asked by the Russian government to investigate the living conditions of workers in the coalmines of the Don basin. The conditions were appalling and Palchinsky's critical report led to his being exiled to Siberia for eight years. Following his pardon, Palchinsky became vocal in his denunciation of big state engineering projects that had no consideration of their environmental and social impact. Criticism of this sort was not tolerated by Stalin's regime, and he was tortured and executed. Alexander Solzhenitsyn wrote admiringly that Palchinsky resisted every pressure and never surrendered. Palchinsky developed three principles for progressing and learning from failure: seek new ideas and try new things; try them out on a scale that does no damage; learn from them and improve.

Our approach of using both contemporary and historical examples continues with a look at the extraordinary fortitude of one of the most famous architects of all time, working in the most trying of circumstances.

Christopher Wren

There is for the British perhaps no more iconic photograph than that of London's St Paul's Cathedral withstanding the

Blitz. On the night of 29 December 1940, the 114th consecutive night of German bombing started a firestorm that killed 160 Londoners, injured 500 and destroyed numerous buildings. And there among the fire and smoke stands the cathedral: resolute and miraculously untouched. This remarkable building has played a significant role in London's, and the nation's, consciousness since it was built in the seventeenth century. The thirty-five-year story of its design and construction is that of extraordinary fortitude on the part of its architect, Sir Christopher Wren (1632–1723).

Imagine the circumstances facing the city of London when it was decided to build the cathedral. It had endured the Great Plague followed by the Great Fire of 1666, which had devastated the population and the infrastructure, including burning the original St Paul's to the ground. The city was being rebuilt, becoming in the process the greatest city in the seventeenth- and eighteenth-century world. But those doing the rebuilding were working in dangerous times, as society was deeply troubled. The English Civil War had recently concluded, during which a king had been deposed by Parliament and then executed. The nation was deeply polarized, both politically and religiously. While Puritans denounced pleasures of all kinds, Quakers ran naked through the streets, joined occasionally by the rambunctious Ranters, an anti-authoritarian sect keen on public ale houses, sexual permissiveness and swearing (somewhat ahead of their time, if some of London's present Saturday night hot spots are anything to go by). A new king had ascended to the throne, continually challenging the powers of the Parliament that had beheaded his father.

It was in these circumstances that Wren took on the task of designing St Paul's Cathedral. He had to manage the competing interests of King Charles II, Parliament, the clergy and the City of London authorities (which had especial powers within its boundaries), all of whom held strong and often opposing views and were deeply suspicious of the other parties. Wren's was a truly 'wicked' problem. His work was frequently criticized, half his salary was withheld for fourteen years, others who were less competent were given authority over him – and yet he persevered. He displayed fortitude throughout the long years it took to build his greatest achievement. His memorial stone at St Paul's reads: 'Here in its foundations lies the architect of this church and city, Christopher Wren, who lived beyond ninety years, not for his own profit but for the public good. Reader, if you seek his monument – look around you.'

Wren, although he might have been astounded to be so described, was in our sense a playful entrepreneur. He was a polymath: an astronomer, anatomist, mathematician and physicist, bringing his expertise together in defining the previously unrecognized role of architect. He was a professor at Oxford University, Government Surveyor-General, a Member of Parliament and one of the founders of the Royal Society (and its president from 1680–82). His personal life was hard: he buried two wives and a child. But levity can be seen in a delightful love letter to his wife, likening his love for her to the constant ticking of a clock, but unlike a clock incapable of breaking.[3] One of Wren's battles with the clergy over the design of the cathedral focused on the latter's insistence on a spire, rather than the architect's desired dome on top of the church. He drew an amalgam with a spire reaching out from a dome that received the king's approval, keen as he was to placate all parties. The king, however, noted under his signature that Wren had the right to make minor changes to the design. As the building progressed, Wren interpreted this dispensation generously and the spire never appeared (Wren waited, no doubt, for his opponents to expire or to see the beauty of his scheme).

Wren did exceptional things because he consorted with the equally gifted. He enjoyed the company of a group of 'new philosophers', including the biologist, physicist and surveyor Robert Hooke and the author and horticulturalist John Evelyn, who met to discuss new scientific and political ideas. In deeply uneasy political and religious circumstances, this group of thinkers met to uncover 'a new way to observe and understand the world'. All the contributors and their families had been

profoundly affected by the Civil War – one had a relative imprisoned in the Tower of London, others had at various stages been
exiled overseas – yet they adhered to the view that 'the pursuit
of reason was above any personal or political animosity'.[4] Wren
could not have achieved his great works without the encouragement and support of his peers.

The fortitude of playful entrepreneurs is supplemented by
greater purpose than simple personal gain. Wren's fifty-six
churches and great cathedral were part of his religious devotion
and his noble contribution to the public good. Yet Wren had to
be a politician to realize his ambitions and, as the following case
shows, politicians can display playfulness, fortitude and even,
to the surprise of many, nobility, as they persist with problem-
solving in the face of fierce opposition.

Norman Fowler

Certain members of Margaret Thatcher's Cabinet could well be
described as players pejoratively, but some deserve to be called
players in the noble sense. Honourably among the latter is
Norman Fowler, a man who saw opportunities and took risks
with the long-established machinery of British government.
Cartoonists lampooned Fowler, who was the UK's Minister of
Health from 1981 to 1987, by representing him as a chicken.
Yet he was a resolute politician determined to push for what was
right in the face of fear and prejudice. When confronting a
crisis, he looked for expert scientific advice, made bold decisions, then worked tirelessly to implement those decisions in the
face of bureaucratic inertia on the one hand and anger and
outrage on the other. He fought direct opposition from the
prime minister, and in a coalition of science, media and interest
groups led the biggest and most innovative public education
campaign ever staged in Britain.

At first sight Norman Fowler is an unlikely champion of
those suffering from AIDS, but as soon as he learned about the
disease he became, and has remained, a passionate advocate for

sufferers. His is a story of how politicians make a difference when they confront difficult challenges, effectively marshal evidence, push for what ought to be done rather than what is expedient, and when their concerns are for people's wellbeing, not lifestyle choices. Fowler reminds us that the noble behaviours of the playful entrepreneur – grace, craft, fortitude and ambition – can be found in the most staid of politicians.

The scale of the challenge Fowler addressed was terrifying. In addition to reports in the early 1980s of young homosexual men dying in San Francisco, the British Foreign Office was reporting an epidemic hitting Africa, where the strange disease was 'spreading like wildfire'. St Mary's Hospital in London opened an AIDS clinic in 1982, expecting a few patients. In no time it had over 400, and doctors there were predicting an increase to 20,000. Thus far, 36 million people have died of AIDS. Tragically, 17 million children have lost one or both parents to AIDS, and despite the massive improvements in medication and public health advice described in Chapter 2, there are still millions of new cases and deaths each year.

The scientific community at the time understood the epidemiology. Suggestions on what to do about it, however, in the words of the UK's Chief Medical Officer at the time, Donald Acheson, caused 'alarm accounting almost to panic'. There was reference to the 'gay plague'. A Member of Parliament suggested people with AIDS should be quarantined permanently in a guarded enclosure on the Isle of Wight, a small island off southern England. Gay men were being turned away from restaurants and from their lodgings. The Chief Constable of Manchester claimed his religion led him to see gay men and intravenous drug abusers as 'scum floating on a sea of corruption'.

Fowler's Health Department began a newspaper campaign informing people about the dangers of AIDS. This was followed by a leaflet, sent to all 23 million households in the country, something that had never been attempted before. There was a very effective television campaign that had a tombstone as its motif. There was continual political opposition to these campaigns, and Mrs Thatcher tried to subvert them all. Essentially, the British government was being asked to publicly go into detail on sexual practices and drug taking, and promote the use of condoms and clean injection needles. The attorney general was concerned about the campaigns causing offence and even creating panic, the Treasury didn't want to pay for them and the conservative press was sharply critical. Many religious and political leaders felt the issue was not one of public health, but of morality.

Fowler's view was straightforward. It was not a time for delicacy. People were dying. His original draft of the campaign was explicit about the sorts of sexual behaviours that were risky. Thatcher hated it, complaining that by telling young people about such unspeakable acts they'd be encouraged to try them out. Her opposition continued on a number of fronts. She used her political allies, such as the fearsome Norman Tebbit, to question his approach. She had a quiet private word with Fowler at 10 Downing Street: 'You mustn't become known as just the minister for AIDS' – code for 'you are ruining your career'; she also vetoed a ministerial broadcast on the dangers of AIDS.

Fowler's frustration grew with the Thatcher government of which he was a part. As a political issue, he notes dryly in a recent book, AIDS promises few rewards.[5] He certainly didn't dither, though. In his autobiography Donald Acheson remembers seeking a meeting with Fowler to talk to him about AIDS for the first time. He recalls: 'Norman's reaction was one of deep concern, and for the rest of my time in Whitehall, with his unfailing encouragement and support, I was able to give the AIDS epidemic a place close to the top of my priorities.'[6]

Fowler visited San Francisco in 1987, and his diary tells of being photographed shaking hands with personable young men with AIDS who would be dead in a couple of months. He visited New York and looked at the babies of intelligent and articulate drug-using mothers who would shortly die. He was deeply moved and harrowed by what he saw, and was taken aback that despite the bigger problem in the US, less seemed to be being done. As Acheson says of the visit, 'At a Federal level from Ronald Reagan down, there was a state of complete psychological denial even seemingly to the very existence of the HIV/AIDS epidemic.' He bemoans: 'The word AIDS hadn't crossed Reagan's lips.' In his diary, Fowler recalls the trip being physically and emotionally gruelling.

Essentially, Fowler's approach emerged because, as he says, he 'didn't have any alternative but to do it that way'. His view was: 'disease was disease, suffering was suffering and we had a moral and human obligation to treat sexual disease just like any other'.

How did Fowler progress his agenda in the face of such opposition? For one thing, he encouraged a bipartisan approach. The first parliamentary debate on AIDS was held on 21 November 1986. Hansard records an incredibly well-ordered and informed debate, which Fowler opened by outlining that the disease was fatal and incurable, estimating it affected 30,000 people in the UK. He asked for as much common ground among the political parties as possible. Apart from the occasional reference to the need to curtail promiscuity, the five-hour debate was essentially non-partisan and graceful with lengthy and well-informed contributions from members of both major parties, resulting in general consensus that the key issues were public education, research and treatment.

Fowler then cleverly circumvented Mrs Thatcher. Realizing that progress was always going to be blocked by the full Cabinet, where too many diverse and unknowledgeable interests would have intermingled to cause gridlock, he encouraged the establishment of a special Cabinet committee to deal with AIDS. Mrs Thatcher would usually have expected to chair any such committee, but on this occasion Willie Whitelaw took the chair: an inspired choice. Whitelaw knew how things worked: he was deputy prime minister and had been home secretary. Whitelaw was a decorated Second World War tank commander, and appreciated the need for action. But what is more, he had been responsible for his men's sexual health when overseas and understood the need for blunt advice and condoms. Fowler calls this innovation in Cabinet 'a great example of what can be done in government ... they all took ownership'. The committee managed to get all the policies through in the space of a couple of months.

Another element in Fowler's strategy was dealing with the media, and he found a lot of support from television companies. He was very concerned about the opinions of religious leaders. Before launching one campaign Fowler asked his chief medical officer to embark on what Acheson described as one of the most memorable experiences of his career, and that was 'to gain, at least the acquiescence, if not the approval, of the Archbishop of Canterbury, the Cardinal of Westminster, the Moderator of the Free Churches and the Chief Rabbi'. All were concerned with the unfolding tragedy and despite the fact that Acheson's message promoted the use of condoms, he received no criticism from them about the government's intentions.

Although Fowler was initially apprehensive about it, he had a secret weapon in the campaign against AIDS: Princess Diana. Fowler and Acheson are full of praise for Diana, the latter saying the 'fearless example of this largely untutored young woman, by allowing herself to be photographed embracing people of all ages infected by HIV ... probably had more influence in dispelling irrational fears ... than all the Government's leaflets and advertisements put together'.

Norman Fowler's book *AIDS: Don't Die of Ignorance* reflects on his campaigns and also on the state of the disease.[7] He argues that his information campaigns were successful. Gallup polling showed that 94 per cent of the public thought the government was right to be doing it. He believes the most successful part of the campaign was introducing new clean needles; consequently the UK has hardly been touched by transmissions through intravenous drug use.

Fowler continues his work on AIDS in a number of organizations. He has been highly influential in making condoms available in prisons and in giving asylum seekers and other non-British citizens free HIV treatment. As his book reveals, he continues to be shocked by the persistent official and personal prejudice shown towards people with AIDS around the world. Fowler's political persona may be that of an effective administrator and back-room political operator, but in our sense he is a player. He displays extraordinary grace in the face of continual opposition and has drawn on the collective skills, knowledge and reputations of many diverse people and groups. He has crafted innovative approaches to a hugely complex problem, his ambition is directed towards the health of the vulnerable and his fortitude is seen in his determination, whatever the odds, to do the right thing. These behaviours have contributed to a positive response to a vexatious issue.

We now turn from someone whose fortitude was displayed at the highest level of government to someone whose resilience was called upon at the highest echelons of the law.

Carla Del Ponte

Carla Del Ponte shows that you can be a player, seeing opportunities and taking risks, even at the height of the legal profession. When she was Switzerland's attorney general, and in the face of fierce opposition, she changed Swiss banking laws to prevent the laundering of criminal proceeds. While in the process of doing so, the Mafia murdered her close Italian colleague and counterpart and she received death threats. Del Ponte then led the international tribunals prosecuting war crimes in Yugoslavia and Rwanda, facing direct opposition from those countries in which the crimes occurred and indifference and occasional hostility from supposed supporters. Among the uncertainties she faced was the daunting challenge of whether it was possible in an international court to reconcile prosecution in common-law and civil-law legal systems. The treacherous political shifts – among those hiding the people she aimed to prosecute and those on whose behalf she was working – made her work profoundly uncertain and liable to disruption.[8] Yet through innovative organizational arrangements she succeeded in getting a head of state, Slobodan Milošević, to answer charges before an international tribunal for the first time ever. Del Ponte describes her career serving the interests of justice as an exercise in asserting her will, consistently and persistently. Her career is an example of how resilience is built in the face of extraordinarily difficult circumstances through the belief that something is right – and justice for victims of war crimes could not be anything but proper and necessary – by strength of character in confronting resistance in the face of disruption and change.

It is hard to imagine a starker contrast in the circumstances in which fortitude emerges than between the rarefied worlds of Norman Fowler and Carla Del Ponte and the unforgiving world of the Australian bush. To illustrate how play is important in a wide range of circumstances we now turn to examples of two men who comply with the stereotypical image of the tough Australian man of the 1950s and 1960s, but whose fortitude sustained persistent experimentation and adaptation in the most challenging of circumstances.

Leslie Thiess

Sir Leslie (Les) Thiess (1909–92) was a tough man in a hard industry, and few of his competitors would have called him playful. Throughout his long career building a large Australian mining and construction company, however, he demonstrated a major component of playfulness in his continuous ability to learn and adapt. Despite personal and business setbacks his eponymous company played a significant role in the building of modern Australia by responding to opportunities, taking risks, learning and evolving.

From a large family of German heritage, with ten brothers and one sister, Les grew up in a regional area of Queensland, Northern Australia. He began an earth-moving business, transporting rocks to build roads in demanding conditions. Four of his brothers joined the company, Thiess Brothers, and together

163

they established a reputation for reliability and for the capacity to take on demanding jobs. Les won a lot of business along with the respect of the American forces based in Brisbane in the Second World War. The US military needed roads, runways and buildings, which Thiess always delivered.

After the war Les realized that the Americans had left a vast amount of materiel – earth-moving equipment, vehicles and scrap metal – in the jungles of Papua New Guinea, 2,000 kilometres to the north. He negotiated the purchase of hundreds of tons of equipment that was moved back to Australia. The Americans said Thiess could have anything on which they hadn't painted a big white mark, which tended to be the working, high-cost machinery. Legend has it that Les and his brothers painted out these marks in the dead of night, and some highly valuable equipment was shipped back to Australia, reconditioned and put to highly productive use.

As part of its post-war reconstruction, Australia embarked on the Snowy Mountains hydroelectric scheme, its largest ever infrastructure project, involving 16 major dams, 7 power stations and 140 miles of tunnel. Thiess was the major Australian company involved in the project and delivered some of its core elements. The work was hard, in freezing conditions, and its dangers were starkly exposed when Les's nephew, Ken, was killed in a workplace accident. Over 120 men lost their lives on the project.

Thiess's 'can-do' approach saw all obstacles dealt with. Wives of the Thiess brothers moved in the heat and the dust and the floods from remote site to remote site, living, cooking and educating their children in tents. When a large bulldozer needed moving right across country in demanding terrain the Thiess family, husbands or wives, just got in it and drove (whether or not it was legal to do so using public roads). When a blockage in a road or a river slowed things down, the Thiess family knew just what to do with a stick of dynamite.

Never one to miss an opportunity, Les Thiess recognized the growing demand for energy in Japan as it rebuilt after its wartime devastation and he resolved to help meet it – bearing in mind that this was only a few years after the hatred stirred by the war, with Australia's relationship with Japan being especially sensitive. Thiess's move into the coal industry was also brave for the business diversification it involved. As the mining interests developed, Thiess found great use in a robust Japanese vehicle made by the re-emergent Toyota company, and Les bought the Toyota dealership in Australia.

Great projects were undertaken, such as building the tunnel under Sydney Harbour and developing the beautiful Hayman Island resort. Les was a trailblazer. He bought a series of corporate jets, a remarkable occurrence at the time. Life was good. The family enjoyed holidays on Les's yacht and the brothers continued their legendary drinking sessions. And then all his fortitude was called upon when a hostile corporate takeover saw his effective removal from the company that he had built. The success and profitability he had created proved attractive to CSR, a building materials company with cash to burn. Long-term institutional shareholders, with whom Les thought he had an agreement, took the money CSR had to offer in what was then Australia's largest corporate takeover. Les Thiess remained as president, but was not a member of the board. Painfully, he lost control of his company.

Ordinary people in such circumstances might have chosen retirement. Les was seventy years old at the time and had plenty of money in the bank. But instead he started up a number of companies and bought into a small local construction company, helping to build it up. Within a few years he bought back into the Thiess construction company – 'dropping ten years in age in the process'[9] – and created consortia with mining interests. After a series of joint venture arrangements, ownership of the Thiess company moved from CSR to Hochtief, the German construction group, to Les's considerable financial advantage. At its peak, Thiess was a company with $7 billion annual sales, and it is now part of the world's largest construction conglomerate outside China.

Les's personal fortitude became embedded and upheld in the culture of the organization, where the term 'blue blood' emerged to capture the beliefs and behaviours of the company's long-term staff. This is certainly not used in the classic meaning of the aristocracy, but in the nobility of hard work and indomitable spirit where no problem is too difficult.

Failure is common in working lives, especially if they involve innovation and risk. The way we deal personally with the embarrassment of failures such as Les's loss of his company, and learn valuable lessons from it, contributes to the development of fortitude. He didn't give up, and alongside his sheer bloody-mindedness he kept his optimism and enthusiasm for learning as part of his engrained entrepreneurial behaviour.

Australians of Les Thiess's generation had a deserved reputation for toughness, so for another example of fortitude, although in very different circumstances, we turn to one of his contemporaries.

Arthur Bishop

The engineer Arthur Bishop (1917–2006) displayed many of the behaviours of the player. He possessed immense intellectual curiosity for and passion about the discipline and craft of mechanical engineering, and displayed dogged persistence in the face of overwhelming odds. In his career he confronted the indifference and arrogance of the British military in the 1940s, as well as the power, introspection and occasional dishonesty of the US car industry in the 1950s and 1960s.

Like many players, his primary motivation was to understand and improve things. He was a man whose need to know how things work was like a hunger, and who was contemptuous of those who made money from money. Bishop's biographer, Clare Brown, says he explained how after the Second World War 'I was being carried forward on a wave of new and exciting opportunities. I didn't think of it so much as a way to make money, but it was an opportunity to make a career out of innovation.'[10]

His engineering career began in earnest during the Second World War, with the building of the Beaufort bomber, used extensively by the Royal Australian Air Force in the Pacific, and the only bomber ever built in Australia. The planes were desperately needed for Australia's war effort, but supply of the British-designed bombers and parts inevitably dried up given Britain's other pressing priorities. When parts such as undercarriages and propellers could no longer be supplied, the challenge was on to build aircraft in a country that did not yet make cars. In the absence of aero-engineering skills, Australia drew on the expertise of people with backgrounds in the less obvious fields of car spares and the railways. They faced extraordinary challenges, but got things done precisely because they did not immediately understand their difficulties they would encounter.

One irritation was that the British were reticent in providing technical information about the bombers they made. In an example of the incredibly distorting power of intellectual property rights, Clare Brown tells how the British manufacturer Vickers refused to send technical drawings to Australia during the war because of its licensing agreement with the German manufacturer, Krupp. In a case of supreme irony, shortly afterwards the Vickers factory was destroyed by German bombs.

In an impressive logistical feat, an aircraft factory was built in Sydney that was up and running within a year. Eventually the Australian-built bombers (700 in all, with their 39,000 parts) was manufactured by an organization of 8,500 people.

Bishop played a central role in the efforts to build the bomber. He designed an important innovation in the landing gear, and developed instruments better than those found in the US and Britain, explaining that he and his colleagues had 'the advantage of having no inhibitions, no sense of what could or couldn't be done'. In 1944, Bishop went to England to promote his undercarriage design and was met with arrogance, scepticism and complacency, but he prevailed after many uncomfortable months. The greatest challenge of his career, however, lay in his attempts after the war to introduce his radical new design for a variable ratio steering gear to the US car industry. It became a ten-year struggle, as he engaged in vicious political battles involving staunch supporters and implacable opponents.

His difficulties in the US were affected by that nation's almost complete ignorance about Australia. He was an outsider, an outspoken and opinionated foreigner, telling the world's most powerful industry that he knew better than its leaders. Bishop had to confront a common challenge of entrepreneurs and innovators when they question existing ways of doing things that are profitable and successful. His steering system was technically better, but existing systems worked, were well established and produced substantial returns to their producers, inducing entrenched resistance to change. He faced the well-known phenomenon of the not-invented-here syndrome: things are of questionable value unless you develop them yourself. Some of the companies Bishop dealt with had no qualms about behaving unethically, reneging on deals, infringing patents and resorting to dirty tricks. The short-sighted and occasionally corrupt behaviour of the car industry at the time is well known, as pointed out by Ralph Nader in his influential book *Unsafe at Any Speed*.[11] The crashes caused by existing steering systems, which could be very dangerous, were ascribed by the industry to 'nuts behind the wheel'.

The frustrations Bishop felt must have been immense, although Brown's biography only records two instances of him not so playfully grabbing antagonists by the throat. He loathed the industry's preoccupations with marketing and styling changes, rather than improved engineering. He had a powerful belief in the social responsibility of engineers.

Bishop resorted to setting up his own businesses to demon-strate what established firms believed impossible and had to make painful business compromises. Eventually, his financial success derived from licences to his patents for the valves on variable ratio gears and their manufacture, as the industry adapted to Bishop's ideas and, rather than wholly adopting them, used them to change existing products incrementally.

Somewhat ironically, despite all the time he spent overseas and the personal cost of continual moving of his family back and forth from Australia to the US and UK, the first opportunity for applying his variable ratio gear was in an Australian car in 1968, fourteen years after he began peddling it around Detroit. Bishop's steering system is now used on 20 per cent of the world's cars.

Bishop's drive and self-belief were extraordinary. A restless inventor throughout his life, he developed heaters, car trailers, air conditioners, a concrete mixer and a rotating house. His name appeared on eighty-five patents, including twenty-five on the design and manufacturing of steering gears. He invested hundreds of thousands of dollars of his own money back into his ideas. In later life he became passionate about small-scale public transporters, developing the concept of Austrans: people movers. When in 2001 Bishop made $7 million from the sale of 30 per cent of his company to Daimler Chrysler, he put every cent of it into Austrans. After his death, Austrans went into receivership and Bishop Steering Technology was sold to a German company.

Like Steve Shirley's, Bishop's career tells us a great deal about the trials and tribulations of the player, and the rewards that ensue when good ideas are persevered with. It also tells us that nothing lasts forever and players don't always get things right, but what matters is persistence and tenacity.

Reflections

Fortitude maintains, sustains and upholds play. Working and innovating in a world of uncertainty implies there will be failure. As Joseph Schumpeter put it, innovation involves the carrot of spectacular reward or the stick of destitution: there will be damage, and fortitude keeps you going. In the work of Christopher Wren and Arthur Bishop the pressures put on them to give up or bend to opposing forces were extreme, but they never stopped moving forward. Despite the challenges to Les Thiess, his is a story of continually upholding deeply held beliefs in improvements and progress through adaptation. Fortitude is sustained by noble objectives, seen particularly clearly in the case of Norman Fowler and his lengthy commitment to address the scourge of AIDS, and in the grit of Carla Del Ponte fighting extraordinary legal battles. Fortitude involves the assertion of will, captured in the words of Winston Churchill who said that, except in convictions of honour or good sense: 'never give in, never give in, never, never, never'.

The fortitude of innovators and entrepreneurs provide examples of people who have persevered in circumstances a lot more trying than those most of us face at work. They give us the opportunity to consider:

- whether to move the point at which we give up on schemes, and the value of continuing further than we have in the past when things aren't going so well;
- how to deal, personally and organizationally, with efforts turning out in unexpected ways; and
- how to see failures as opportunities to learn and build the basis for eventual success.

6

Ambition

The object of strong desire or aspiration.
   The ardent desire to attain rank, influence, distinction or other preferment.

Ambition underlies the behaviour of all players. The ancient Greek philosopher Heraclitus said that big results require big ambitions. It is ambition that stretches people to do extraordinary things. The intrepid eighteenth-century sailor and explorer James Cook, for example, said that 'ambition leads me not only farther than any other man has been before me, but as far as I think it possible for man to go'. The motto of John Christie, founder of Glyndebourne, the opera house and company – 'doing not the best we can do but the best that can be done anywhere' – nicely summarizes the ambitions of those striving to be at the forefront, the leaders, innovators and entrepreneurs, of their fields. Glyndebourne, now in its third generation of family leadership, continues to uphold the motto.

This chapter is about players with a wide range of backgrounds and variety of motivations for their actions, but with one unifying noble behaviour: they are all determined to meet the high ambitions they have of themselves, and use their advantages to give back, and in doing so to make the world a better place. Their activities reflect Rousseau's view in *Emile* that the purpose of life is to do good, and 'life is not breath, but action, the use of our senses, our mind, our faculties, every part of ourselves which makes us conscious of our being. Life consists less in length of days than in the keen sense of living.' The following people's ambitions motivate actions guided by a keen sense of living and giving.

Jeremy Coller

Jeremy Coller is one of Britain's most successful private equity entrepreneurs. His ambitions are very much more than pecuniary: he has the extraordinary ambition of ending animal factory farms and their misuse of antibiotics before he dies. Although Jeremy does not intend to die for another forty years or so (he plans to live to be ninety-eight), some time ago he asked a friend to write his obituary. His friend noted his uncommon influence on the finance industry, but Jeremy was shaken by the lack of contribution to his life-long concerns about animal factory farms. He vowed to use his considerable influence and wealth to do something about it. He says he's made many sacrifices over the years to build his company, especially in his family life, but the devotion to his business has paid off in the way he can now be a champion for the causes he strongly believes in.

Jeremy was instrumental in developing the 'secondary market' in private equity, which provides liquidity to investors wishing to exit early from their private equity investments. He completed Europe's first secondaries transaction in 1988 when he was working for ICI pensions, and he created his own company in 1990, which in 2012 completed its sixth fund, worth $5.5 billion. In 2015, Coller Capital closed its seventh fund with commitments of $7.15 billion. Headquartered in London, with offices in New York and Hong Kong, Coller Capital has won numerous awards in the venture fund industry and has the largest investment team dedicated to private equity secondaries in the world. In 2002, he formed the Jeremy Coller Foundation which funds the Coller Institute of Venture at Tel Aviv University, and the publication of the *Private Equity Findings* journal. Always fascinated by scientists and inventors, he wrote an entertaining book entitled *The Lives, Loves and Deaths of Splendidly Unreasonable Inventors*.[1] A forceful, engaging and reflective man, and a lifelong vegetarian, he loathes animal factory farming, believing it causes four problems: it spreads drug resistance (80 per cent of all antibiotics in the US are used in animal factory farms; the figure is 50 per cent in Europe); it exacerbates undernourishment and hunger (one-third of the world's grain harvest is fed to farmed animals, and it takes on average around 6 kilograms of plant protein to produce 1 kilogram of animal protein); it consumes scarce resources (livestock production uses one-quarter of the world's fresh water and uses 30 per cent of the world's land surface, and it takes more than 1,000 litres of water to produce 100 calories of beef); it contributes to global warming and pollution (livestock produces 37 per cent of human-induced methane).[2] He also points to the sharp increase in factory farming over the past twenty years, evidence of meat consumption increasing cancer and cardiovascular disease and the worrying legislation in the US that makes it illegal to film or photograph inside animal farms.

The approach taken by the Jeremy Coller Foundation is threefold: to influence legislation on the use of antibiotics; influence capital flows away from factory farms; and measure and benchmark animal welfare. The increasing demand for environmental, social and governance (ESG) criteria in investment decisions is seen in the following: in 2002, 16 per cent of investors demanded ESG investment restrictions in Coller Capital funds; this figure grew to 29 per cent in 2007 and 80 per cent in 2012.

It is striking when conversing with Jeremy just how open he is about the behaviours needed to succeed, both noble and questionable, and the personal costs of the investment in time and energy needed to build a highly successful business. He refers to the Faustian pact of rewards requiring obsessiveness in business. Super successful people have periods of obsession, he contends,

173

when they have to sacrifice a bit of themselves. He talks about being 'imprisoned by your own expectations, and motivated by a fear of failure'.

Jeremy wanted to be an academic, and took his A-levels three times before studying for a Management Science degree and a Master's in Philosophy. But he recognized his limitations in this regard and his much greater strengths as an entrepreneur. His especial skill, according to one of his contemporaries, is seeing value where others do not, and Jeremy himself talks about the need for mastery of risk. Entrepreneurs, he says, are not fearful of uncertainty and change and are comfortable with, and capable of calibrating, risk. On the one hand he refers to behaviours such as the importance of will power, self-confidence and tenacity, and the importance of being relentless and ruthless when you know you are right and everyone else is wrong: 'if you know where you are going the world parts for you'. On the other hand, he talks about self-knowledge, about being genuine and authentic and the need to give time and knowledge to others. Ambition, he says, is driven by usefulness and knowing what it means to be useful, including for the greater good, which in his case is fighting to end the factory farming of animals.

As the above dictionary definitions of ambition suggest, there are associations with prestige and self-aggrandisement, but the word also suggests selfless and public-spirited concerns. Alfred Nobel, for example, had no interest in personal wealth, and left the bulk of his huge fortune to establish his eponymous prizes. Jeremy Coller's book says of Nobel: 'wealth for its own sake did not interest him; the determination to succeed and a highly developed sense of responsibility to those with whom he was involved were the greater motivation'. There are certainly many ambitious people for whom the accumulation of money is deeply distasteful. Steve Shirley says that money is elusive and – like happiness – if you pursue it too avidly, it will elude you.

The great economist John Maynard Keynes was especially critical of those for whom personal financial advance and 'the love of money as a possession', where people place value on ends above means, was divorced from the 'paths of virtue and sane wisdom'. In an essay exploring 'Economic Possibilities for our Grandchildren', Keynes bluntly exclaimed, 'the extraction of usury is a misdemeanour, and the love of money is detestable', and suggested even more strongly that it is a 'disgusting morbidity, one of those semi-criminal, semi-pathological propensities which one hands over with a shudder to the specialists in mental disease'.[3]

Keynes was certainly not opposed to free enterprise and appreciated what he called the animal spirits of investors and risk-takers (and he was a highly successful investor for his Cambridge college). He simply despised those whose ambition rested with the accumulation of money for money's sake. Keynes's biographer, Lord Robert Skidelsky, has similar views, which he shared with us: 'Ambition used to be a noble thing. To make your mark on the world, leave your footprint, ambitious for your community, ambitious for success. Now ambition is associated with money and greed.' Keynes might have raised an eyebrow about the relentless personal acquisitiveness, and occasional questionable practices, of businessmen such as Andrew Carnegie and Bill Gates, and it would be interesting to learn his views on the private equity world of Jeremy Coller – but he would have whole-heartedly applauded the philanthropy of all three.

In this regard the ends justify the means, when the ends are laudable and the means are legal. Making vast amounts of money by sailing close to the wind is fine, if the eventual intention is to put that money to good use. 'Good' in this case means outcomes that improve human experience. There are those, however, for whom social and personal advance are indistinguishable, and this is apparent in a number of entrepreneurs whose businesses are built on the beneficial application of science.

Elizabeth Iorns

Elizabeth Iorns is the co-founder and CEO of Science Exchange, a Silicon Valley start-up providing match-making services for scientific research and business. Connections between scientific research and industry are often challenging to initiate and maintain, and Elizabeth's company brokers scientific equipment so that universities and businesses can work productively together. Born in Australia in 1980, Elizabeth grew up in New Zealand and undertook her PhD in cancer biology at the renowned Institute of Cancer Research (ICR) in London. She then moved to the University of Miami in a post-doctoral position and became a member of faculty at its School of Medicine.

The creation of the company grew out of her disillusionment with the way medical science is conducted. She sees enormous waste in the utilization of scientific equipment. In her estimation, scientific facilities are only used at 30–40 per cent of capacity, yet often as a condition of the granted award of the equipment they need to operate at 100 per cent.

While at ICR she was impressed at the way a relatively small organization could assemble multidisciplinary teams very quickly, and cites the example of an idea moving from basic research to clinical application in only three years. In Miami, however, Elizabeth argues the new school was hampered by the need to create many new protocols and systems that led to a frustrating situation where there was funding for research that couldn't be undertaken.

While at Miami, she and two partners came up with the idea of Science Exchange, and applied for funding to Y Combinator, which makes biannual small-scale investments in a number of start-ups, offering them advice and connections. In her 2011 round of funding there were 64 start-ups with 164 individuals supported. Her academic boss, who was head of department, supported the idea and gave her three months to visit Palo Alto, taking over responsibility for the PhDs she was supervising.

A number of factors led Elizabeth to step out of a medical research career, the major one being the strength of her concept and a desire to improve the conduct of science. Her ambition was to create a business driven not by financial returns, but by the goal of improving the quality and efficiency of scientific research. Science Exchange has created a market, but one that is based on what she calls a 'clearly defined exchange of values'.

The Science Exchange's business model is based on providing companies with the use of under-utilized science facilities more effectively and productively than companies can source such facilities directly. This makes short-term contracts for service easier to arrange. Businesses' experience of collaboration with universities can be poor: they often have to renegotiate every contract and there may not be much expertise and professionalism in universities on how to manage business services. The Science Exchange is designed to overcome the rigidities of university systems and give companies a better experience of connecting with scientists. Universities benefit from revenue streams for contract research and researchers have more opportunities to experiment and exercise their skills; businesses receive quality-assured access to the best researchers and equipment.

Although there have inevitably been sleepless nights, Elizabeth feels she has been lucky and her journey has been drama-free compared to most entrepreneurs. She has had the support of two co-founders: Dan Knox, an economist, and Ryan Abbott. She says they had a great combination of skills. Knox already knew what it was like to work for a start-up and had taken the Executive MBA in entrepreneurship at MIT. Abbott brought important technical skills (but he has subsequently left the company). The company was planned very carefully. The time at Y Combinator convinced them they were onto something. The founders initially raised $1.7 million, and in short order there were 5,000 users of the Exchange. By 2015 it had raised $10.5 million from venture capitalists and business angels. In Elizabeth's view, Y Combinator gives you the opportunity to be honest about what might go wrong and how to learn from it. Its network of mentors provides perspective. She is confident that she has developed a whole range of new entrepreneurial skills that she wouldn't have developed in academia.

Reviews are taken after every transaction in the Exchange. To date, over 98 per cent say they would use the laboratory again and 60 per cent actually have used it again. Elizabeth claims this is high for the nature of the experiments that are being performed.

Elizabeth says there is huge latent potential in the supply side. One thousand laboratories are now part of the network, and she suggests this could double within a year. Science Exchange has attracted a number of major pharmaceutical companies on the demand side. Each pharmaceutical company works with about 500 vendors, and each time Science Exchange works with a new company it bring its network into the platform.

Elizabeth is still leading the company's operations, but tries to find time for strategy. She now works part time at Y Combinator (which has a strong reputation in software) to help with its life sciences and biotechnology areas to build its brand.

And now to another scientist – a man right at the top of the profession – and to his extraordinary ambitions within the practice of science.

Chris Toumazou

New Bond Street is one of London's swankiest addresses. The world's most exclusive and expensive stores are there, such as Cartier, Asprey and Bulgari. And then there is a new company called GENEU – pronounced 'gene you'. This company offers the world's first DNA test for personalized skincare. By taking a swab from your mouth, within minutes your DNA is tested on a microchip and an individualized programme of anti-ageing skincare can be prescribed. It may be a surprise that the person fronting the marketing of such a high-profile fashion-oriented enterprise is Nick Rhodes, previously of the band Duran Duran. It may be even more surprising that the person behind GENEU's technology is someone who left school without many qualifications and who trained as an electrician. Chris Toumazou also happens to be a very eminent academic whose inventions have reduced the size of mobile phones, aided deaf children, improved home monitoring of people with renal disease and whose design for an artificial pancreas is currently being tested.[4] He is also the founder of a rapidly growing company – DNA Electronics Ltd – that is applying its molecular diagnostics technology to real-time testing of medical conditions such as sepsis.

Chris is of Greek Cypriot heritage. His parents ran fish and chip and kebab shops in Cheltenham. He left school at sixteen with hardly any qualifications. School didn't inspire him, he says, but it did encourage him to try and look ahead and prepare beforehand to impress others, often in the hope of avoiding bullying. He says it challenged him to achieve and be the best. The expectation was that he would move into the family business, but he was always interested in electronics and he enrolled in a City and Guilds course as an electrician. He did well in this and then enrolled in an Ordinary National Diploma, equivalent to an A-level. This was sufficient for him to gain an interview for an electrical engineering degree programme at Oxford Brookes University. Accompanied by his extended family to Oxford, and into the actual interview itself by his father, he was offered a place and began his undergraduate studies.

He excelled and it was not long before he was encouraged to undertake a PhD where, along with his supervisor Professor Lidgey, he turned his mind to a new approach to circuit design based on current rather than voltage. Lidgey describes this as a hugely productive time, with lots of academic papers being produced, and says, 'We were like two children in a toyshop.' Always enthusiastically tinkering with circuits, Chris says his supervisor introduced him to a totally new 'playground of electronics'.

Chris's work focused on analogue circuit design. Most organic signals – eyesight, sound, speech – are analogue, and transferring these into digital signals for products such as mobile phones requires a lot of interfaces taking up space and energy. By moving focus away from voltage to current Chris designed analogue circuits for ultra-low-power electronic devices that require two orders of magnitude less power to use.

After his PhD, Chris moved to Imperial College London, where his academic progress was stellar, becoming at the age of thirty-three Imperial's youngest ever professor. With over 700 research publications and 50 patents to his name, he explains his success as a mixture of theoretical understanding with an intuition for what is practically possible. He also says he was given great freedom to pursue his interests, encouraged, for example, to go to conferences whether or not he was presenting his research, just to meet people.

His work quickly attracted sponsorship from a number of industries working at the interface between analogue and digital technologies. These included the mobile phone sector in Thailand, where his research produced digital and analogue handsets. Over time Chris became more and more interested in the medical field. A Canadian entrepreneur approached him about improving cochlear implants for children who were born deaf. At that time the digital circuitry required, in Chris's words, a great box the size of a car battery. After two years he produced the world's first analogue chip that could be fully implanted in a child's ear. This very much smaller chip is now used by tens of thousands of children.

Chris's interest in medicine was intensified when his nine-year-old son lost his kidneys through a congenital disorder and spent three years on a dialysis machine. He was appalled at the primitive nature of the technology supporting his son's care, such as frequent manual temperature and blood pressure checks, so he invented a small processor – embedded in what he calls a Sensium patch – attached to the skin. It can measure key indicators such as heart rate and temperature and send that information from home to hospital. The body monitoring system has been approved by the US Food and Drug Administration and is now increasingly being used in the US and UK.

Chris worked at breaking down the disciplinary barriers between engineers and medical researchers. He says he especially enjoys pulling disciplines together, and describes how inspiring it is to work beyond your own team. He jokes that medical researchers looked at engineers as simple technicians, but says his approach tolerates no prima donnas. The objective, he says, is to make sure people in one discipline are not intimidated by those in others. His interdisciplinary approach accorded exactly with the strategy of Imperial's rector at the time, Sir Richard Sykes, who encouraged him to start an Institute of Biomedical Engineering. Estimating that the cost would be £20 million, Sykes put in half the money and asked Chris to find the rest. Sykes says through a mixture of charm and credibility Chris had no problem raising the money. His reputation in business was based on his track record of developing technology that demonstrably worked, such as in mobile phones and hearing implants. Chris reports that his parents were especially proud to meet the Queen when she opened the Institute.

A major result of Chris's inventiveness is the 'lab on a chip'. Only 0.1 per cent of an individual's DNA differs from anyone else's. It is this tiny proportion that tells us about our characteristics, such as whether we have a predisposition to genetic diseases or a tolerance to drugs. Essentially, Chris created a chip that could recognize a genetic mutation in a DNA sample placed on it. The chip can reveal whether you have a predisposition to a disease or whether you can metabolize a medicine. This can be done in minutes and allows doctors to tailor prescriptions individually. By reducing over- and under-dosing, fewer hospital visits are needed and enormous savings are made in the health system. The process also saves on the costs of having to send samples to laboratories.

As well as DNA Electronics Ltd, Chris has started three other companies to commercialize his inventions: Toumaz Technology Ltd, Applied Bionics PTE and Future Waves. He says his companies have made him money, but that was never what motivated him – he is driven by innovation and putting his ideas to valuable use.

References to play litter Chris's description of what he does. He calls his work a 'playground of innovation', where people from different disciplines – engineering, medicine, science – can work together. He tells us to look at children in playgrounds, how they meet and share language and speech with others they have only just met. This approach allowed extensive collaboration with medical researchers and clinicians, leading to the design of the artificial pancreas. Chris says he has the advantage of understanding the analogue language of biology, while a co-developer and medical colleague says Chris has the ability to ask questions that the medical profession would not ask itself.

The process of discovering the lab on a chip follows Chris's approach of not aiming to address particular problems, but rather to discover a solution and then set the problem around it. He experiments with ideas – such as the extraordinarily imaginative decision to put DNA on a microchip – and then asks, 'What have we created here? What use is it?' It is at this point that the need for expert advice in complementary areas becomes apparent.

Much comes down to leadership, he says, especially in the way you provide an environment that gives others the freedom to operate and innovate. He describes his model as PPR: start with the *people*, put in the right *process* and the *results* will come. As ideas progress in the playground and reach a commercial stage, planning and funding needs to be put in place. Much of the funding for Chris's enterprises has come from very wealthy individuals. He says there is a cost to this, as such people inevitably want to be involved, need to be kept informed and feel some ownership of the scientific and commercial developments. However, Chris feels these costs are worth bearing compared to the alternatives, such as venture capital investments. The reasons are twofold: first, they allow him greater freedom to do what he thinks best, and second, these investors know what it is like to grow businesses and take risks.

The freedom Chris enjoys motivates his aim to give the same to the people running the companies he's started. His leadership style is to encourage a culture where people are comfortable in their independence. One of the measures of his success in this regard is that when these people have high-profile visitors that bring them great kudos, they still choose to invite him along, proud to be sharing the limelight with him.

His approach to dealing with investors is to ensure that they use his ideas in ways that give them a sense of ownership.

Chris's ambitions extend beyond the need to sate his intense scientific curiosity and include his aim to improve public health and be a successful entrepreneur. To celebrate the Queen's Diamond Jubilee in 2013 Chris was appointed to the highly prestigious position of Regius Professor at Imperial College London. He is a fellow of the Royal Society and has received numerous other high-level academic recognitions. To illustrate the way he spans the worlds of scholarship and business, he won the 2014 European Inventor of the Year Award for his lab on a chip.

Albert Einstein said that imagination is the preview of life's coming attractions, and Chris combines focused practicality with an imagination that foresees and welcomes the most extraordinary disruption. In his TEDMED talk of 2012, Chris imagines a future where a doctor will message your biological record, query your organ and debug your DNA. Quite a preview!

To illustrate the wide application of behaviours supporting play, having explored the nobility of ambition in the sciences we now turn to ambition in the arts.

Léonard Gianadda

On 31 July 1976, a private plane crashed at Bari, Italy, leading to the death of Pierre Gianadda. Pierre died a week later from injuries he sustained when helping his fellow passengers from the ensuing fire. Out of this tragedy comes an example of noble ambition on the part of Pierre's brother, Léonard – an extraordinarily entrepreneurial ambition, cast by bereavement, in the world of the arts.

Léonard Gianadda was born in 1935 in Martigny, Switzerland. His grandfather Baptiste emigrated from Italy to Switzerland in 1889 at the age of thirteen, travelling through the imposing St Bernard Pass on foot. Baptiste was an economic refugee, hungry and in search of work. He went to night school, studying design and French, and went on to found a successful construction company. Léonard's father Robert was an entrepreneur in Martigny, and the family was sufficiently wealthy to allow his sons Léonard and Pierre to spend many happy years in their early twenties travelling in the US, Cuba, Canada, Russia, Africa and the Middle East.

Léonard's first job was as a reporter and press photographer. In 1960 he changed careers and qualified as a civil engineer. He became a successful and wealthy engineer and constructor, building the bridge that spans the Rhône at Riddes in 1985. He built the second bridge at Gueuroz in 1994 – his grandfather had built the first – and numerous buildings in and around Martigny, including more than 1,500 apartments.

In the spring of 1976, while planning to build a rental house on a plot of land he owned in Martigny, Léonard discovered the remains of a Gallo-Roman temple, the oldest in Switzerland. He entered discussions with the local authority about preserving the remains within a museum he wanted to construct. But Pierre's tragic death changed Léonard's career forever. The forty-one-year-old Léonard was very attached to Pierre and decided to establish the Pierre Gianadda Foundation, inaugurated on 19 November 1978, the day Pierre would have turned forty. Léonard invested 3 million Swiss francs to start the foundation, with the vision to preserve the temple and other local ruins. He also wanted to celebrate Pierre's love of photography and art, so decided that the foundation should exhibit contemporary art and photography and provide a concert hall for the very best chamber musicians, set within a sculpture garden.

Léonard's first exhibition was a flop. But a short while later he organized a successful Picasso exhibition, followed by one on Paul Klee. Léonard, a larger-than-life character, now manages to convince private collectors to loan their paintings for specially curated exhibitions. The foundation also has two permanent exhibitions, one on the engineering and design genius of Leonardo da Vinci and the other an impressive collection of historic motor vehicles. By Léonard's eightieth birthday in

August 2015, nearly 10 million people had visited the foundation. Léonard has become a stalwart of the international art world, raising private and corporate sponsorship to run a critically acclaimed centre for the arts, and receiving numerous international awards and recognitions.

Léonard also created a publishing house, producing detailed explanatory catalogues for exhibitions on Turner, Kandinsky, van Gogh, Manet and Toulouse-Lautrec. He also acquired a fine collection of modern sculpture by Rodin, Miró, Moore, Chagall and Ernst. The list of musicians who have performed at the foundation is similarly impressive, with performers such as Yehudi Menuhin, Daniel Barenboim, Alfred Brendel, Yo-Yo Ma, Mstislav Rostropovich and Cecilia Bartoli. Léonard became friends with the artist Henri Cartier-Bresson and Jacqueline Picasso.

Léonard Gianadda has become an entrepreneur in the art world, playfully combining paintings, sculptures, music and exhibitions to create a rewarding experience for visitors. In his brother's death he found a new ambition in life. His desire to give back is seen in other ways, and his social conscience, raised during earlier travels with Pierre, remains with him. He feels passionately about Europe's refugee crisis, and in 2015 he offered five apartments to Syrian families.

Play, in our sense, can be a means and feature of what in contemporary business is called 'pivoting'. Most usually applied to the world of start-up companies, and the common need to pivot to new business models as such firms grow, as with Paul Drayson's PowderJect, it also applies to careers. Léonard Gianadda pivoted into the world of the arts, and we now turn to someone who pivoted in his career so as to focus his attention on his concern for environmental sustainability.

Keith Tuffley

Keith Tuffley, an Australian, had a very successful twenty-five-year career in investment banking. When the economic crisis unfolded in the late 2000s, he took stock of his career and where his future ambitions would take him. Keith wanted time to be with his wife and four children, a chance to explore the world in a different way, and to give back to society. The family decided to move from London to a quiet, rural setting and they now live in Switzerland. Keith is passionate about the environment and sustainability and wanted to find ways to help businesses change to more sustainable practices. His career shift allowed him to pursue this interest along with what to many would seem a series of extreme adventures.

Applying his financial experience, Keith became founder and chairman of NEUW Ventures SA, based in Lausanne, Switzerland: an entrepreneurial investment company that finances new businesses which aim to reduce the human ecological footprint and accelerate the transition to a sustainable economy. NEUW Ventures chooses companies where sustainability is both a fundamental part of their business strategy and a core driver of long-term financial performance. Keith is also a director of the Great Barrier Reef Foundation and of Bush Heritage Australia, a governor of WWF-Australia, a member of the board of We Mean Business and a member of the Corporate Advisory Panel of the World Forum for Natural Capital.

In 2014, Keith became the managing partner and CEO of The B Team, a new foundation focusing on sustainable business. The B Team was formed by an extraordinary group of entrepreneurs, including Richard Branson and Ratan Tata. Keith once again finds himself travelling, splitting his time between Switzerland, London and New York, attending international meetings such as COP21 in Paris and helping to bring business leaders together to address issues of climate change and sustainability.

Keith also wanted to explore his personal interests in a wide range of adventure activities and sports, in a way that publicizes and promotes sustainability and environmental causes. In 2013 he undertook his Grand Tours Project, becoming the first amateur to cycle every kilometre of the Tour de France, Giro d'Italia and Vuelta a España, on the same day as each race and in one season. As a keen mountaineer, Keith has climbed most of the 4,000-metre peaks in the European Alps, and has led climbing, sailing and skiing expeditions to the Karakoram ranges in Pakistan, the Chilean Andes, the New Zealand Alps and the Antarctic Peninsula. In 2016 he skied to the North Pole, and in the winter of that year set off on a trip to cycle and ski 640 kilometres to the South Pole on a route never taken before, dragging a sledge across an uncharted 150-kilometre glacier. Keith pursues these as personal challenges, but also as a way to further the cause of environmental sustainability through various associated initiatives that attract commentary.

From the ambitions of those from the disparate worlds of private equity, science, business, environmental sustainability and the arts we now turn to someone completely different: to a woman working in a very different era, doing very different work, but with the same ambition to do good.

Maria Dickin

Looking at photographs of Maria Dickin (1870–1951), the word 'playful' does not jump immediately to mind. 'Austere' might be more appropriate. But Dickin was an extraordinary woman who innovated to become one of history's greatest advocates for animal welfare.[5]

From a large, religious family, Dickin married a well-to-do accountant and lived comfortably in Hampstead Heath in London. Deciding she wanted more in her life, she started visiting the slums of the East End of London to see if there was anything she could usefully do. She was horrified and dismayed at the poverty she saw, but most particularly in the way this affected animals. She saw dogs and cats with horrible diseases and broken limbs, cruelly overworked horses and goats and rabbits kept in appalling conditions, which she said 'made me indescribably miserable'. She wrote a book called *The Cry of the Animal*, and decided to do something about the horrors she had seen. A deeply religious woman, a spiritualist, the *Oxford Dictionary of National Biography* refers to her 'semi-obsessive concern about the sufferings of others in the powerful combination often found in reforming pioneers at their moment of creative vision'.

Poor people loved their pets and needed healthy animals to eat and help them work, but they could not afford expensive veterinary care. In the face of opposition, and a notable lack of financial and practical support, Dickin created the People's Dispensary for Sick Animals (PDSA) and in 1917 opened her first free animal dispensary in a Whitechapel basement lent to her by a sympathetic clergyman. The crowd needing to have animals treated was so large the police were called to maintain order. Larger premises were found soon after that allowed the charity to treat a hundred animals a day.

Dickin was also ambitious to help animals outside of London. Her view was:

> I must have dispensaries throughout the whole of East of London ... no, throughout the whole of London, then I became very bold – why not – throughout England – then the British Isles, the British Empire?

As a first step, she converted a gypsy caravan, designing and equipping it as a horse-drawn mobile clinic that freely dispensed medicine and advice during its travels. Her husband donated the horse. She eventually had a fleet of these clinics that travelled throughout the country. By 1921 the PDSA had seven dispensaries, treating 40,000 animals a year. By 1923 there were sixteen dispensaries and Dickin had designed a motor caravan dispensary. By 1935 Dickin had established five PDSA hospitals, seventy-one dispensaries and eleven motor caravan dispensaries, and over a million animals a year were being treated.

In 1928, the PDSA Sanatorium was opened to offer large-scale treatment of animals and to act as a training school for PDSA technical staff. It was the first of its kind in Europe.

The PDSA opened dispensaries in Morocco, Egypt, Greece, South Africa and Palestine.

Opposition from the fee-charging veterinary profession was inevitable, and Dickin was criticized by the Royal College of Veterinary Surgeons and the Ministry of Agriculture. In 1937 she wrote a letter to the Royal College:

> If you are so concerned about proper treatment of the sick animals of the poor, open your own dispensaries ... Show owners how to care for their animals in sickness and health. Do the same work that we are doing. Instead of spending your energy and time hindering us, spend it dealing with this mass misery.

Eventually, two Acts of Parliament cemented the role of the PDSA, but vets' hostility threatened the movement for the rest of Dickin's life.

In another example of playfulness, in 1934 Dickin launched the Busy Bees, a special club for children. Busy Bees were taught how to look after pets properly, and raised funds for the charity. Dickin was Queen Bee of the Busy Bees and was eventually succeeded in the role by the famous children's author Enid Blyton.

During the devastation of the London Blitz during the Second World War, PDSA Animal Rescue squads helped to save and treat over a quarter of a million pets buried and injured by bombs. The Dickin Medal was established in 1943 to recognize the courage of animals who worked alongside British forces, and it has become widely recognized as the animal equivalent of the Victoria Cross. Recent recipients include animals trained to detect arms and explosives in the Gulf and Afghanistan, and those aiding search and rescue after 9/11 in New York.

Today, PDSA offers pet care, advice and insurance. It is the UK's leading veterinary charity and the largest private employer of veterinary surgeons and nurses.

Dickin's journey required great fortitude. She referred to the strain endured by herself and by PDSA staff during its early years, which she dealt with by combining energy with firmness. She was recognized with an Order of the British Empire in 1929 and a Commander of the British Empire in 1948. But she did not seek personal recognition. No large donations from her were publicized and at no stage did she use PDSA literature for self-advertisement. Her photograph did not appear in an annual report until 1949. Her intent was serious, but she was not averse to being playful – exemplified by the conversion of gypsy caravans and organizing children – in realizing her ambition to relieve animal suffering.

Fred and Gabi Hollows

Some playful innovators and entrepreneurs – such as Maria Dicken, Norman Fowler, Jeremy Coller and Jenna Tregarthen – are motivated by the desire to alleviate suffering, and that is certainly the case with Fred and Gabi Hollows. They are the complete opposite of those Keynes excoriated as being only interested in money, showing how scale of ambition need not be limited by scale of available resources. Fred and Gabi Hollows's charitable foundation has the ambitious aim to end avoidable blindness.

Over 30 million people in the world are blind, and four out of five of them don't need to be. Fred and Gabi Hollows began working together in an Aboriginal community in central Australia in 1976. As a result of poor social and economic conditions and lack of healthcare facilities, eye diseases, especially trachoma, are particularly prevalent in Aboriginal communities. Fred was an eye surgeon, while Gabi was an orthoptist, specializing in eye movement disorders. Fred developed a relatively simple and cheap operation for treating cataracts by inserting intraocular lenses: that is, taking out old cloudy lenses and replacing them with plastic ones.

Fred Hollows died in 1993, but by means of the Fred Hollows Foundation Gabi proceeded to increase the scale of activities. Eye surgery costs hundreds of dollars, which is often prohibitive in poorer nations. The Foundation helped reduce the cost to

$25 at 2015 prices. It has restored the sight of more than 2 million people, mainly in poor countries such as Nepal, Eritrea and Vietnam. Fred Hollows had a saying: 'Every eye is an eye. When you are doing the surgery there, that is just as important as if you were doing eye surgery on the prime minister or king.' The foundation works in twenty-five countries, including North Korea. In 2016, along with its local partners, it conducted over 1 million eye surgeries and treatments, including 137,000 cataract operations; trained over 78,000 eye-health workers, from highly skilled ophthalmologists to nurses, community health workers and teachers; and built, upgraded or equipped 120 eye-health facilities including laboratories for the manufacture of low-cost intraocular lenses. The foundation's approach to building local factories and developing local skills reflects the old Chinese saying: give someone a fish and you feed them for a day; teach someone to fish and you feed them for life.[6]

Ambition becomes virtuous in players only when their ardent desire for advantage has both a social and personal component: when Josiah Wedgwood embarked on his innovator's journey he did so for 'fortune, fame and the public good'. Personal and social advance were for him complementary. The great Quaker companies in England – from Rowntree and Cadbury in chocolate to Lloyds and Barclays in banking – were founded on religious notions of social engagement and mutual advancement. This bond between personal and social progress was partly altruistic and partly good business sense. Opportunities to create economic value increase when the society from which they emerge is better engaged in and rewarded by their realization. Cadbury built a model village – Bourneville – with 300 well-designed houses for its staff on a pleasant estate, realizing that a happy workforce was a productive workforce. The Lever brothers, who created the soap company that later became Unilever, were social reformers, insisting on shorter working days and health benefits for their workers. They built another model employee village – Port Sunlight – with architecturally designed, high-quality housing and community facilities. These business leaders were deeply interested in the health – physical and moral – of their employees.

Public health has long been the target of ambitious, socially minded players, as seen in the case of Joseph Bazalgette.

Joseph Bazalgette

Joseph Bazalgette (1819–91), the great Victorian engineer, saved hundreds of thousands of lives by building a sewer system in London, and influenced city infrastructure worldwide. The photographs of Bazalgette, and the shamefully small statue of him on the London Embankment, which he also designed and built, show a kindly face. A father of ten, he was a short man, with impressive whiskers and steely grey eyes, and is reported to have conveyed great presence. His obituaries tell of his stoicism and determination in the face of extraordinary pressures. In his book *The Great Stink of London*, Stephen Halliday describes him as 'a man of heroic patience and exemplary persistence in the face of frustrations'.[7] He was a member of the establishment, and he was certainly a workaholic, often working until 1 a.m. and on other occasions leaving for work at 2 a.m. The pressures of his work and his chronic asthma could understandably make him irascible, but he displayed many of the noble behaviours ascribed to the playful entrepreneur.

Bazalgette's predecessor in the sewer project died in post, aged fifty-two, as a result of what was described as 'harassing fatigues and anxieties of official duties'. Bazalgette dealt with these pressures and at the same time took risks, trying out new innovations – such as using a new kind of untried cement and accepting the best rather than the cheapest tender – even where the cost of failure was going to be devastating to his aims, and he resolutely seized opportunities at massive scale if they were going to improve public health. He was collaborative in his approach, and managed to hold together a highly unstable coalition of powerful interests comprising politicians, financiers, businesspeople and the media.

Bazalgette's challenge was daunting. London literally stank in 1858, and the awful stench of human waste pouring into the River Thames was so disgusting it nearly led to the evacuation of the Houses of Parliament. What came to be known as the 'Big Stink' was caused by people beginning to use water closets rather than have their 'night soil' collected by cart. The untreated sewage flowed directly into the River Thames (and often into neighbours' basements). The sewage was washed upstream in the tidal river to fester, before returning on the tide to bring misery to the long-suffering population. The smell was only part of the problem. Periodically tens of thousands of Londoners were killed in epidemics caused by water-borne diseases. In three outbreaks between 1831 and 1854, over 31,000 Londoners died of cholera.

The solution was a hugely ambitious, complicated and highly innovative engineering project, led by Bazalgette. He built a series of large sewers – 82 miles in length – across London to intercept the sewage before it reached the river and move it downstream, outside London and beyond the Thames's tidal reach. He built the Victoria, Albert and Chelsea embankments on either side of the river to speed its flow downstream. Bazalgette's intercepting sewers used gravity and the motive power of household wastewater to remove the collected waste at a gradient of 2 to 4 feet a mile, down great oval-shaped, 11-foot-high tunnels. This gradient was calculated to optimize flow: too steep and the surface would wear out, too flat and material wouldn't move. The engineering difficulties were compounded by the need for the new infrastructure to go above and below existing roads, railways and rivers. In all, the sewerage project employed 20,000 workers using picks and shovels, used 318 million bricks and involved the excavation of 3.5 million cubic yards of earth.

The concept of the system was to move the sewage down to points in the Thames where it could be released during high tides and washed out to sea. As gravity moved the sewage down-wards, massive pumping stations were needed at the end of the intercepting sewers to raise all the waste up to a level where it could be released into the river. These pumping stations were substantial engineering achievements. The southern intercept pumping station alone had four James Watt steam engines, then the largest in the world.

At this time London had no unified governance, and was administered by 300 different bodies, deriving powers from 250 local Acts. When it came to sewage, there were numerous commissions that were not obliged to coordinate their activities with those of neighbouring districts, and district surveyors had no powers to instruct builders to connect houses to public sewers, so Bazalgette had to skilfully craft a way through this maze of bureaucracy.[8]

His changes also had to deal with vested interests in private water, railway and wharf companies. The very thought of public investment in infrastructure enraged powerful voices, with conservative politicians, lawyers and clergy describing public investments as infringements of personal liberty and offences against private property. *The Economist* railed against the principle of large-scale public investments in public sanitation.

The technical problems to be conquered were extreme. At the same time as new sewers were being built, Bazalgette oversaw the reconstruction of 165 miles of old sewers of varying sizes, shapes and levels. He also oversaw 1,100 miles of new sewers constructed by local parishes that would feed into his intercepting sewers.

Bazalgette suffered a series of disasters: a gas pipe ruptured, killing a local resident and a tunnel collapsed, killing three miners; in all there were ten fatalities during construction of the sewers. He also dealt with a bricklayers' strike. A lot of his time was spent managing various schemes put forward by private companies that proved irresistibly attractive to politicians as they promised opportunities to turn sewage into money. Bazalgette had to deal with a chief commissioner of works who continually rejected his plans and a fifty-five-member board with various factions. Yet he had even more powerful opponents. Prime Minister Gladstone wanted to get his hands on the highly valuable land on the new embankments for government buildings, so Bazalgette faced continual inquiries and dispute resolution cases.

This was an expensive project, inevitably so because it was being undertaken in densely populated urban areas. Furthermore, it was very difficult to estimate costs as the idiosyncrasies of work in each area made standardized and historical estimates inaccurate. Bazalgette began with a budget of £3 million, but across his projects he probably oversaw budgets of £20 million – around £1.5 billion at present prices. Bazalgette's sewers served the capital until well into the twenty-first century, but he wryly noted 'how difficult it is to induce the present generation to expend its capital in providing for the requirements of after generations'. The sewers were funded by loans arranged by Parliament, and the embankments were funded by redirecting most of the duty paid on coal and wine imports. As Bazalgette put it, this funding stimulated many improvements while they 'touch but lightly the pockets of the poor'.

He faced all these difficulties, uncertainties and pressures with fortitude and tact, but he did not deal with them alone. A characteristic of his leadership was his great ability to select able colleagues, including those with whom he had previously had disputes. He gracefully bore no grudges.

Bazalgette was energetic and persistent in his 'playful performance', or what today would be called public relations. He spent a great amount of time explaining his plans and practices to various members of boards and commissions. He engaged in protracted public discussions over his plans and was continually summoned to give evidence to Parliament. The project received a lot of attention from the press and Parliament, and numerous visits to the works were encouraged from politicians and opinion formers. Some visits included 500 to 600 people. When the southern pumping station was opened, four days were devoted to visits by VIPs, and on the fifth day all the workers who built it, along with their wives and families, were invited to view the facility and were given a meal.

The Victoria Embankment was opened to great fanfare by 6 members of the royal family, 23 ambassadors, virtually every member of both Houses of Parliament and 10,000 ticket holders. As it was in London, and alcohol was involved, the occasion deteriorated into a drunken brawl between hooligans and the police.

The sewer system was only one of Bazalgette's contributions. He oversaw the creation and extension of London's parks, such as Battersea, Victoria and Clapham Common. He was given responsibility for sorting out the growing traffic problems caused by delays associated with paying tolls on privately owned bridges. He purchased eleven bridges for the government, removed the tolls and improved almost of all them, as well as designing new bridges at Putney, Hammersmith and Battersea. He oversaw the creation of new streets, such as Shaftesbury Avenue and Charing Cross Road. His department developed plans for 3,000 streets and saw 40,000 people rehoused from appalling slums. He was involved in the first use of electric lighting by a public authority.

The sewer system was, and still is, a technological marvel, and one of history's most important civil engineering projects. Peter Ackroyd, the biographer of both London and the River Thames, says that Bazalgette's work can be considered one of the new wonders of the world. Bazalgette was motivated by a Victorian sense of public duty and disquiet at the way the world's greatest city at the time, the centre of the largest empire the world had ever known, could not deal with its own human waste. The smell abated, but the project made a greater contribution. At the time of the sewer's construction it was believed that health improvements would result from removal of the smell – the miasma – a view promoted by health advocates such as Florence Nightingale. As was discovered by the redoubtable Dr John Snow, the cause of much prevalent disease in fact lay in germs in the water supply. After the opening of the Bazalgette sewerage system there were no more terrible cholera epidemics in London. His civic-mindedness is clear from his presidential address to the Institute of Civil Engineers in 1884, when he spoke of his concern for sanitation in cities around the world and the importance of engineering for the health, comfort and longevity of mankind.

In 2016 a new £4.2 billion super-sewer system, known as the Thames Tideway Project, began being built in London. It is one of the largest construction projects in Europe. Its aim is to relieve pressure on the existing Bazalgette system, which overflows into the Thames when storm water washes down London's streets. This means that millions of tonnes of sewage and pollutants wash into the Thames every year. The company leading the Tideway project is called Bazalgette Tunnel Ltd.

Shelley Harrison

To continue with the theme that play can be motivated by the pursuit of private gain and public good, we turn to the case of a man who has the ambition of ensuring that research in universities contributes to business opportunities and to social and healthcare advances. He has provided remarkable opportunities for experimentation, learning and fun, including by children, in conditions that are literally out of this world.

When Julie Blackburn talked about her experiment, just about everyone who listened ended up in tears. A school student with spina bifida, Julie explained how, along with some classmates at an Atlanta school for children with disabilities, in 1999 she had sent some painted lady caterpillars into space. The opportunity had been provided by SpaceHab, a company that gave school-children the chance to design experiments undertaken in NASA's Space Shuttle. Julie talked about the success of the experiment, proving caterpillars could metamorphose in microgravity. She exclaimed her amazement and delight that although she would never leave her wheelchair her mind could construct an activity that had taken place beyond the Earth.

Shelley Harrison was in the audience that day. He was CEO and then chairman of SpaceHab, and he describes Julie's speech as extraordinarily moving. Shelley's CV is long and distinguished. He founded Symbol, the company that brought laser scanning to barcodes and was eventually sold for $4 billion. He is a serial entrepreneur and successful venture capitalist, and has been involved in building numerous businesses in the US, Taiwan, China and Israel. When he talks about his career, and his meetings with heads of state and the CEOs of the world's great companies, the stories are fascinating and compelling, but he is most animated when he talks about giving back and making a contribution. So through the efficiency of barcode readers Symbol has contributed to improvements in global productivity, and SpaceHab allowed numerous experiments to be undertaken during eighteen space missions, while enthusing hundreds of thousands of children around the world about space and science. Shelley also gives back through decades of work with his alma mater universities, assisting their ventures and international partnerships.

With a PhD in electrophysics, particular expertise in microwaves and experience of working in the world-famous Bell Labs, Shelley foresaw the opportunities for barcodes in supermarkets to track and manage stock. He left his university lecturer job in 1971 and started Symbol along with his wife and Jerome Swartz, a fellow researcher. Susanne Harrison has been a partner in all Shelley's ventures and he often refers to how her judgement about people and businesses has bettered his own. Their work progressed on the laser barcode reader and also on the process of printing barcodes, where there had been little advance since their invention at IBM. Shelley recalls his first sales visit, which happened to be to a manufacturer of toilet rolls. The person he was pitching to was fascinated by the description of the technology, but after an hour asked with a smile whether he was going to be sold something. He kindly suggested that it might be helpful to have a demonstrable technology, a defined market need, some idea of what value the product could deliver and what its price would be.

The business principle behind laser reading and barcodes is automated data entry, reducing opportunities for human error.

Shelley says businesses respected what Symbol was aiming to do with inventory control, but had to teach him how to make money. After a lot of hard work, and with an expanding list of blue-chip customers, Symbol grew successfully, and after its second initial public offering in the 1980s, Shelley retired. He admits that despite much practice he is not very good at retiring: he has retired five times.

In his forties at the time, and after a relatively short period of inactivity in business, he became involved in another company that was at the forefront of local area networking on microcomputers. He helped build the business and then bought stock in it, ruminating afterwards that it would probably have been best to do this the other way around. Eric Schmidt eventually ran the company before he left to be executive chairman of Google.

The next stage of Shelley's life involved working closely with his alma maters New York University and the Polytechnic University (which subsequently merged). He founded PolyVentures, located on the university campus, which provided venture capital funds for start-ups and early-stage high-technology investments. Over thirty investments were made from this fund into companies in the US, Taiwan and Israel, some of which were acquired for billions of dollars. His desire to give back to the institutions that gave him his education continues in his active promotion of global research collaborations between universities in the US, China, Europe and Israel. He has extensive experience of working with Taiwan, Hong Kong, Singapore and China, and speaks Mandarin. After one successful deal his Taiwanese partner promised him a gift, which Shelley says he still relishes to this day: he was taught tai chi.

In the early 1990s a scientist from the Smithsonian Institution approached Shelley and described the inefficiencies of the large, unpressurized payload bays being under-utilized in the Space Shuttle. Experiments in microgravity are particularly valuable in physics and medicine, and these were undertaken in the crew areas and were therefore very small scale. Tired, in his own words, of 'managing other people's money', and intrigued by his visitor's suggestion that this project could be his new 'mission', Shelley became involved in SpaceHab, a commercial company paid to do experiments in space.

His business skills came to the fore in the development of SpaceHab. The company was having difficulty negotiating with NASA, which flew the shuttles, and the large defence companies that built them. It took a personal meeting with President Clinton in the Oval Office to break one of the log-jams holding the company up. Developing the company involved close liaison with the leaders of partner companies in Europe, Japan and Taiwan. Attracting investment in the US was challenging as the project was so risky (although this was mitigated when Lloyds of London agreed to insure the missions), but Shelley says that many people were motivated by a patriotic desire to maintain a lead in space.

Talking to the many astronauts involved in the company's eighteen missions, Shelley asked them what they did with their spare time. They replied that they looked out of the window, gazing at the beautiful blue sphere, comparing it to emptiness of space and noting the irrelevance from that position of national boundaries drawn on a map. Knowing the astronauts personally made the circumstances of the last mission, the disaster of the Challenger, especially difficult to bear. After Challenger, despite the pleasure and joy he got out of the opportunities SpaceHab provided to children, Shelley lost his enthusiasm for the project and gradually disengaged.

He still talks of his pride in the work at SpaceHab: of the important experiments undertaken; of developing the first commercial entity working in space; and of the opportunities it gave children to get excited about space and science. He says that when children all around the world started talking about their experiments on the internet they also started discussing their lives, aiding international understanding. On two occasions, SpaceHab was given the challenging technical task of delivering critically important equipment to the Mir space station, making the company highly celebrated in Russia.

Shelley is still involved in financing companies and in shepherding their growth. He works on building international partnerships in leading universities and actively promotes an urban living laboratory studying health and the environment in four major cities.

Shelley's story begins with his school days, and this perhaps explains his concern to give back. Because of his family circumstances, his schooling was fractured and he attended seven schools during his first eight grades of study. As a result, he failed all but one course. Summoned to meet the head teacher with his father, he was asked to explain not why he failed so many courses, but how he managed to get an unprecedented score of 100 per cent in his studies of the Talmud. Shelley considers that this achievement reflected his logical thinking and reasoning abilities. He reflects on this instance and others when, during his life, he has had to argue to be given a chance in the absence of evidence for his ability. The fact that people in education gave him that chance, and helped focus and direct his innate logical thinking, explains his lifelong and continuing concern to connect others and provide them with opportunities.

Reflections

Ambition motivates, encourages and adds reasons to play. The ambitions of the highly successful people whose stories are told in this chapter merge personal and social progress. They are motivated by the ambition to create something, solve a problem or sate their curiosity. They may have commercial or charitable objectives, and they may pursue these with varying degrees of personal modesty, but all have a civic-minded concern to give back. There can be a range of motivations behind these ambitions, such as the desire to alleviate suffering and disease in people and animals, patriotism or putting the wonders of science to practical use. The scale of these ambitions – to end factory farming, to build immense city infrastructure, to change the way logistics are managed – and the worthiness of their objectives are conducive to play: they attract behaviours that are optimistic, explorative and collaborative. They also feed the fortitude of those, like Maria Dickin, who fight entrenched interests. Ambition can produce delightful outcomes, such as allowing a wheelchair-using child the excitement of constructing an experiment outside the Earth's boundaries. When it extends the purpose of playful work beyond the advance of the individual it can stimulate effort and curiosity that can be highly socially progressive.

These innovators and entrepreneurs give us an opportunity to assess our ambitions at work, and reflect upon whether:

◆ our motivations and efforts, and those for whom we work, match our expectations of ourselves and what we want from life; and
◆ we have the right balance in our working life between its rewards in salary and status and its contribution to community and society.

Part 2 of the book now concludes by revisiting and testing lessons about play and noble behaviours in the most unlikely of organizations.

The case of MI5

An opportunity arose to explore the behaviours supporting play in an organization that at first sight seems unlikely to be playful: the national security service, responsible for keeping citizens safe from terrorism. Britain's internal security service, MI5, is playful in a number of senses: it is entrepreneurial in the way it manages opportunities and risks in highly uncertain circumstances; the manner by which its employees explore, learn and adapt is crucial to its success; and the organization also finds ways of having fun. Baroness Manningham-Buller, director-general of MI5 from 2002 to 2007, provides many insights into these behaviours.[9]

During a thirty-three-year career with MI5, Eliza Manningham-Buller was responsible for intelligence on the IRA, which had embarked on a deadly bombing campaign on mainland Britain, and al-Qaeda. She says security intelligence is an occupation besieged by ambiguity and uncertainty, and there are no military or security options that are certain to succeed. Eliza went to Washington the day after 9/11 and describes the immense anxiety, tension and sense of vulnerability there. The prospect of chemical, biological or radiological terrorism looked more likely. Bin Laden had instructed followers to find and use nuclear material.

There is massive uncertainty in such circumstances. Terrorist groups learn and change, and Eliza says they now have at their disposal tools once only available to the state, so it is crucial that security agencies learn and adapt quickly. Unpredictability is compounded because dealing with the extraordinary and continually evolving challenge of terrorism depends on information that is fragile and relies on 'the rich plethora of incomplete intelligence, sometimes fragmentary, sometimes false, often contradictory'. Eliza uses the analogy that intelligence work is like trying to do a jigsaw: 'You don't know what the picture looks like. You don't have the box. And you've got four or five pieces. You are trying terribly hard to get more pieces, but chances are quite high that you don't get enough.'

Excruciating choices on what to pursue have to be made on this basis, and crucial advice must be provided to ministers on the basis of imperfect information. These are not ordinary decisions: they have life-or-death consequences. It might be remembered that the IRA's mainland campaign during this period killed 175 people, including senior politicians, and injured many thousands. It twice came very close to murdering two prime ministers. So while the ability to make decisions in unpredictable circumstances based on incomplete information applies to the playful entrepreneurs discussed throughout this book, MI5 provides an extreme example. Eliza says living with uncertainty is something she is very used to, and leading the intelligence agency meant helping others live with such uncertainty.

The learning and adaptability of the organization in such circumstances was underpinned by a sense of fun. Christopher Andrew's definitive history of MI5, *The Defence of the Realm*, describes Eliza Manningham-Buller thus:

> Her insistence on high standards . . . which some of her staff found intimidating, was balanced by a sense of fun which made her many friends. Manningham-Buller later became the first Director General (perhaps the first head of any intelligence agency anywhere), to give a talk to staff entitled, 'Fun at Work'.[10]

In the popular imagination (well at least in ours), play in security agencies is associated with the tricks and toys of 'Q' in the James Bond films. Disappointingly, Eliza reveals that operatives do not come to work in bullet-proof Aston Martins with ejector seats, but tend to cycle. Yet there is a sense of fun. 'When I joined in 1974, the service was informal. That was unusual at the time in government and institutions. There was a great culture of humour and fun. It helps keep things in perspective and defuses tension . . . If you walk along an MI5 corridor you will find people having fun.' She also points out that the fun element of play is only possible when pressure is not at its most intense, but is a very necessary way of relieving pressure as soon as possible.

We asked Eliza about the behaviours that supported play, that made people work so hard to common purpose in such trying circumstances and where there was a need for continual change and adaptation. To begin with ambition, MI5 has the stark, overriding and unifying objective of preventing British citizens being hurt and killed by terrorists: a focused and motivating ambition if ever there was one. When it came to personal ambition within the organization, she professes her career advancement was unexpected. She explains that in her early career MI5's view on female officers was to look for docile women who did sensible work in backrooms – it certainly wouldn't have dreamed of having a woman as head of the service (there have now been two). Eliza also talks about her ambitions for those she has led and worked with, referring to 'the privilege of working with motivated colleagues on a common purpose', while always being aware of the potential dangers of those in the field being interrogated and killed, emphasizing the need for exceptional care in risky circumstances.

Progressing to the top of an organization such as MI5, and dealing with the stresses and strains of a job where lives are at stake, requires immense fortitude. It is especially needed when you know a terrorist attack is imminent, but do not know enough to pre-empt it. Eliza required fortitude to condemn the US's use of waterboarding to glean information, and to oppose the British government's proposal to extend the period terrorist suspects could be held without charge.

We asked her how such fortitude is sustained, and she says it is to do with self-confidence and also rationality, and it is helped by support from colleagues and family. Eliza added that she has never minded admitting she didn't know what to do, seeing this as a strength, not a weakness. She says increasing openness involves courage, especially in an organization based on secrecy, and when MI5 began providing information on jobs, careers and current threats on its website it incurred opposition. Eliza describes in her BBC Reith lectures a disturbing dream in which she was threatened with prosecution under the Official Secrets Act. One of her achievements has been to institute family days to open up the service. Previously families and friends knew nothing of what went on in MI5 and why its people worked so hard, often under great pressure. During visits families learned of the organization's achievements and saw some tools of the trade, instilling a sense of pride in what their loved ones were doing. This, she says, helped de-stress the working environment.

When asked about grace, Eliza cut immediately to its core, saying it is about good manners, showing warmth and the ability to be self-critical. It encompasses attitudes to failure, as she says no one gets things right all the time. People can make perfectly reasonable judgements that turn out to be wrong. The point is to keep learning and trying to improve, and to have people around you who are prepared to adapt and to question your decisions and approach. The people she wanted were not those threatened by change but those who found it exciting: 'People who are very insecure are keen on control. You want a culture where people know it's ok to challenge and that they are expected to question.'

Grace can also be displayed in recognizing and respecting difference. Eliza argues that the relationship between different international intelligence communities starts with the understanding that they often have different views from one another. Agreement is not necessary to cooperate on intelligence, and protecting British citizens would be impossible if we were restricted to talking to those whose values we share. Sometimes this involves talks with those who are dangerous and threatening to your own position.

Raised on John le Carré novels, our notions of craft in intelligence relate to tradecraft: concealed devices, dead drops and honey traps. Yet craft infuses every aspect of intelligence gathering; as Eliza says, intelligence work isn't a science. It involves the construction of a view based on imperfect information. Intelligence, in Eliza's words, is information that is deliberately intended to be concealed. Returning to the jigsaw analogy, the craft lies in combining bits and pieces here and there that are never complete or certain, to make an assessment. Decisions are made based on judgements, she says, and stuff happens that you cannot predict and plan for. The key is to have people on your staff who are flexible, swift and can adapt quickly. Facts and intellect are always complemented by discernment and experience.

She says leadership is difficult, but points to the importance of having time for reflection and learning: 'This is one of the most important attributes for good leadership. It is obvious, but many testosterone-fuelled CEOs run from one task to the next, not caring to stop and reflect.'

Although we are looking at a highly untypical organization, MI5 provides many insights into playful work. Eliza Manningham-Buller shows how playfulness in an organization working in the most uncertain and stressful environments is supported by its approaches to leadership, collaboration, trust and openness. All the noble behaviours are displayed in the most demanding of workplaces.

PART 3

Being playful

7

Work and organization

Studs Terkel begins his book *Working: People Talk About What They Do and How They Feel About What They Do* thus: 'This book, being about work, is by its very nature about violence – to the spirit as well as the body.'[1] His remarkable collection of people's experiences includes many sad stories as health and will are broken through relentless, dismal and often cruelly destructive work. Terkel wrote the book in 1974 and we might hope that the world of work has changed considerably since then. In the developed world many of the dangerous and repetitive jobs he describes have been automated. We have certainly come to expect more. Roman Krznaric claims that our recent material prosperity has freed our minds to expect much more from the adventure of life, and this includes the expectation of fulfilling work: a job that provides a deep sense of purpose, and reflects our values, passions and personality. Young people especially, it might be argued, want stimulation in their work. Yet these completely understandable and reasonable expectations arise in circumstances that are fundamentally uncertain and turbulent, and for many work continues to be drudgery, ungratifying and unfulfilling. A survey undertaken for the Royal Society of Arts shows that three-quarters of people think the quality of their work needs to be improved, making it more satisfactory, rewarding, meaningful and purposeful.[2]

Almost everyone you speak to nowadays complains about the increasing pace of life and the insecurity and anxiety of work. People feel more and more time-poor in an era where the demands of work are intensifying. Time is a scarce and precious resource. The relentless pursuit of efficiency and productivity across all of the economy has been fuelled by the collection of performance data and the use of targets, incentives and penalties, placing more and more pressure on people as they are constantly compared and measured. The advent of social media has amplified the quantities of data about individuals and increased the number of attributes that can be measured. Knowingly or unwillingly, people are sharing data from technology such as mobile phones and wearable devices, and a few are beginning to experiment with implanted near-field communication devices, raising the spectre of even more measurement and surveillance. The massive increase in the availability of data of all sorts is very likely going to increase the range and number of metrics still further. *Fortune* magazine's 'manager of the century', Jack Welch, named in 1999, sacked the bottom 10 per cent of performers each year in his company, General Electric. Enron went one better, sacking the bottom 15 per cent.

Innovation in the financial sector has resulted in faster, worldwide flows of money in search of quicker returns, adding to a sense of impermanence and instability. The twenty-four-hour news cycle curtails the ability of decision-makers to focus on anything but the immediate. Lack of time can result in stress and aggressive behaviour. We seem to be on shorter fuses. We suffer road rage, see parents behaving badly at children's sporting events and lose our tempers with the endless frustrations of online services and the increasing bureaucratic incursions into our lives. Free time – to relax, think and play – is often seen as a luxury afforded to the few.

Everything seems more volatile. We are confronted with the dilemmas of genetically modified food, human organs grown from stem cells or 3D printed, fracking to release gas deposits and children born with three genetic parents. The incidence of extreme weather events is increasing. There's great uncertainty about where our personal data is stored and who has access to it. As well as technological change, globalization threatens established businesses and jobs. For many, productivity is associated with working harder and innovation means even more unwelcome change. Overseas companies whose names we hadn't heard of a few years ago now own major utilities or their products feature prominently in all our shops. Governments strive for stability and consistency, yet party politics and personal ambition often seem to trump the public good. Growing societal and political introspection and disillusionment add to the fragility of community cohesion. There is despair at seemingly insurmountable problems, such as the global refugee crisis or the increasing polarization of society's divisions, as political differences become more entrenched and confrontational. Politicians struggle to produce the long-term policy settings that encourage productive investments. Financial markets remain fragile. Rather than supporting the allocation of capital to productive new investments that create and sustain jobs, the financial system is geared more to developing ever more sophisticated mathematical tools to trade existing assets. Concern for environmental sustainability places new obligations on governments, businesses and individuals, but there are many opportunities for prejudice to shout down the science of climate change. The list of challenges – 'wicked problems' – seems endless.

Companies are struggling to adjust from the age of mass production and mass consumption. We are moving away from hundreds of markets with millions of customers to millions of markets with hundreds of customers, or even fewer. Markets that address individuals – in sectors as diverse as healthcare, financial services and clothing – are becoming a reality. Drugs are being designed to match our particular genes, the nutritional content of our food will likely be programmed to individual requirements and our jeans are being made to fit our idiosyncratic shapes – not with the dual measures of waist and leg, but with thousands of data points. Companies are challenged to provide individually tailored goods and services at mass-production prices. This puts increasing pressure on those doing the work to deliver on these expectations. And while we might think these changes are good for us as consumers, we have to deal with the overwhelming number of choices. Selecting a mobile phone plan or a pension scheme from all those available can be confusing and harrowing. This predicament is brilliantly caught in Kathryn Bigelow's Oscar-winning film *The Hurt Locker*, when a bomb disposal expert who makes life or death decisions daily is paralyzed with indecision when confronted by the vast choice of breakfast cereal in a supermarket.

The uncertainties confronting work may be more acute for younger generations. Thomas Friedman puts it this way:

> My generation had it easy. We got to 'find' a job. But, more than ever, our kids will have to 'invent' a job. Fortunately, in today's world, that's easier and cheaper than ever before. Sure, the lucky ones will find their first job, but, given the pace of change today, even they will have to reinvent, re-engineer and reimagine that job much more often than their parents if they want to advance in it.[3]

Kate Dodgson has written about how the pressures on millennials are now so strong they can lead to a 'quarter-life crisis'.[4]

Whatever age you are and no matter what job you have, work is such an important element of our lives that we need to ensure as far as we can that it is rewarding and enjoyable. In 1943, the psychologist Abraham Maslow developed a hierarchy of human need and his insights endure today. He argued that our most basic needs are physiological: air, water and food. These are followed respectively by our need for safety, social belonging and esteem. At its pinnacle is our need for self-actualization, which Maslow describes as the desire to accomplish everything that one can and to become the most that one can be. This aspiration applies to the work we do.

Being a player

To deal with the challenges of change and uncertainty and do worthwhile and gratifying work, we can learn from the people whose stories are told in this book. Working in a wide range of circumstances and coming from a wide range of backgrounds, these innovators and entrepreneurs show how to make choices and take advantage of opportunities in the uncertain conditions and complexity surrounding modern work. They show how to adapt to risks and be agile in the face of uncertainty. Turbulence and change is their world: it is what they do. Innovators and entrepreneurs play as they explore, directing their ambition, curiosity and effort to experiment and tinker with ideas to be applied at work: this is the way they identify and nurture new ideas to achieve their objectives, express their freedom and have fun at the same time.

Playful entrepreneurs personify Emile's cheerfulness and charm. They have a sense of adventure, enjoyment and pleasure, and talk freely about the dignity, happiness and even love associated with work. They play by the rules, although they may occasionally sail close to the wind and these rules may be interpreted playfully: think of Wren's subversion of his agreement to put a spire on the top of St Paul's or Thiess's 'liberation' of equipment from the Papuan jungle that he was not strictly entitled to. Their work balances the pursuit of individual objectives with public good in ways that are personally agreeable, rewarding and inspirational to others. As Paddy O'Rourke, English teacher and director of a major construction firm, puts it: work is about purposefulness for yourself and usefulness for others.

Playfulness is supported by a number of behaviours that can inspire everyone to play more, thereby making work more valuable, rewarding and distinctive. Few have the scientific brilliance to diagnose DNA on microchips, or the business genius to see the possibilities of barcodes before anyone else, but everyone can learn from the innovators and entrepreneurs in this book; everyone can share their behaviours and motivation. When asked by the *Financial Times* about the relative importance of talent or ambition, the scientist Professor Brian Cox replied: 'You have to find something you're fascinated by and love doing. Most people, I think, are able to do great things if they find something.' As Aristotle put it: 'pleasure in the job puts perfection in the work'.

The players here are not shallow self-seeking celebrities purporting to have the answer to every problem. Some are not well known, although some of the younger entrepreneurs interviewed will undoubtedly have considerably higher profiles in future. But each person in their own way offers some insights into how to deal successfully with a rapidly changing and unpredictable world. Collectively they tell us about the virtues of play in all its manifestations of endeavour, contributing to and comprising good purpose.

There is much to admire in the imagination of Thomas Heatherwick, the openness of Gerard Fairtlough and Rajeeb Dey, the ideals of Gerald Chan and Leonard Gianadda, the sustained vision and commitment of Shelley Harrison and Eliza Manningham-Buller, the urbanity of Richard Wheatly, the tenacity of Les Thiess and Arthur Bishop, the determination of Paul Drayson, the modesty of Don Strickland and Sean Bowen, the enthusiasm of Jenna Tregarthen and Elizabeth Iorns, the concern of Jeremy Coller, Alexsis de Raadt St James, Keith Tuffley and Maria Dickin and the public-spiritedness of Joseph Bazalgette and Norman Fowler. There is much to respect in the personal modesty of Steve Shirley, who is so open about herself and her failings, in the example of Ove Arup and his encouragement to act honourably at work and in the collective grace of all the hardworking people at Bletchley Park.

If we were to try to capture a single quality of all the people who feature in this book, it would be generosity of spirit. For Steve Shirley this is the 'importance of giving people the freedom to pursue their own fulfilment'.

The personal journey of the player is not always smooth. Many talk of the dramatic ups and downs of their work and its disruption to family life. Many great innovators, such as Tommy Flowers, one of the most influential people in the history of computing, are under-appreciated, which in his case led to him ending his life in poverty. Yet all these players make a positive difference, and the alternative – the world of Robert McNamara, which aimed to avoid contact with people and ideas – is bleak indeed and can lead to a tragic reassessment of your contributions in later life.

Many of the innovators and entrepreneurs have combined a number of the behaviours described as noble, for example by mixing great ambition with considerable grace. Yet there are also many great innovators – Edison, for example – who are not known for their grace towards others. Two of the most notorious recent entrepreneurs, Steve Jobs and Elon Musk, have been driven by greater ambition than the accumulation of wealth: Jobs wanted to make beautiful products whose design brought pleasure as well as functionality and Musk wants to make this planet more ecologically sustainable and other planets habitable (he says he wants to die on Mars, but not on impact). Neither has been renowned for their patience and tolerance; both are famed for the extreme demands they place on employees.[5] They, and other well-known recent leaders such as Andy Grove at Intel, are famously not consensus builders: they push hard to achieve what they want and if they fail they try to do so quickly, recoup and try again. The examples we have used show that there is another path to great achievements which is less combative and dismissive of others. In the competitive worlds of innovation and entrepreneurship, it is possible to succeed by being a decent and nice person at work.

There is nobility in perseverance and the preparedness to carry on despite setbacks, and in the personal ability to cope with failures. Self-confidence and strong belief in your objectives are supported by an absence of hubris and the recognition that you can't win all the time. Sean Bowen's high-level experiences as a sportsman taught him about the value of competitiveness, but also of teamwork and the ability to deal with the inevitable occasional loss. Players at work will unavoidably have some ups and downs, but it is always worth remembering the dictum of the great West Indian cricketer Sir Vivian Richards, who said that form is temporary but class is permanent.

Despite the typecast view of the entrepreneur simply being a relentless and soulless pursuer of personal advantage and profitable opportunities, the behaviours revealed here provide an antidote to hyper-competitive, zero-sum leadership and management styles. The occasional fleeting successes of this 'nature is red in tooth and claw' behaviour mask the damage it does and hide the ways real value is produced. The lessons from the people we describe show how it is possible to cope with, and indeed embrace, instability and complexity so that we can become well-grounded and comfortable in the confusing and unpredictable circumstances that surround us without losing our humanity, humility and humour. As the history of work reveals, choices do exist, and we can turn things to our advantage and find elements of stability and contentment amidst all the changes surrounding us.

There are, of course, national and cultural differences in interpretations of playfulness, even between places that may seem quite similar. So, for example, behaviour that might be seen as self-confidence in Silicon Valley may be considered arrogant in Europe. An element of showmanship, proclaiming one's own achievements, may seem natural in some countries, but British reserve may see it as hubris, and some Asian cultures might consider it offensive. Despite the many enduring differences between nations, virtually every country in the world aims to progress by becoming more innovative and entrepreneurial. The virtues of play and noble behaviours are universal and can be usefully encouraged everywhere. Our lengthy experiences of working in Asia, for example, have shown us that even in the most hardworking corporate environments, say in large Korean *chaebol* or rapidly globalizing Chinese companies, there are opportunities for play. We continually see examples of people enjoying subversive, mischievous fun at work in the most hierarchical of societies and organizations.

Can all the noble behaviours reside in one person? Some examples appear here, but such people are very rare. More commonly, some people have particular behaviours in abundance; others may display small amounts of each. The issue for us as individuals is to consider how to cultivate and improve our practice of them all. Apart from decisions we may make about behaviours we would like to improve, we may want to assess potential employers or employees according to their behaviours, and we may choose to overcome deficiencies in ourselves by partnering with others who possess more of those we lack.

Being a playful organization

It is easier to be a player in a playful organization. Many organizations behave well towards their staff and stakeholders. They have broad mandates from their leaders about the objectives of the organization that move beyond the short-term bottom line. They have good and open communications that encourage people to participate in decisions and they are concerned about their environmental impact and the quality of the jobs people do. They protect and help improve their supply chains, give back to their communities and are highly collaborative internally and externally with high degrees of trust. These are good indicators of well-run organizations but, as we have seen, playful organizations go further: they actively encourage play, and provide supportive spaces and technologies to allow it.

People in playful organizations are given permission to play and get excited about doing things differently. They are also subject to discipline and rules. This is the paradox of play at work: liberty within boundaries. Play is an enjoyable personal experience, and is found in companies that encourage intimacy and sharing. It is self-fulfilling and fun, and allows opportunities to explore. Chris Toumazou encourages a culture in his companies where people are comfortable in their independence. Play allows intelligent participation in shared activities at our own discretion. Sean Bowen offers 'play days' to his staff. But play also frames and orders activities within accepted boundaries and conditions. There is tolerance of failure, for example, but sanctions for repeated failure. There are times and circumstances where play is inadvisable. Fun is off the agenda when a crisis hits MI5. There is a need, as shown by Edison, for balance.

The question remains as to whether play comes at the expense of profit, and whether businesses whose prime motivation is shareholder return can ever act playfully, in the sense of allowing slack in the use and availability of resources. Other questions arise about playfulness in large organizations. It might seem easier to instil playfulness in smaller organizations and teams, but what happens when size increases? And maybe younger organizations can be more playful than older ones?

As well as seeing playfulness in a wide range of smaller and younger organizations, long-established, large, profit-oriented companies, such as IBM, play. IBM has a useful model encouraging bottom-up initiative and innovation, with top-down approval and sanction. Play is also found in the austere worlds of parliament and court and in the deadly serious world of anti-terrorism.

There is a strong and persistent belief in some management circles that organizations need to separate creative tasks from standardized work, exemplified by Taylorism. Many large organizations either separate experimental and playful activities from regular, repetitive operations or progressively move over time from looser, self-determined work to more constrained forms of organization as uncertainty about markets and technologies diminishes. This separation can take the form of so-called skunkworks, semi-sanctioned groups working on adventurous projects and protected from stifling company processes and procedures. One part of the company explores new knowledge, which other parts exploit. One part is playful, others are not. There are different perspectives on this separation. One view points to the way it ignores the importance of play and creativity in all parts of an organization and the need for close connections between the conception and execution elements of work. Howard Gardner says of companies that 'spin off' creativity, for example, that 'Experience shows this divide-and-conquer strategy rarely lasts – if creativity does not infiltrate the DNA of an organization, it is unlikely to be passed on to the next generation.'[6] Another view suggests that standardized work is more susceptible to replacement by machines, and what is needed is for organizations to consider how best to retain playfulness in areas where people's work is distinctive from and complementary to technology. It is certainly the case that organizations need to consider the benefits of inclusiveness, as shown in the fire engineering case, and the potential dangers of play becoming an exclusive activity for some while it is denied to others.

Playfulness in an organization is always to some extent bounded by the purpose it serves – the objectives of a design company differ from those of a chemical factory – but there are still choices to be made about how work is conducted. One organization may more successfully allow the exercise of people's playfulness than another, even when they are in the same areas of business or operation. We have seen companies where work is conducted differently in different workspaces even though they are producing exactly the same product. Organizations are playful not in the sense of what they do, but in the behaviours they endorse in the people that work for them. Styles of leadership and culture can make a significant difference and we have seen playfulness in many different work situations. The lessons drawn from playful innovators and entrepreneurs are broadly applicable: organizations can choose to be playful, designing and promoting playful cultures and practices, and players can choose to work for those that demonstrate and encourage playfulness.

Choices can be made to design work that is playful. Dr Nick de Leon is head of the Service Design programme at the Royal College of Art, and is thinking about how to design work in the future. He argues that the way work is constructed at present is an afterthought and by-product of the way organizations, and the business processes that support them, are created and operate. The tendency described in Chapter 1, of work being progressively objectified since F.W. Taylor, and continuing with the quality control and lean production movements, has continued more recently, de Leon argues, with the increase in outsourcing and development of the 'gig economy'. There has also been a relentless focus on efficiency and delivering value to customers, using a number of tools such as design thinking, that have diverted attention away from whether the workers delivering these benefits are actually valued themselves. In de Leon's terms, rather than the way we work being determined by the present structures and priorities of organizations, we should begin with the way we want to work and construct organizations sympathetic to those aims.

Constructing playful work would begin with questions such as: What does it look and feel like? What does it mean to us? What are its consequences? Elements of play could be prioritized: Does work encourage exploration and express freedom? Is it fun? Does it allow learning and adaptation? De Leon's approach would be to use recently developed tools, such as design thinking, which he has been using to create complex services, and apply them to the design of work. These tools are commonly focused on delivering good experiences to customers, and are often co-created by engaging all the stakeholders involved (although not always those actually delivering the services). By applying these tools to the design of work, the importance of issues such as collaboration and worker discretion over decisions come to the fore. This redesign of work includes the definition of tasks, introducing and integrating new employees and review and appraisal processes. In this way concern and effort dedicated to those receiving good experiences will be similarly directed to those delivering them.

Our entrepreneurs tell us about the qualities of leadership needed to encourage play. The personal qualities of decency and consideration for others displayed by many of them are seen particularly in the behaviours of Ove Arup and Gerard Fairtlough.

The absence of hubris and ability to reflect on one's own behaviour are notable, and are captured by Eliza Manningham-Buller readily admitting to her staff what she doesn't know. Don Strickland confessed to his staff that he couldn't come up with a solution to a major problem, and successfully sought their advice. He also generously allocated them substantial shareholdings that he could have acquired himself. Virtually all people and organizations, going back to Joseph Bazalgette, promote and prioritize collaboration and recognize when they need structure and discipline in what they do, and when they need flexibility and innovation. Leadership is especially difficult when problems are profound but pressures to perform are short term, and leaders today need to steward organizations in exceptionally trying circumstances. In *Team of Teams*, General Stanley McChrystal explains how in the most complex and unpredictable conditions – fighting insurgent terrorism in Iraq – he came to realize that the old military command-and-control leadership did not work, and that he had to engage a wide community of people in decision-making, using what he calls systemic understanding and grounded shared consciousness. He says the war was not one of planning and discipline, but of agility and innovation, and the role of the senior leader was no longer that of controlling puppet-master, but rather that of the empathetic crafter of culture. McChrystal and his colleagues have created a consultancy company to advise organizations on how to adapt in the face of extreme uncertainty, and there is considerable and growing demand for such services. Part of the future conversation about leadership, we contend, should encompass play. Encouraging play isn't the only answer to the challenges leaders face, but it can be a valuable means of future-proofing their organizations by improving their abilities to adapt.

From a personal perspective, it is worthwhile asking whether organizations for which you work or might want to work are supportive of the behaviours you want to practise. Since the global financial crisis of 2008 in particular, there has been a healthy scepticism about the extent to which companies in key sectors behave nobly. There are perennial questions about ethical investments, fair trade in supply chains, tax avoidance, sexism and corporate corruption. But apart from making huge fortunes that allow their owners and senior managers to be philanthropic, can businesses be motivated to give back in the sense of having broader objectives than profit for share-holders, in the manner of the innovators and entrepreneurs in this book?

The closest thing that businesses have to a mechanism that encourages giving back is their policy towards corporate social responsibility, or, more recently, 'shared value'. The former includes charitable donations, and businesses valuably support many worthwhile causes. The latter is more pragmatic. Opportunities to create economic value increase when the society from which businesses emerge is better engaged in and rewarded by their realization. Even the doyen of corporate strat-egies for competitive advantage, Harvard Business School's Professor Michael Porter, has come to recognize that the crea-tion of economic value rests ultimately on the development of shared, social value.[7] Essentially these approaches argue that obligations to shareholders to provide a return on their invest-ments are best met when there are efforts to invest in the social and business communities of which they are a part and through concern for the environment. This is not public interest in the sense of many of the stories here, but self-interest. The concern for profit and community are not necessarily mutually exclusive.

People can assess the extent to which these behaviours are real or based on rhetoric, and make choices about whom to work for accordingly. They can decide their preferences for organizations that make profits and then give some away to good causes or make investments in good causes to produce profits.

The capacity of organizations to play – and provide oppor-tunities for playful work – often reflects choices they make about their location and the use of their physical spaces.

Playful locations and spaces

Virtually all the people written about here have lived in vibrant places. We are lucky ourselves to live and work in Brighton, Brisbane and London. These are playful cities that create a cosmopolitan mosaic of different people and cultures, sparking and cross-pollinating ideas. San Francisco in the US and Copenhagen in Denmark, along with many other locations around the world, are similarly playful places with diversity and energy. The buzz or vibe of Detroit during the Motown era, the Liverpool of the Beatles or Seattle with its garage bands, were places of palpable playful energy. Playful places also build on traditions of quality and craft. Paul Smith, one of Britain's most successful fashion designers, talks about continued attachment to, and inspiration from, his home town, Nottingham, and its reputation for manufacturing beautiful lace, and of nearby Leicester, famous for its knitting.[8]

History shows the importance of location for creativity and innovation. The great works of Christopher Wren and Josiah Wedgwood were dependent upon their local networks. It is no coincidence that, because of the patronage of the Medicis and a few other families, both Leonardo and Michelangelo, along with many other scientists, poets, philosophers, financiers, painters and architects, were attracted to work in Florence in the fourteenth and fifteenth centuries. There, in the words of Frans Johansson, 'they found each other, learned from one another, and broke down barriers between disciplines and cultures'.[9] Playful locations are valuable because, in the words of Ralph Waldo Emerson, they 'give us collision'. Collision in this sense is a metaphor for an exchange of energy. Players seek and welcome such collisions, and they occur most when locations offer a density of diverse organizations and people that create opportunities for playful work. Following the Great Exhibition of 1851, Prince Albert recognized the value of an agglomeration of talented people in one place to 'bring together arts and sciences for the betterment of humanity for a thousand years'. In today's world, Rudy Burger, a leading venture capitalist, told

225

us that the one word that defines the success of Silicon Valley is *density*: of capital, talent, buyers and lifestyle.

Organizations such as IDEO, Airbnb or the Heatherwick Studio actively stimulate playfulness. Physically, they provide stimulating spaces, and hold a cornucopia of objects, artefacts and images intended to encourage free thought, conversation and interaction. References are made to the use of toys and toyshops, replicated in the form of hackspaces and makerspaces. Walter Isaacson quotes Steve Jobs as saying creativity comes from spontaneous meetings and random discussions, and says he designed the Pixar building to promote encounters and unplanned collaborations: 'If a building doesn't encourage that, you'll lose a lot of innovation and the magic that's sparked by serendipity.'

There have always been places and spaces where ideas flourish – for example the coffee houses of eighteenth-century Britain where ideas were fomented and shared, encouraging wide-ranging discussions of philosophy, politics, science and business – and they played an important role in stimulating innovators such as Josiah Wedgwood. Clubs and places for meeting like-minded people remain important today. They are spaces to relax and think seriously, where serendipitous meetings occur and ideas are transacted and worked upon. Recognizing this, companies have opened new-style offices-as-clubs and a fresh range of rental and free spaces for entrepreneurs have sprung up, looking and feeling just like clubs. There are numerous hackspaces available for technologists, some with specific remits: the British mapping agency, Ordnance Survey, for example, runs Geovation, a hub for entrepreneurs working with spatial data. Organizations don't always get it right. In a major legal practice where efforts were being made to encourage greater creativity, we were invited to see the 'playroom', which consisted of a bare room with four beanbags.

In his book *The Lab*, David Edwards brings a slightly broader perspective to bear. He argues that existing ways of dealing with big, difficult problems need new forms of experimentation, merging art and science to allow 'cultural incubation' in what he calls 'artscience labs'.[10] These labs can be found in various forms in cities around the world, including IDEO and the MIT Media Lab, and he uses the example of Le Laboratoire in Paris, which is responsible for giving the world 'Le Whif', chocolate you can inhale.

Artscience labs combine aesthetic and analytical thinking, bringing together, for example, Harvard professors in mathematics and neuroscience with Japanese composers and Indian artists. Their creation, Edwards argues, is necessary for moving the innovation process away from one that produces lifestyle conveniences benefiting a few individuals to one that benefits society collectively. In the artscience lab model, art and design moves from research and education to social and cultural change, with public dialogue taking place in between through cultural exhibition instead of academic publication. It is the place to experiment with the riskiest ideas.

The somewhat frivolous 'Le Whif' involved serious knowledge of olfactory function, aerosol science, culinary arts and commercial and manufacturing expertise. These new labs are places that, like Heatherwick Studio, curate creative processes, and encourage our abilities to play and have fun with experimentation. In Edwards's view they function as an innovation funnel involving repeated experimentation, public exhibition and critique of prototypes, and the evolution of highly motivated, differentially skilled and often youthful teams. Public engagement is crucial. Edwards shows that this new form of laboratory involves scientists and science addressing social and cultural challenges by engaging artists in circumstances where hypothesis matters more than utility, surprise more than functionality and imagination more than commercial viability. The labs look for ways to value the process of experimentation, not just its products. In many cases these experiments, and the engagement of multiple and diverse parties, are supported by technology.

Playing with technology

Technology has always profoundly affected what we do at work and how and why we do it. Richard Sennett in *The Craftsman* argues that the medieval view of humanity's place in the world changed as a result of three tools: the telescope, the microscope and the scalpel. Technology will continue to have a deep effect on our lives and the ways we play, but that effect is not predetermined by the intrinsic nature of the technology itself, which is developed and used by people. We should never be fatalistic about its impact: we have options. Douglas Adams, author of *The Hitchhiker's Guide to the Galaxy*, once observed how age determines our approach to new technology. If a technology exists when we are born it is ordinary and part of our normal life. If it is developed when we are between the ages of fifteen and thirty-five it is exciting and we think about developing a career in it. If it appears when we are over the age of thirty-five we consider it an abomination that disrupts the natural order of things. This is witty and amusing, but it is wrong. There is no reason anyone of normal ability of any age or background cannot embrace technology and use it to his or her benefit. As Mark's study of CNC machines showed years ago, when computers were put onto machine tools the assumption was that their operators had neither the skills nor the ability to program them. Yet machinists of all ages, used to mechanical devices, became expert at computing and, by possessing knowledge of the manufacturing process that programmers did not have, soon captured the 'clever bits' of the work, improving the efficiency of production.

The new technologies of today result from the actions of innovators and entrepreneurs and are used as a tool to assist them. There are powerful technologies available to help play at work. They undertake repetitive and tedious tasks, allowing for more interesting work. They facilitate experiments and prototyping, making them faster, cheaper and often more effective. Michael Nielsen in *Reinventing Discovery* claims that these technologies improve the way discoveries are made. Brynjolfsson

228

and McAfee in *The Race Against the Machine* say technologies such as data visualization, analytics, high-speed communications and rapid prototyping have augmented the contributions of more abstract and data-driven reasoning, increasing the value of jobs using them. The Executive Office of the President's report on AI and automation considers how these technologies will create jobs and suggests that employment will grow in areas where humans engage with existing AI technologies, develop new AI technologies, supervise AI technologies in practice and facilitate societal shifts that accompany new AI technologies, for instance in planning for driverless cars and cybersecurity.[11]

Such technologies help visualize problems and data, and as the great physicist Richard Feynman showed, there is much advantage in playing with images. Christopher Wren had a talent for discovering visual means to represent complex ideas.[12] Once problems are visualized, they take comprehension of issues beyond that of the specialists used to working with particular forms of data and information, such as blueprints, technical drawings and software code. This allows more diverse people to participate in finding and then applying solutions to problems. As in the case of fire engineering, these digital technologies allow radical new ideas to emerge and to be shaped to the satisfaction of groups with widely different responsibilities and perspectives.

New technologies also allow different forms of communication and engagement between workers. IBM, for example, has run a number of 'Jams', using a web portal to involve tens of thousands of people in raising and prioritizing new ideas for use in the company. Social media provides new ways of collecting and disseminating ideas, and indeed, as seen in the way authors such as Philip Pullman and David Mitchell are using Twitter, technology changes the way we can tell stories, and may be used increasingly to influence how work is done.

Of all the technologies to have affected modern life and work the internet has been the most influential, and it continues to evolve apace, particularly with the continuing innovations in mobile devices, cloud computing, the internet of things, AI and blockchain. There are now more mobile phones than people in the world. Features that we use now on our mobiles were unimaginable a few years ago, such as finger-vein pulse monitors that utilize the camera and torch to assist health diagnosis and monitoring. Yet, in common with most radical technologies in history, there are downsides. There is a great deal of uncertainty about who has access to data, who owns it, where it is stored and what happens to personal privacy and security. People worry about whether they will be able to access their bank accounts if they lose their passwords and about the amount of personal information they'll lose if their phone is stolen. We have yet to see the full social and cultural ramifications of mobile devices, yet it is with disquiet that we see how their use distorts our children's language, makes them immune to the dangers of driving and texting at the same time and encourages them to reveal things on social media a parent really doesn't want to know.

Overall, we are optimistic about the technologies of the future, counterbalanced with a degree of caution. Technology can assist in dealing with society's problems, but our capacity to adapt and change is crucial to our ability to benefit from it while mitigating its downsides. We cannot control the future, nor can we tame the uncertainties that surround us with technologies such as AI, and to try to do so would limit progress. We can, however, recall the early reactions to mechanization in the Industrial Revolution, and expect technology, and those designing and diffusing it, to fit with social expectations, and for society to dictate the terms by which technology is used. The circumstances of political and industrial control following the Industrial Revolution in which technology repressed workers have become more enlightened, with recognition of its empowering role. Technology can allow us, in David Hume's words, to 'carry improvements into every art and science', and can facilitate the 'new bohemianism' of Clark Kerr and his colleagues. The experimental and learning-orientated playfulness demonstrated by innovators and entrepreneurs allow us to be better informed and more active participants in guiding technology's contribution to finding answers to many complex and perplexing challenges.

Play relies on a number of 'noble' behaviours that inspire, shape, sustain and motivate it.

Being noble

Grace is recognition of your own shortcomings and the abilities of others, and the demonstration to others of your trust and reliance on them. It exudes a calm aura that inspires others and suggests that although circumstances are uncertain and pressurized we'll get through it together. Grace reflects self-knowledge and the recognition that you can't do everything on your own, and that others have knowledge and skills of great value that you don't yourself possess. This is particularly relevant when they have broadly different backgrounds and skills. Heatherwick Studio, IDEO and Arup are very practised at bringing diverse skills together to produce things. Chris Toumazou takes great pleasure in breaking down barriers between academic disciplines. Working with people like yourself may be easier, but it is unlikely to stimulate the ideas and innovation that results from working with people with different backgrounds, perspectives and skills. When allied to great ambition and purpose, as shown in the case of Bletchley Park, a kind of collective grace can emerge.

Experience of failure or loss, and how you deal with it, provides lessons in grace. Alexsis de Raadt St James gracefully used her personal tragedy to improve the lot of others facing the same situation. A splendid artistic foundation emerged from the Gianadda family's bereavement. Innovators push the boundaries, working in areas where failure is common if not inevitable. Innovators try everything to avoid failure, which is commonly a terrible blow to their ambitions and views of their self-worth, but gracefully accept that when it occurs it is no one else's fault but their own, and it provides an excellent opportunity to learn, think about new ways of doing things and keep your ego in check. Steve Shirley puts it well in her autobiography: 'Modesty in the art of surrender is the key to many kinds of success.'

Whether it is Thomas Heatherwick's 'making', or Chris Toumazou's 'mixing theoretical understanding with an intuition for what is practical', craft involves the ability to mould connections. Scientist Stephen Hawking said that science is beautiful when it makes connections between different observations, and entrepreneurship is often about joining the dots, or as Schumpeter puts it, new combinations. Play contributes to such melding and blending of novel combinations of ideas. Successful play at work is an exercise in crafting connections and combinations; it is a way of liberating curiosity from the confines of narrow professions, disciplines and experiences, and framing and fashioning innovations.

Craft is a source of immense pride. Just as the ability of the potter to shape a lovely vase or of the furniture maker to make a beautiful chair is deeply satisfying, so too is the ability to put an innovative idea to use and construct a solution to a problem, especially when the idea is adventurous and novel and the problem is contentious and vexatious. As with manual craft, craft in its modern sense combines intellect and intuition as products, services and solutions to problems emerge with identified purpose. Even where data is crucial in informing decisions, intuition and experience have to be brought in. Reliance on 'the numbers' will, as the case of Robert McNamara shows so tragically, lead to perverse decisions. As McNamara himself said, 'rationality will not save us'.

Being able to cope with failure is a feature of fortitude: to persevere when all seems against you. It is still an awe-inspiring experience to visit St Paul's Cathedral in London, over three centuries after its construction. It is even more remarkable when the difficulties experienced by its architect, Christopher Wren, are taken into account. All innovators have times when their willingness to continue is tested, and they have to draw on their reserves of energy and willpower. Steve Shirley is an exemplar of resilience. The difficulties in her business were immense and compounded by the distressing challenge of her son's autism. Yet she persevered, motivated by the concern to build a company of women for women, and to honour those who saved her from the Nazis by showing that hers was a life worth saving. Such fortitude is necessary to maintain and uphold play – to continue to explore, experiment and have fun – when conditions are bleak and unconducive.

Great innovators give back. Their ambitions extend well beyond personal objectives, such as proving something to themselves or satisfying their curiosity, or even gaining great wealth. Some want to give back to their profession or discipline. Elizabeth Iorns is motivated to better use scientific equipment. As she put it, she's aiming for an exchange of values to improve science. Jenna Tregarthen wants to help people overcome eating disorders. Arthur Bishop believed strongly in the social responsibility of the engineer. Gerald Chan's 'philanthropic capital' targets an area of medical science that he has worked in and supported all his life with the aim of benefiting society. Joseph Bazalgette and Norman Fowler took great career risks to meet their objectives of improving public health. Shelley Harrison devotes his time and energy to giving back to the higher education system that gave him his opportunities in life. Jeremy Coller is dedicated to his lifetime's ambition of ending the use of antibiotics in animal farms. Keith Tuffley is pursuing his enthusiasm for the environment, supporting many causes and promoting them through his extraordinary endeavours. MI5's ambition is to keep people safe from terrorism. Giving back is rewarding: Steve Shirley says the money she has let go has brought her infinitely more joy than the money she has hung on to. Such ambitions set great examples to others and help encourage and give further reason to play.

Jeremy Coller's decision to ask his friend to write his obituary provided the opportunity to reflect on his life's progress before it comes to an end. Atul Gawande has written an insightful book about the less than cheerful matter of dying. What he says has profound implications for how we work:

> As our time winds down, we all seek comfort in simple pleasures – companionship, everyday routines, the taste of good food, the warmth of sunlight on our faces. We become less interested in the rewards of achieving and accumulating, and more interested in the rewards of simply being. Yet while we may feel less ambitious, we also become concerned for our legacy. And we have a deep need to identify purposes outside ourselves that make living feel meaningful and worthwhile.[13]

Gawande refers to the work of Josiah Royce, whose *Philosophy of Loyalty* argues that we find meaning in our lives by giving devotion to a cause of our own choosing, and for which we are prepared to make sacrifices.[14] Self-interest, according to Royce, is short term, restless and insatiable, and we benefit more by devoting ourselves to a cause greater than our own advancement.

In his *Notes*, Leonardo da Vinci encourages people to make their work in keeping with their purpose. As Jonas Salk is quoted by the Academy of Achievement:

> It's necessary to have a purpose in life . . . So number one is to have a purpose. It can be different at different times in your life . . . Take good care of that purpose. Let that be your guide. This requires respecting our own individuality, our own uniqueness and that of others. The idea of being constructive, creative, positive, in trying to bring out the best in one's own self and the best in others follows.[15]

Along with generosity of spirit we can add greater purpose and cause beyond our own advancement in defining the essence of the player. We may be at work for over 80,000 hours in our lives. No one wants that time to be meaningless: we want to make a contribution, to be recognized and rewarded in ways beyond financial gain.

Some reflections

As Darwin knew, to adapt is to survive. To adapt we need to learn and make choices. We need to do this because to balance stability and change, continuity and disruption, security and insecurity, is a continuing and unresolved challenge as progress is made. The world of work is and will always be a confusing and contradictory place and we will always yearn for some semblance of order in it and influence over it. Authority and bureaucratic structures might present an illusion of command, but, as found in the Soviet Union, control is impossible in a world that is continually evolving and surprising us with the unexpected. As an alternative, the innovators and entrepreneurs whose stories we tell offer some tried and tested playful behaviours that encourage adaptability and help them to survive and thrive in challenging conditions. In the words of Isabel Behncke, play is our adaptive wildcard. Fortunately, play is not a hardship for most people. As Rousseau knew with Emile, we naturally play, and learn as we do so. Play is intrinsically rewarding, giving us pleasure and contentment, and it comes easily to us. Humans are social animals and love social interactions: play brings us together. Ronald Reagan said, 'I've heard that hard work never killed anyone, but I say why take the chance.' The play and rewards of innovators, which as we've seen often involve hard work, show that it is not such a hard choice and it is a chance well worth taking.

Our focus has been on behaviour. Going back to the ancient Greeks and their thinking about 'virtue ethics', there is a strong view that nobility exists in our moral characters, rather than in our behaviour. Nobility in this view lies within a person rather than in their actions. We are not philosophers asking who we are and want to be, nor psychologists studying the many influences on our characters. We are interested in what people do.

Our interest in writing this book lies with the behaviours that encourage playfulness and thereby lead to actions that have positive consequences.

Innovators and entrepreneurs aren't always noble in all their behaviours, even the ones written about here. Their imaginations may inflate their actions and contributions in their minds. Memory plays tricks and some high achievers are neither short of ego nor averse to highlighting their generosity. Others involved in the making of their stories may question how these stories are being told. In the examples discussed, it is not a case of saying that if you are working in complex and uncertain circumstances 'this is what you need to be like', but rather 'these are behaviours worth considering'. They don't offer prescriptions but opportunities for reflection, and we capture some of the practices encouraging playful work to assess yourself against in the appendix, 'Make it playful: A manifesto for those seeking more agreeable work', at the end of the book.

Some of the behaviours of the players we've discussed may not have been squeaky clean on the way up – many an obstacle will have been robustly and energetically dealt with in ways that others may find discomfiting – but they would not be playful in our sense unless they took their risks with a generous spirit and eventually gave back, usually with good humour. Play, in the end, is about making things, people, organizations and the world of which we are a part better and more enjoyable.

The innovators and entrepreneurs described here hold lessons for those wanting to become innovators and entrepreneurs themselves, and also for those who simply want better and more rewarding work in their current and future workplaces. Their stories provide opportunities for anyone in work to ask some important reflective questions, such as the following.

- Is our work laudable and useful, matching the expectations we have of ourselves?
- Do we give and receive respect to and from co-workers and the organizations we work for?

- Do we have the satisfaction of using our skills and expertise to create new opportunities and solve problems?
- Can we push the boundaries and take risks to improve what we do without fear?
- Is our work energizing and fun?
- Does our work improve opportunities to learn and improve ourselves?

We have been interested in the nature of work, rather than the important question of its extent. There are great threats confronting large sections of the workforce. Driverless cars and trucks, for example, are a present-day reality and who knows what their future consequence will be for the millions of truck, van and taxi drivers around the world. Home working using cloud computing may provide welcome flexibility, but could also lead to social isolation and exploitation. We have no answer to the question of future employment levels: there are too many complex and interacting factors that could influence outcomes. The world may, however, become split into workers remaining in the industrial age, whose jobs are under continual threat from automation, and players in the modern age with discretion and choice at work and whose skills remain in demand. Under these circumstances huge challenges arise over increasing inequality and the distribution of wealth. Technological disruption is exacerbating social inequalities, and we need to think seriously about better social security nets and the virtues of a social wage. We may need to fund people to work, without necessarily being employed, in a manner that allows them to help others or practise their skills in ways that they find meaningful and rewarding. To this end, education may also need to change from readying people for a (probably non-existent) job to preparing them to create self-defined work.

These are questions well beyond the remit of this book. Here it is enough to claim that since much of the threat to jobs arises from new technologies, the securest jobs in the future will be those that do what machines cannot, or can combine and augment distinctly human advantages with those of machines. We do powerful things beyond the reach of machines: we are great problem solvers, and sometimes there is virtue in bloody-mindedly pursuing something in the face of all known evidence, which could lead to failure or spectacular success. It is our abilities to empathize, intuit, sympathize and imagine, relishing the charm of our freedom and cheerfulness of our interest, that will become ever more important as a way to distinguish the value of being human. We alone can think and behave morally, by making ethical decisions about right and wrong. Machines are being created that can learn and adapt, and some exploration and experimentation can be automated. But it may be a long time before machines match the way these things are done when they are motivated by the delightful personal liberty and the basic human instinct to socialize, contribute and have fun. At a time when technology's incursion into the world of work is causing immense personal and organizational disruption, Emile's greatest gift may be to show how distinctive it is to be human.

Postscript

Emily left her management consultancy job. After being promoted to director she found nothing changed. There was still no joy in the work. She had started various support groups and tried to get the company to address gender equality and move away from their focus on narrow performance metrics: to assess people's broad contributions, not simply their sales figures. She always felt there was sympathy for her concerns among the top levels of the company, but there seemed to be an engrained inability to address the problems. The play antibodies were too strong. As 'voice' did not work, and she couldn't bear to work there anymore, she had no alternative but to 'exit'.

To recharge her batteries Emily took a short break before searching for work. Money was much tighter, and a number of luxuries at home were dispensed with. Having previously been decisive in her career choices, she was surprised to discover that she had no particular urge to join a specific company or work in any particular industry. She was confident in her skills and their attractiveness to potential employers. She was numerate, could write well, was good at searching for information and judging its value, and she was an excellent listener, which contributed to her success at building empathy with others. Emily had numerous deep conversations with her friends about their work, how and why they did it, its rewards and disappointments.

She decided to pursue a childhood dream of running a small café. Located in an up-and-coming area, Emily started the business with a friend, and she threw herself into her love of cooking by trying new dishes and recipes. The business thrived, but Emily wanted to explore more options in her life. Having made the choice to leave one way of working, she wasn't going to restrict herself by immediately locking herself into another. She'd made the calculation when talking to her headhunter friend that she wasn't prepared to sacrifice her large salary for a similar although more substantial leadership role. She sold her share of the business and got a job as a tutor at the local university. While she enjoyed the interactions with students, she was appalled at the levels of bureaucracy the university demanded, which deadened the rewards she felt. Through a chance meeting at a party, she joined a public relations company. The work was varied. One day she was working with a music band 'young enough to be my children, but richer than all my friends put together', the next she was promoting an interior design company.

All these experiences were enjoyable in their way, but Emily felt they weren't exactly what she wanted. When she did find the job she was always after, it was in the most unlikely of places. She started to work in the health sector, in a struggling hospital renowned for its mindboggling inefficiencies. She had experienced the highs and lows of the health system, having seen the consequences of its neglect of her mother and extraordinary professional care devoted to one of her children when he was seriously ill. The challenges were immense. Facilities were run down, budgets were being cut and there were sharp divisions between medical and administrative staff. Things were so bad that the hospital was threatened with closure. Emily threw herself into her work, using all her skills. She decided there was no one single answer to the problems confronting the hospital, but there were hundreds of small ones. She facilitated lots of discussion about the problems with all those involved. This process developed a momentum of its own, and soon groups of staff were sorting things out themselves without her involvement. A group bonus scheme was introduced to reward collective effort.

Emily used her technology skills to replace the dozens of antiquated information systems with one new and effective one. She used the technology to ask the hospital's staff, supporters and patients for ideas on how to improve services, and then reported back to them on their implementation. Her business skills were applied to sell some of the good ideas for medical products and services that had emerged in the hospital. Incentives were introduced to come up with innovative ideas, with social recognition and financial rewards for those who did so. Emily drew on all her experiences: catering improved; staff enrolled in more educational and training courses; wards were nicely redecorated owing to her interior design connections; and many well-known bands were persuaded to perform at fundraisers. Staff turnover reduced and patients got better quicker.

Emily had turned into a player: a queen on her own chessboard, rather than a pawn on someone else's. Prepared to sacrifice salary and standard of living for quality of life she had become mistress of her own destiny, expressing her freedom, and rather than facing constant constraints to her decision-making she had the opportunity to explore and experiment. She decided to put play above pay. Emily knew her work to be valuable, and knew it was widely respected. She knew the challenges confronting the hospital would never be resolved, and there was no shortage of institutional roadblocks and operational uncertainties confronting her, but she had a clear objective to which she was totally committed: a better hospital. Her ambition matched her accumulated skills and knowledge and the expectations she had of herself. This was achieved by improving work, and letting people explore new ways of doing things and experiment with their own answers to problems. She gave the people working there permission to be enthused and engaged. Emily had regular confrontations with the local authority and health regulators but endured them because of her greater purpose. She was infuriated by the intransigence of some staff, but this was outweighed by the rewards of seeing the satisfaction people got when things changed for the better through the application of their own ideas. Her board of governors was initially horrified at the thought of commercializing ideas funded by the government, but was soon placated when the profits began to roll in. The obstacles put in her way by local government and national health system procedures continually tested her, but she persisted because she wholeheartedly believed in what she was doing.

She still worked long hours and had some sleepless nights worrying about the risks she was taking. But she loved her job and, being more content, was more capable of dealing with everyday challenges. She liked and respected the people she was working with and their shared values around making sick people well. She relished the messy complexity of all the organizational, financial and technological problems she had to deal with, because shaping their resolution was something she could influence, was pleasantly rewarding and meant things got demonstrably better. Once a month she took an 'Emily Day', where she switched off the phone, didn't look at emails, but spent the day going to the cinema or visiting galleries and museums and thinking about her work and how she could improve it. There were still many meetings with poor audio-visual equipment, and she still occasionally laddered her tights beforehand, but she walked into them energized, with a spring in her step and a twinkle in her eye. Appreciating Emile's gift, she successfully brought play into her work.

Endnotes

Prelude

1. Rousseau (1762).

1 Work

1. Cappelli, Hamori and Bonet (2005).
2. Deloitte (2014).
3. Krznaric (2012).
4. Plato (1967 & 1968).
5. There are, of course, those driven by less laudable motives, such as parental pressure.
6. Dodgson, Gann and Salter (2005).
7. Brynjolfsson and McAfee (2011); Ford (2015).
8. Johnson (2016).
9. Sutton-Smith (2001).
10. These, and all other definitions used subsequently (in italics) are taken from the *Oxford English Dictionary*.
11. The criterion for selecting people and organizations to study was based on the extent to which we thought they were *interesting*: did their stories hold our attention and offer insights that we believed were of value? Our methods of study included historical and documentary analysis and interviews. When we interviewed (those we interviewed are denoted in the text by the use of their first names) we used an open-ended approach. We cross-referenced whenever possible to assess the validity of what we were being told, but also relied on our judgement to decide whether what we were being told was plausible or exaggerated. While such an approach is not infallible, we'd like to think that between us, after thousands of such interviews conducted over a combined period of over sixty years, we are reasonably attuned to spotting when the wool is being pulled over our eyes.

12. Uglow (2002).
13. Weber (2009).
14. Kane (2005), p. 13.
15. Thompson (1967).
16. Schiller (2004).
17. Krznaric (2012), p. 37.
18. Babbage (1832).
19. Hume (1742).
20. Carlyle (1829).
21. Sennett (2008).
22. Hobsbawm (1952).
23. In most trades this was between father and son. Extensive craft practised by women, such as quilting and needlework, tended to be less industrially structured and market focused. The formal organization of crafts tended to exclude women.
24. Morris (1884a).
25. Ibid.
26. Morris (1884b).
27. Morris (1888).
28. Ibid.
29. MacCarthy (2010).
30. Quoted in Montgomery (1989).
31. Schmidt is one the best-known case studies of work in the management literature.
32. Wrege and Hodgetts (2000).
33. Kamata (1983).
34. Beynon (1973).
35. Braverman (1974).
36. Kerr, Harbison, Dunlop and Myers (1960).
37. De Botton (2009).
38. McChrystal et al. (2015).
39. Emily's day is a composite of the experiences of one person who wishes to remain anonymous. Many people who have read this story have said: 'I've had days like that!'

2 Play

1. Shirley (1993).
2. Shirley and Askwith (2012).
3. Schrage (2000); Schrage (2014).
4. Krznaric (2012).
5. Dodgson, Gann and Phillips (2013).
6. Kelley, with Littman (2001).
7. IDEO (2012).
8. Van Kralingen and Van Kralingen (2007).
9. Cassidy and Boyle (2010).
10. Galbraith (1977); Bauman (2007).
11. Kane (2005).
12. Bateson and Martin (2013).
13. Cleese (2001).

14. Behncke (2011).
15. Shapley (1993).
16. Halberstam (1972).
17. Lacey (1986).
18. Halberstam (1986).
19. McMaster (1997).
20. Halberstam (2007).
21. McNamara (1995).
22. Ibid.
23. March (1976).
24. Mukherjee (2010).
25. The videos are made by Videoarts: www.videoarts.com.
26. Millar (1968).
27. Huizinga (2014).
28. Jack (2010).
29. http://www.bbc.com/future/story/20131127-secret-to-thinking-like-a-genius, accessed 18 February 2014.
30. Feynman (1997); Feynman (2005).
31. Lewis (2016).
32. Temple (2012).
33. Millard (1990).
34. Bragg (2007).
35. See, for example, Criscuolo, Salter and Ter Wal (2014).
36. We exclude regular human failings, such as being boorish and self-centred, within the normal behaviour distribution curve. Steve Jobs was notoriously rude, and Edison had scant regard for personal hygiene.
37. Sutton-Smith (2001).

3 Grace

1. Dodgson (1991).
2. Fairtlough (1994); Fairtlough (2007).
3. Smiles (1892).
4. Ronson (2012).
5. Byrne (2005).
6. Isaacson (2014).
7. Dawkins (2006).
8. Uglow (2002).
9. See, for example, Csikszentmihalyi (2003).
10. Schultz (2010).
11. https://www.arup.com/publications/speeches-and-lectures/section/ove-arup-key-speech?query=key%20speech, accessed 3 November 2017.
12. When the authors were asked to write a short introduction about innovation, we chose to begin the book with Wedgwood, in the belief that he is one of history's greatest innovators: Dodgson and Gann (2010).
13. Dodgson (2011).
14. Gardner (2006).
15. A disgraceful Hollywood film – U-571 – was made about this event. In the film the hero was American. At the time of these events the US had not yet entered the war and there were no Americans involved in this action.

16. McKay (2010).
17. http://www.bloomberg.com/news/2014-09-08/harvard-gets-record-350-million-gift-for-public-health.html, accessed 3 November 2017.
18. Kahneman (2012).
19. Beinhocker (2006).

4 Craft

1. Adamson (2013).
2. Nielsen (2012).
3. The term 'wicked problem' emerged first with Rittel and Webber (1973), and has been used in many contexts subsequently.
4. There is a large literature on the ways designers design. See for example Vincenti (1990) and Salter and Gann (2003).
5. As has their hierarchy: the term 'at sixes and sevens' may reflect a fourteenth-century row over the precedence of the guild of tailors and skinners.
6. See, for example, Verganti (2009).
7. Arlidge (2014).
8. http://jalopnik.com/ask-mclaren-chief-designer-frank-stephenson-anything-yo-1159093256, accessed 9 April 2014.
9. Heatherwick (2012).
10. *Wired,* 7 October 2013.
11. Thomke (2003).
12. Rees (2012).
13. Executive Office of the President (2016).
14. Dodgson, Gann and Salter (2007).
15. Simulation tools are based on digital models that represent key parameters and relationships in a system, and that provide an abstraction with some explanatory power related to cause and effect. Simulation technology simplifies reality, enabling analysis of how parts of a system work together. These virtual environments can enable experiments that would often be physically impossible or prohibitively expensive to undertake in reality; Dodgson, Gann and Salter (2005).
16. Design thinking is an approach to designing that systematizes the integration of market and technological opportunities and has been popularized by Stanford University's d.school.
17. Tregarthen, Lock and Darcy (2015).
18. Rusbridger (2013).
19. See, for example, various interviews at the National Theatre on directing and rehearsing, such as https://www.youtube.com/user/NationalTheatre/featured, accessed 3 November 2017.

5 Fortitude

1. Ormerod (2005).
2. Harford (2011).
3. Tinniswood (2002).
4. Hollis (2009).
5. Fowler (2014).
6. Acheson (2007).

7. Fowler (2014).
8. Del Ponte and Sudetic (2009).
9. Priest (1981).
10. Brown (2003).
11. Nader (1965).

6 Ambition

1. Coller and Chamberlain (2009).
2. Coller Foundation (2014).
3. Keynes (1930).
4. See, for example, https://www.ncbi.nlm.nih.gov/pmc/articles/PMC4135321/, accessed 26 October 2017.
5. Information for this section comes from Brian Harrison, 'Maria Dickin', *The Oxford Dictionary of National Biography*, and the PDSA website – www.pdsa.org.uk – where information about the charity and how to donate to it can be found.
6. For further information on the Hollows Foundation and details on how to make donations, see www.hollows.org.
7. Halliday (2001).
8. A Metropolitan Board of Works was created to provide some overall responsibility for sewerage infrastructure. This body eventually morphed into the London County Council and then the Greater London Council, which was eventually disbanded in 1986 by Margaret Thatcher, who resented its political power.
9. The quotes that follow come either from our discussions with her, from her book *Securing Freedom* (Profile Books, 2012) or the series of Reith Lectures she gave on the BBC, http://www.bbc.co.uk/radio4/features/the-reith-lectures/transcripts/2011/, accessed 7 February 2018.
10. Andrew (2009).

7 Work and organization

1. Terkel (1974).
2. https://medium.com/@thersa/why-we-need-to-talk-about-good-work-728d7d82877c, accessed 7 February 2018.
3. Friedman (2013).
4. Dodgson (2017).
5. Isaacson (2015); Vance (2015).
6. Gardner (2006).
7. Porter and Kramer (2011).
8. Breward and Wood (2012).
9. Johansson (2006).
10. Edwards (2010).
11. Executive Office of the President (2016).
12. Hollis (2009).
13. Gawande (2014).
14. Royce (1908).
15. Salk (1991).

Bibliography

Acheson, D. (2007), *One Doctor's Odyssey*, Arima Publishing.

Adamson, G. (2013), *The Invention of Craft*, Bloomsbury.

Al-Khalili, J. (2012), 'The Life Scientific, Martin Rees', BBC Radio 4, 6 March.

Andrew, C. (2009), *The Defence of the Realm: The Authorized History of MI5*, Penguin.

Arlidge, J. (2014), 'Jonathan Ive Designs Tomorrow', *Time*, 17 March.

Babbage, C. (1832), *On the Economy of Machinery and Manufactures*, Echo Library, 2000.

Bateson, P. and Martin, P. (2013), *Play, Playfulness, Creativity and Innovation*, Cambridge University Press.

Bauman, Z. (2007), *Liquid Times: Living in an Age of Uncertainty*, Polity Press.

Behncke, I. (2011), 'Evolution's Gift of Play, from Bonobo Apes to Humans', TED talk, posted March 2011, accessed 3 October 2015.

Beinhocker, E. (2006), *The Origin of Wealth*, Harvard Business School Press.

Beynon, H. (1973), *Working for Ford*, Allen Lane.

Bragg, M. (2007), *Twelve Books That Changed the World*, Sceptre.

Braverman, H. (1974), *Labor and Monopoly Capital: The Degradation of Work in the Twentieth Century*, Monthly Review Press.

Breward, C. and Wood, G. (2012), *British Design from 1948: Innovation in the Modern Age*, V&A Publishing.

Brown, C. (2003), *Driven by Ideas*, UNSW Press.

Brynjolfsson, E. and McAfee, A. (2011), *The Race Against the Machine*, Digital Frontier Press.

Byrne, J. (2005), 'Working for the Boss from Hell', *Fast Company*, 1 July.

Cappelli, P., Hamori, M. and Bonet, R. (2014), 'Who's Got Those Top Jobs?', *Harvard Business Review*, March.

Carlyle, T. (1829), 'A Mechanical Age', *Edinburgh Review*, http://www.indiana.edu/~hist104/sources/Carlyle.html, accessed 8 February 2018.

Cassidy, J. and Boyle, B. (2010), *The Klutz Book of Inventions*, Klutz.

Cleese, J. (2001), 'Creativity', Video Arts, YouTube, accessed 26 October 2017.

Coller, J. and Chamberlain, C. (2009), *Splendidly Unreasonable Inventors*, Overlook Press.

Coller Foundation (2014), *Global Sustainability: Animal Factory Farming*, Coller Foundation, May.

Criscuolo, P., Salter, A. and Ter Wal, A. (2014), 'Going Underground: Bootlegging and Individual Innovative Performance', *Organization Science* 25, 5, 1,287–305.

Csikszentmihalyi, M. (2003), *Good Business: Leadership, Flow, and the Making of Meaning*, Basic Books.

Dawkins, R. (2006), *The God Delusion*, Transworld Publishers.

De Botton, A. (2009), *The Pleasures and Sorrows of Work*, Penguin.

Deloitte (2014), 'Agiletown: The Relentless March of Technology and London's Response', Deloitte LLP.

Del Ponte, C. and Sudetic, C. (2009), *Madame Prosecutor*, Other Press.

Dodgson, K. (2017), *Not My Jam: The Quarter Life Crisis: Why It's Happening to Us and How We're Dealing With It*, Kindle edition.

Dodgson, M. (1991), *The Management of Technological Learning*, De Gruyter.

Dodgson, M. (2011), 'Exploring New Combinations in Innovation and Entrepreneurship: Social Networks, Schumpeter, and the Case of Josiah Wedgwood (1730–1795)', *Industrial and Corporate Change* 20, 4, 1,119–51.

Dodgson. M. and Gann, D. (2010), *Innovation: A Very Short Introduction*, Oxford University Press.

Dodgson, M., Gann, D. and Phillips, N. (2013), 'Organizational Learning and the Technology of Foolishness: The Case of Virtual Worlds in IBM', *Organization Science* 24, 5, 1, 358–76.

Dodgson, M., Gann, D. and Salter, A. (2005), *Think, Play, Do: Innovation, Technology and Organization*, Oxford University Press.

Dodgson, M., Gann, D. and Salter, A. (2007), '"In Case of Fire, Please Use the Elevator": Simulation Technology and Organization in Fire Engineering', *Organization Science* 18, 5, 849–64.

Edwards, D. (2010), *The Lab: Creativity and Culture*, Harvard University Press.

Executive Office of the President (2016), *Artificial Intelligence, Automation, and the Economy*, Washington, DC, December.

Fairtlough, G. (1994), *Creative Compartments: A Design for Future Organizations*, Greenwood Press.

Fairtlough, G. (2007), *The Three Ways of Getting Things Done*, Triarchy Press.

Feynman, R. (1997), *Surely You're Joking Mr. Feynman*, W.W. Norton and Co.

Feynman, R. (2005), *Don't You Have Time to Think?*, Penguin.

Ford, M. (2015), *The Rise of the Robots: Technology and the Threat of a Jobless Future*, Basic Books.

Fowler, N. (2014), *AIDS: Don't Die of Prejudice*, Biteback.

Friedman, T. (2013), 'Need a Job? Invent It', *New York Times*, 30 March.

Galbraith, J.K. (1977), *The Age of Uncertainty*, BBC/Andre Deutsch.

Gardner, H. (2006), *Five Minds for the Future*, Harvard Business School Press.

Gawande, A. (2014), *Being Mortal: Medicine and What Matters in the End*, Metropolitan Books.

Halberstam, D. (1972), *The Best and the Brightest*, Random House.

Halberstam, D. (1986), *The Reckoning*, William Morrow and Co.

Halberstam, D. (2007), *The Making of a Quagmire*, Rowman and Littlefield.

Halliday, S. (2001), *The Great Stink of London*, The History Press.

Harford, T. (2011), *Adapt: Why Success Always Starts With Failure*, Farrar, Straus and Giroux.

Heatherwick, T. (2012), *Making*, Thames and Hudson.

Hobsbawm, E. (1952), 'The Machine Breakers', *Past and Present* 1, 1, 57–70.

Hollis, L. (2009), *The Phoenix: St Paul's Cathedral and the Men Who Made Modern London*, Weidenfeld & Nicolson.

Huizinga, J. (2014), *Homo Ludens*, Martino Fine Books.

Hume, D. (1742), *Of Refinement in the Arts, Part II, Essay II*, Library of Economics and Liberty.

IDEO (2012), *The Little Book of IDEO*, IDEO.

Isaacson, W. (2014), *The Innovators: How a Group of Hackers, Geniuses, and Geeks Created the Digital Revolution*, Simon and Schuster.

Isaacson, W. (2015), *Steve Jobs*, Abacus Books.

Jack, A. (2010) 'Carbon Breakthrough Wins Nobel Physics Prize', *Financial Times*, 5 October.

Johansson, F. (2006), *The Medici Effect*, Harvard Business School Press.

Johnson, S. (2016), *Wonderland: How Play Made the Modern World*, Riverhead Books.

Kahneman, D. (2012), *Thinking, Fast and Slow*, Penguin.

Kamata, S. (1983), *Japan in the Passing Lane*, Pantheon Books.

Kane, P. (2005), *The Play Ethic: A Manifesto for a Different Way of Living*, Pan Macmillan.

Kelley, T. with Littman, J. (2001), *The Art of Innovation*, HarperCollins.

Kerr, C., Harbison, F., Dunlop, J. and Myers, C. (1960), 'Industrialism and Industrial Man', *International Labor Review* 82, 3, 1–15.

Keynes, J. (1930), 'Economic Possibilities For Our Grandchildren', http://www.aspeninstitute.org/sites/default/files/content/upload/Intro_Session1.pdf, accessed 8 February 2018.

Krznaric, R. (2012), *How to Find Fulfilling Work*, Macmillan.

Lacey, R. (1986), *Ford: The Men and the Machine*, Little, Brown and Co.

Lewis, M. (2016), *The Undoing Project: A Friendship That Changed the World*, Penguin.

MacCarthy, F. (2010), *William Morris: A Life for Our Time*, Faber and Faber.

Manningham-Buller, E. (2012), *Securing Freedom*, Profile Books.

March, J. (1976), 'The Technology of Foolishness', in J.G. March and J.P. Olsen, eds, *Ambiguity and Choice in Organizations*, Universitetsförlaget, Oslo, 69–81.

McChrystal, S., Collins, T., Silverman, D. and Fussel, C. (2015), *Team of Teams: New Rules of Engagement for a Complex World*, Portfolio.

McKay, S. (2010), *The Secret Life of Bletchley Park: The WWII Codebreaking Centre and the Men and Women Who Worked There*, Aurum Press.

McMaster, H.R. (1997), *Dereliction of Duty*, Harper Perennial.

McNamara, R. (1995), *In Retrospect*, Times Books.

Millar, S. (1968), *The Psychology of Play*, Penguin.

Millard, A. (1990), *Edison and the Business of Innovation*, Johns Hopkins University Press.

Montgomery, D. (1989), *The Fall of the House of Labor: The Workplace, the State, and American Labor Activism, 1865–1925*, Cambridge University Press.

Morris, W. (1884a), 'Art and Socialism', lecture delivered before the Secular Society of Leicester, 23 January.

Morris, W. (1884b), 'A Factory as It Might Be', *Justice*, 17 May.

Morris, W. (2008), *Useful Work Versus Useless Toil*, Penguin.

Mukherjee, S. (2010), *The Emperor of All Maladies: A Biography of Cancer*, HarperCollins.

Nader, R. (1965), *Unsafe at Any Speed*, Pocket Books.

Nielsen, M. (2012), *Reinventing Discovery: The New Era of Networked Science*, Princeton University Press.

Ormerod, P. (2005), *Why Most Things Fail*, Faber and Faber.

Plato (1967 & 1968), *Plato in Twelve Volumes*, Vols 10 and 11, trans. R.G. Bury, William Heinemann Ltd.

Porter, M. and Kramer, M. (2011), 'The Big Idea: Creating Shared Value', *Harvard Business Review*, January–February.

Priest, J. (1981), *The Thiess Story*, Boolarong Publications.

Rittel, H. and Webber, M. (1973), 'Dilemmas in a General Theory of Planning', *Policy Sciences* 4, 155–69.

Ronson, J. (2012), *The Psychopath Test*, Picador.

Rousseau, J. (1921), *Emile*, trans. Barbara Foxley, J.M. Dent and Sons.

Royce, J. (1908), *The Philosophy of Loyalty*, Macmillan.

Rusbridger, A. (2013), *Play It Again: An Amateur Against the Impossible*, Jonathan Cape.

Salk, J. (1991), Academy of Archievement Interview, 16 May, www.achievement. org/achiever/jonas-salk-m-d/#interview, accessed 12 February 2018.

Salter, A. and Gann, D. (2003), 'Sources of Ideas for Innovation in Engineering Design', *Research Policy* 32, 8, 1,309–24.

Schiller, F. (2004), *On the Aesthetic Education of Man*, Dover Publications.

Schrage, M. (2000), *Serious Play: How the World's Best Companies Simulate to Innovate*, Harvard Business School Press.

Schrage, M. (2014), *The Innovator's Hypothesis: How Cheap Experiments Are Worth More Than Good Ideas*, MIT Press.

Schultz, K. (2010), *Being Wrong: Adventures in the Margin of Error*, Portobello Books.

Sennett, R. (2008), *The Craftsman*, Allen Lane.

Shapley, D. (1993), *Promise and Power: The Life and Times of Robert McNamara*, Diane Publishing Company.

Shirley, S. (1993), 'The Journey to Empowerment', *Proceedings of the Lunar Society* 5, 1–9.

Shirley, S. and Askwith, R. (2012), *Let IT Go*, Andrews UK Ltd.

Smiles, S. (2012), *Thrift*, CreateSpace Independent Publishing Platform.

Sutton-Smith, B. (2001), *The Ambiguity of Play*, Harvard University Press.

Temple, J. (2012), *London: The Modern Babylon*, BBC Arts.

Terkel, S. (1974), *Working: People Talk About What They Do and How They Feel About What They Do*, New Press.

Thomke, S. (2003), *Experimentation Matters*, Harvard Business School Press.

Thompson, E.P. (1967), 'Time, Work Discipline and Industrial Capitalism', *Past and Present* 38, 56–97.

Tinniswood, A. (2002), *His Invention Most Fertile: A Life of Christopher Wren*, Pimlico.

Tregarthen, J., Lock, J. and Darcy, A. (2015), 'Development of a Smartphone Application for Eating Disorder Self-Monitoring', *International Journal of Eating Disorders* 48, 7, 972–82.

BIBLIOGRAPHY

Uglow, J. (2002), *The Lunar Men: Five Friends Whose Curiosity Changed the World*, Faber and Faber.

Van Kralingen, R. and Van Kralingen, R. (2007), *De Groeimotor: Meerwaarde Innovatie van Markten & Merken*, Pearson Prentice Hall NL.

Vance, A. (2015), *Elon Musk*, Virgin Digital.

Verganti, R. (2009), *Design Driven Innovation*, Harvard Business School Press.

Vincenti, W. (1990), *What Engineers Know and How They Know It*, Johns Hopkins University Press.

Weber, M. (2009), *The Protestant Ethic and the Spirit of Capitalism*, IAP.

Wrege, C. and Hodgetts, R. (2000), 'Frederick W. Taylor's 1899 Pig Iron Observations: Examining Fact, Fiction, and Lessons for the New Millennium', *Academy of Management Journal* 43, 6, 1,283–91.

Index

INDEX

Make it playful: A manifesto for those seeking more agreeable work

Work and play are mostly separate parts of our lives, but there is much to gain when they are combined. Making work more playful improves the meaning, purpose and experience of a major element of everyone's life. Play helps mitigate work's uncertainties and monotonies, and accentuates the distinctiveness of human endeavour compared to the ever-expanding capacities of machines. Playful work is characterized by:

- *the expression of freedom*, when we have discretion over what and how work is done;

- *having fun at work*, no matter how hard it is, because it is interesting, energizing and rewarding;

- *preparedness to explore and experiment*, which indulges our curiosity and allows us to take risks by trying and testing new things without fear of damaging reputations and careers if they don't work out as expected; and

- *opportunities to learn* about ourselves and the world, enabling us better to adapt to uncertain and turbulent circumstances.

Playful work is supported by behaviours that are 'noble' in the sense of being admirable and virtuous. We should aim to cultivate these behaviours in ourselves and seek to work with and for those who demonstrate them.

Grace

Playful work is encouraged by:

- being respectful, trusting, encouraging and collaborative;

- displaying modesty and avoiding hubris;

- accepting constructive criticism;

- recognizing personal shortcomings and celebrating the abilities of others; and

♦ crediting success to joint efforts, but taking responsibility for failure.

Craft

Playful work is encouraged by:

♦ expressing our creativity and putting our experience and knowledge towards outcomes that are rewarding for us and pleasing to others;

♦ having the occasion and tools to combine different abilities and perspectives and utilize and develop our skills;

♦ engaging with problems that interest us and are pleasurable in their solution and meaningful in their results; and

♦ claiming with justification that what we do is a source of pride.

Fortitude

Playful work is encouraged by:

♦ moving the point at which we give up on schemes, continuing further than we have in the past when things aren't going so well;

♦ coping and adjusting when efforts turn out in unexpected ways; and

♦ seeing failures as opportunities to learn and on which to build the basis for eventual success.

Ambition

Playful work is encouraged by:

♦ making sure our motivations and efforts, and those of our employer match our expectations of ourselves and what we want from life;

♦ having the right balance in our working life between rewards in salary and status, and contribution to family, community and society; and

♦ recognizing the great rewards that come from giving back to the societies and communities of which we are a part.

265